Frontier Cultures

Frontier Cultures

A Social History of Assamese Literature

Manjeet Baruah

Routledge
Taylor & Francis Group
LONDON NEW YORK NEW DELHI

First published 2012 in India
by Routledge
912 Tolstoy House, 15–17 Tolstoy Marg, Connaught Place, New Delhi 110 001

Simultaneously published in the UK
by Routledge
2 Park Square, Milton Park, Abingdon, Oxfordshire, OX14 4RN

First issued in paperback 2015

Routledge is an imprint of the Taylor & Francis Group, an informa business

© 2012 Manjeet Baruah

Typeset by
Star Compugraphics Private Limited
5, CSC, Near City Apartments
Vasundhara Enclave
Delhi 110 096

All rights reserved. No part of this book may be reproduced or utilised in any form or by any electronic, mechanical or other means, now known or hereafter invented, including photocopying and recording, or in any information storage and retrieval system without permission in writing from the publishers.

British Library Cataloguing-in-Publication Data
A catalogue record of this book is available from the British Library

ISBN 13: 978-1-138-66238-4 (pbk)
ISBN 13: 978-0-415-50080-7 (hbk)

For my parents

Contents

Preface   ix
Acknowledgements   xv

Part I: Situating the Problem

Introduction   3

1. The Valley, Frontier and the Question of 'Order'   15
2. Buranjis and Sankari Culture: Language and Narrative in Pre-colonial Textual Traditions   41
3. Language Shift and Narrative: Pre-colonial Continental Crossroad to Colonial Frontier   76

Towards a Conclusion   98

Part II: Literature and Socio-spatial Relations

Introduction   109

4. Language and Narrative: Negotiating between Difference and Contradiction   113
5. Narrative and Social Base: The Irony of Breakdown   140
6. Reinventing Frontier Narrative   155

Conclusion   169

Appendix:
    (a) An Outline on Text and Social Origin of Author in Assamese Fiction   173
    (b) Translations of Essay and Letters Published in *Bahni*   185

Bibliography   193
About the Author   201
Index   202

Preface

It was not too long ago that I completed my doctoral research. The question I began with was: What was the mode in which Assamese fiction between 1940 and 1980 dealt or engaged with the question of identity in general, and 'Assamese' identity in particular? When I completed my research, I concluded that the focus in this regard during the period was not in the content, but in the narrative structure, i.e., plot, use of language, etc. devised to deal with the issue. The fictional narratives certainly comprised the primary data. But I did not find it difficult to gather the supporting analysis strewn around. The question of identity in a frontier seems to always remain a 'burning issue', and on which there is almost a social predilection or even a sense of commitment to write. I thought that I had also reaffirmed to myself, in a way, that as a generation which grew up with reiterations of identity as the single-most important cause of Assam as a volatile frontier, it was indeed to be found as a problematic everywhere.

By the time I had completed my research programme, there was another perspective that had started majorly doing the rounds, and some significant names were supporting the approach, that of 'borderland'. Until then, people had analysed the issue of the north-east Indian frontier as a problematic embedded in the making of an Indian 'frontier' inherited from the British. As seen through the 'borderland' approach, there was nothing necessarily Indian about it. The entire frontier, as per the approach, had historically been a transitional zone or corridor into East and South East Asia, and functioned thus also for South Asia. Therefore, the argument proposed (and almost celebrated) that the problematic of volatile frontier was simply a matter *within*, and had nothing to do with the *without*. If the issue of identity has ripped apart internal cohesion within the frontier it is largely due to its nature of being a continental crossroad and problems of state formation in this context.

Ironically, it was also during this time that one of the Government of India policies began to be discussed widely in the region as well as in Delhi among the communities from the region: the Look East Policy. The policy was devised in the early 1990s. But it acquired its sound bytes (if one may use the term) only during this period. The basic premise of the policy was that the northeast frontier area has had historical ties with East and South East Asia due to being a zone of transition. Why not tap it for economic benefit? If the frontier had not seen development for half a century, why not use this historical relation and geographical situation to reverse the reality of lack of development? Logically, to any discerning mind, the question was why this historical relation and geographical situation was used only for generating militant guerrilla outfits to fight the Indian state rather than for economic benefit.

If logic is at all relevant, then another dimension that was silent in the policy but needs to be spelt out is that the historical relation and geographical situation of a zone of transition can legitimately be tapped for economic benefit, but using the same context for a different political imagination other than being an Indian frontier would be 'criminal'. It is here that the 'intellectual' 'borderland' approach provides the analytical premise, viz. a zone of transition can only remain a zone of transition, irrespective of political imaginations. Problems and volatility of state formation are embedded in its very nature. The approach goes silent from here, and the logic of the Look East Policy could take over thereafter.

Despite my doctorate in my pocket, I was left with a sense of unease. If identity is so important, so much so that even literary narratives could only explore and engage with it but were unable to step beyond it, then why has it remained a problem? The question that rocked me was that if identity is so important and if its consciousness is a concrete reality, why could the region not come up with a common politics for almost eight decades now? It was then that I realised how misguided a researcher I had been, misguided in my own assumptions and by productions from intellectual enterprises which seemed to support me. It was then that I realised that identity cannot explain itself. The more I investigated thereafter, the more I came across details of how people who had articulated identity were not articulating identity per se. They were trying to grapple with the reality of a frontier, of a zone of transition and how they wished to find a common politics for the entire region. In other words, while in my doctoral research I had argued (and even proved!) that identity articulated itself in all its dimensions through the (modern Assamese) literary narratives, I now began to realise that these narratives were after all devices to create a platform for a common politics for the region, or at least its possibility. Language and narratives were instruments of identity politics and identity formation; but more than that they were also seen as instruments or devices which could help overcome the contradictions of ethno-nationalist identities in the region. For example, even from the late 19th century in the Brahmaputra Valley, people were aware and conscious, and were writing that the issue of identity posed one against the other. They were also discussing how languages and narratives may not only accommodate the fact of diverse identity but may also (seek to) *represent* that diversity or multiplicity and thereby create a common ground in cultural forms. In other words, there were conscious attempts at transcending the framework of identity in cultural productions.

But if this was so, why did all such initiatives fail? Does this then prove that a common politics from within a 'frontier' or a 'borderland' is impossible, and therefore attempts at creating narratives which can stand for diversity or multiplicity have been nothing more than futile exercises?

As I probed the issue, slowly and steadily three things dawned on me. First, differences across communities per se are not contradictions. When differences in modern times have entered into a relation with each other in the region, they became contradictions. These differences existed even prior to the 19th century, but they were not bound in a relation of contradiction during that period. This transformation of differences into contradictions was crucially related to changes that the region underwent when becoming a 'frontier' in the 19th century — spatially, socio-culturally, economically and politically. It continues to be a frontier even today. What created the relations of contradiction? During the pre-colonial period, the differences were mediated by shared mapping of socio-spatial relations. Since the 19th century, the erosion of the shared mapping left only the differences, and disourses which developed based only on differences converted them into contradictions for one another. Second, language, language use or narratives have never been of identity per se. They have always been of, and therefore, on the *relation* of identities in the region. One can go a step further and say that in the modern period, the moment identities enter into a relation with each other through the devices of language and narratives, they transform into contradictions. Therefore, in these cultural forms, the relation of differences becomes in reality a relation of contradiction. Third, it was in the very recognition of this relation of contradiction that conscious attempts were being made not only to produce narratives ('literature') but also develop forms of its practise. The most phenomenal practitioner of this method was the cultural icon and peasant leader Bishnu Rabha, especially his cultural productions, from the 1930s to the 1950s. In his approach, it was assumed that text per se cannot accommodate *and* represent the diversity or the multiplicity of the social base at the same time. But if the objective is to create a common politics in the region and make literature accommodate the diversity of its social base, then text has to be placed alongside its practise, and a combination of the two can accommodate and *represent* people. But there was yet another dimension to Rabha's literary practice. To Rabha, what the narrative practice accommodates and represents is not people, but a given political relation among peoples. People in all their diversity or multiplicity can never be accommodated and represented in a form. But a political relation that binds them can indeed be, and for that, literary narratives need to stop looking only for 'readers' (i.e., being language based) but enter the grassroots through the practise of performances, readings and political movements. Rabha's emphasis was on how to recreate the shared mapping of socio-spatial relations in the context of the 20th century. To him, it held the key to a common politics from within.

The contemporary discourse of identity (vis-à-vis study of culture) begins with the assumption that identity is the founding element of research (and of which I too have been guilty). The discourse of borderland argues the improbability of a historical continental crossroad like the region to be able to conceive of a common politics from *within*. However, both the approaches ignore the major attempts by people like Rabha to create that very common politics from within the region and use culture to achieve the end. This study focuses only on the Brahmaputra Valley as case study. However, the problem of relation of contradiction applies as much to it as to other parts of the frontier. Finally, I would say that if in my doctoral programme I worked with identity as the proverbial atom of the politics of language use and narratives, and if as a result I was unable to 'think' of a means of how the volatility in the cultural relations among the peoples in our frontier can be addressed meaningfully, then I do abandon that premise. Now I write with a conviction that a common politics from within is indeed possible and culture, rather than being an issue of conflict and contradiction, can be one of the most powerful means to create that politics. The book is about the history of such attempts, its failures, and the possibilities that such attempts hold in envisioning alternative futures for the region.

Acknowledgements

Writing a book is never a lonely existence. I started with books, libraries and travelling through heat and dust or cold. My family, friends and teachers, their memories and dreams were my greatest encouragement; and my professional duties made it a crowded and busy time indeed. The publishers, with their meticulous reviews and editing, opened my eyes to how much more is involved in writing and communicating. I thank them all.

Now that the book is complete, I feel a sense of emptiness, thus the need to keep writing. I am reminded of my beloved teacher and a great writer from Assam who used to tell me: Beware of the lonely aftermath and keep writing to avoid its dangers.

Part I

Situating the Problem

Introduction

Dialectics focuses on the relation between the different or the contradictions. It concentrates on the process through which the concrete comes into existence, whether in the Hegelian or the Marxist sense. Whether that relational process is seen as dialogue or as class struggle among the opposites, leading to the concrete, dialectics does not deny the reality of the concrete. But it also emphasises the historical processes through which the structures of the concrete come into existence. With regard to understanding the north-east India frontier in general and the trans-Brahmaputra Valley in particular, could dialectics be seen as a useful framework to conceptualise the region? Also, what has been the general approach to study the area, and could the framework of dialectics make a critical departure from such approaches in understanding the region?

The Brahmaputra Valley is the largest valley in the entire north-east frontier region.[1] The other two valleys in the region are Imphal Valley (Manipur) and Barak Valley (Assam). The Valley, formed by the river Brahmaputra and with an average width of 80 km, comprises a major geographical portion of the state of Assam. The north-east frontier region shares an extensive international border. It has Bhutan, Tibet and China to the north; China and Myanmar to the east; and Bangladesh to the south. It shares approximately a mere 3 per cent of its territory with India, connecting it to the state of West Bengal. Except for the three valleys, the rest of the region is mountainous, the lower Himalayas and the Patkai Mountains comprising the main geographical features. The Brahmaputra originates in the Himalayas in Tibet and flows through China, entering the lower Himalayan area in the present Indian state of Arunachal Pradesh, then through the Brahmaputra Valley in Assam

---

[1] The term 'north-east frontier region' is used as the closest appropriate term for the region. Prior to colonialism, the region was not 'north-east frontier'.

and finally empties into the Bay of Bengal after merging with the Ganga in Bangladesh.

Colonial anthropologist Waddell, more than a century ago, wrote on the trans-Brahmaputra Valley,

> This hilly region standing up between China, India, Tibet and Burma has come to be the last refuge of scattered detachments of the more primitive hordes from each of these countries. Driven into these wild glens by the advance of civilization up the plains and the lower valleys these people have become hemmed in among the mountains, where pressing on each other in their struggle for existence they have developed into innumerable isolated tribes, differing widely in appearance, customs and language (Waddell: [1901] 2000: 1).

Commenting on the Brahmaputra plains, Waddell wrote, 'Its history, up till the British occupation, was one of long tale of violent intertribal conflict, invasion and cruel extermination' (ibid.: 2). Waddell's study was based on his fieldwork conducted in the 1880s and 1890s. Nearly a century and a quarter later Sanjib Baruah wrote, 'Contemporary North east India's linguistic and cultural diversity reflects the resilience of a historic non state space despite powerful odds' (Baruah 2009: 8). Baruah situated his thesis on Scott's *The Art of Not Being Governed: An Anarchist History of Upland South East Asia* (2009). Baruah's approach was not an isolated contemporary case. He was part (and still is) of an emerging and influential discourse of 'borderland' that views the entire region as a transnational problematic. The problem, as this discourse identifies, is in making an essentially transnational non-state zone part of modern (nation) state-building process. Baruah's earlier study (1999) makes the point even clearer; he locates the solution to the problem of 'independence' or 'secessionist' movements of the region against the Indian state in an increasing presence of India within the fabric of the region, i.e., the region needed to be made more Indian. By becoming more Indian the inter-community conflict in the region could also be eradicated.

If Waddell's and Baruah's arguments are compared, two points stand out. Both arguments are premised on a similar assumption — that the region comprises different groups of communities, historically isolated from one another and feuding with one another. The nature of the historical geography of the region, including the Brahmaputra Valley, played a major role in it. Where they differed was while Waddell discussed how in the making of a colonial frontier out of the region, selective and strategic control over communities and territory was followed, Baruah argued that to fashion the region into a national frontier, an-all encompassing existence of India was critical. Baruah, however, was unable to explain what constituted that 'India' or the nature of the critical Indian presence that is required. We could argue that in the range that exists between Waddell and Baruah, there are two basic problems. On the one hand there is an uncritical assumption that *isolated* and *different* communities have been an essential feature of the region. While for Waddell they were isolated and different and were constantly engaged in inter-tribal conflict, for Baruah they were different ethnic groups constantly engaged in inter-ethnic conflict. In other words, 'tribe' was replaced by 'ethnic', while the discourse remained the same. On the other hand, both Waddell and Baruah highlighted the stabilising role that the state system from without can play within the region, precisely due to the context mentioned above. For Waddell it was the colonial state while for Baruah it could be the Indian state. As is evident, both highlight the need of a factor from without to negotiate in (and stabilise) the differences among the communities of the region. While in the first case difference was treated as the only concrete reality, in the second case the naturalness of the state system (from without) was assumed to be the concrete reality from which the 'non-state' that the region constitutes needed to be understood.

In contrast, we would try to approach these same issues, i.e., their assumed concrete realities, from the point of relation or dialectics of socio-spatial relations. Therefore, we would argue that it is not the 'tribe' or the 'ethnic' distinct from one another which helps understand the historical formation of the region. On the contrary, it is the historical socio-spatial relations among the communities of the region which help explain it. For the pre-colonial period, these socio-spatial relations exemplify how shared relations across differences were consciously mapped. One of the points that we would highlight is that awareness of difference across communities was not specific to the modern period alone. For example, the Buranji chronicles or the neo-Vaishnava performance literature of the pre-colonial period amply demonstrated the awareness of difference. But importantly, the pre-colonial textual traditions also highlighted how shared domains were in place wherein the different could participate by remaining different. This dialectical nature of socio-spatial relations was central to the reproduction of both differences and the shared domains among the communities within the area. The range of scholarship from Waddell to Baruah generally overlooked these shared domains which were critical to socio-spatial relations of the pre-colonial period.

In the course of my discussion, I will also argue that the 19th century witnessed a major shift in these socio-spatial relations. The shift was in the erosion of the shared domains among the communities. It was a result of massive spatial re-organisation in the valley as well as due to the socio-economic re-organisations carried out in the making of the colonial frontier. The shift could also be seen as one from a crossroad to the frontier. The Brahmaputra Valley had become the strategic space where this making of the frontier was carried out. The erosion of the shared domains had its impact on the dialectics of socio-spatial relations. Whether in terms of the colonial discourse or in terms of identity discourses by the late 19th century, from the relation and coexistence between the shared and the different, the focus had now shifted to notions of 'order' and lack of order. Spatial changes which were part of the colonial project of making a frontier such as converting the foothills of the Brahmaputra Valley into the largest tea-producing area of the world or practising policies of ethnic space, i.e., attempting to territorially demarcate every community or divide the hills and valley into distinct orders of society were seen in colonial reports as instituting 'order' in the region. Spaces and societies which were brought within the colonial control were part of 'order' while those that were left outside came to be termed as 'savage'. It is notable that pre-colonial textual traditions did not use such frameworks as order or savage to distinguish space and societies. The use of such notions began from the colonial period onwards. The impact of notions of 'order' could be clearly seen in the identity discourses of the period among the colonised as well, such as the 'Assamese', 'Ahom', 'Plains Tribe' and others. Therefore, a comparison of the textual traditions of the pre-colonial and the colonial or the postcolonial periods in the Brahmaputra Valley clearly proves the shift in the mapping of differences among the communities.

In recent years, a substantial body of research on identity discourses in the valley has come up. This has two common features. It begins its discussion from the 19th century onwards and primarily focuses on identity consciousness and politics based on it as practised by different groups. However, if the approach to the issue is altered to include how inter-community relations and relations of space were mapped in the pre-colonial period and how such mapping changed since the 19th century, it could be shown that more than identities per se (whether tribe or ethnic) as necessarily the concrete realities, it is the changing nature of historical socio-spatial relations among communities which holds the key to explaining the problems of the present. It is evident that whether in the pre-colonial or since the colonial period, the idea of difference among communities was central. But the shift between the two periods was in the nature of mapping the difference as part of inter-community/space relations. This shift, as I will show, was due to the transformation of the trans-Brahmaputra Valley from a continental crossroad into a frontier.

Socio-spatial Transformations and the Debate on 'Border'

One of the dominant approaches to the study of 'border' has been that 'border' constitutes a socio-cultural or political condition of flux. The 'mainland' or 'centre' is considered to constitute 'order'. For example, between the 14th and 16th centuries, the area of modern Bihar (middle-to-east Gangetic basin) is analysed as a 'border' or outpost between political systems of Bengal and Delhi, and the political organisation of society is seen as a condition of flux, until it got incorporated into the centralising Mughal forces in the 16th century (Ahmad 2008: 74–88). The fluidity of frontier (present-day Bangladesh) has also been discussed vis-à-vis the 'rise of Islam and the Bengal frontier' (Eaton 1994). To take another example, the cultural forms at the American–Mexican border, especially of the Chicano people, have been interpreted in terms of flux, thus explaining why diglossic or multiple narrative modes characterise their cultural productions (Gentzler 2008: 143–79). This, Gentzler argues, poses a challenge to the traditional concept of translation as involving a 'source text' and 'target text'. There is also a substantial body of literature on the (universal) phenomenon of land reclamation and the appropriation of frontiers into agrarian *systems*, whether in the pre-modern or in the modern period.

Two other historiography traditions can also be referred to here, viz. the historiography around the Turner thesis on the American frontier and that of continental crossroad on the US–Mexico border. In both the traditions frontier is seen largely in terms of process, yet to become demarcated territoriality. Once territoriality gets defined, a 'region' comes into existence. In this regard, Wrobel contends that when the process is complete, a frontier becomes a constituting region of the nation (1996: 401–29). However, it would be interesting to recall Turner himself in this matter, 'As successive terminal moraines result from successive glaciations, so each frontier leaves its traces behind it, and when it becomes a settled area, the region still partakes of the frontier characteristics' ([1920] 2010: 15) It is also an approach to be found in Eaton's classic study (1994) of the 'Bengal frontier'. Where the framework of continental crossroad differs from it is that it drops the element of the 'settled area' and its implications of order. Thus it is the fluidity, whether socio-cultural or economic, which is focused upon through frameworks such as trans-regional or transnational. It is argued that concepts such as trans-regional or transnational can explain the socio-spatial indeterminacy that characterise a frontier or borderland. For example, Truett and Young, in their Introduction, remark on the implication of the US–Mexico border coming up in 1854, 'Ever since the border was mapped in 1854, the borderlands have supported a complex web of historical relationships that transcended — even as they emerged in tandem with — the US and Mexican nations. Residents of borderland often see their history differently' (2004: 2). They further state,

> By understanding contradictions between the ideal nation and social reality at the point that national identity was being forged, we can better historicize the nation. What have nations meant for those living at (or moving across) their most tangible territorial limits, and how can the histories of these continental crossroads help us re-think the world we live in today.

It is evident that in the two historiography traditions, the idea of order and nation were closely connected.

Returning to the geographical theatre that the study is primarily concerned with, an example of 'border' and the condition of flux which gets institutionalised is the 6th Schedule of the Indian Constitution, arranged especially for the north-east India frontier in 1950 (when the Constitution came into effect). Under the provision, autonomous self-governing councils were provided for the 'tribal' communities of the region. The basic argument that guided the policy was that the British had not brought the entire frontier region under direct administrative control, i.e., under direct colonial jurisdiction. The large number of different communities were allowed to self-govern based on their respective customs and practices. As a result, these communities continue to exist and operate as distinct peoples. Thus autonomous councils, it was assumed, would provide for continuing with the practice, but under the overall framework of the Indian Constitution and sovereignty. Gradually, the structural integration with the larger Indian nation state would become possible. However, if the objective was to ensure a mechanism whereby the sovereignty of the Indian Constitution and the concept of Indian nation were implemented in the frontier and the gradual integration of the frontier people with the rest of the country was achieved, it still remains debatable.[2]

The approaches surveyed above are not intended to be exhaustive but only indicative. In contrast to these, my contention is that this near universal approach of systemic centre vis-à-vis peripheries in flux needs to be revisited, especially in historical analysis of culture formation at geographical boundaries. At the core of the approaches surveyed here is the question of order. While the former is seen as embodying order, the latter is seen as either lacking or challenging order. In terms of why the latter lacks or challenges order, the answer is traced to the factor of its location, whether geographical or socio-political and cultural, which (a) prevents it from constituting into an order; and (b) makes integration into national orders difficult.

In my discussion on Waddell and Baruah, I outlined how a continental crossroad or frontier need not be seen in terms of indeterminacy of order, the indeterminacy assumed to be due to

---

[2] The Armed Forces Special Powers Act, enacted in 1959 by the Indian Parliament for the north-east Indian frontier, is a peculiar instrument in this regard. It allows for the suspension of effective functioning of the Constitution until conditions are created that it can effectively function. The Act, which gives unprecedented power to the Indian army in governance, is still in operation in most parts of the frontier. The Act also came into operation in the Kashmir Valley since the 1990s.

multiplicity of differences, which in turn is located in historical geography. With the trans-Brahmaputra Valley as a case, I also argued that continental crossroad and frontier may be two different kinds of formations. I located the difference between them in the nature of socio-spatial relations that constitute them as region formations. As a continental crossroad, the prime characteristic of its socio-spatial relations was how the different and the shared domains across the difference existed and reproduced each other. As a frontier, the change was in the erosion of the shared domains (whether ideational or of material conditions), resulting in the development of discourses wherein the different came to be treated as the concrete reality. As I will try to show in the study, the erosion of the shared domains or shared mapping transformed the differences into contradictions. One of the fundamental assumptions underlying the development of the discourses of contradictions was the binary opposition seen between order and lack of order, also formulated in the codes of civilised and savage by the colonial state and the colonised alike.

The dialectical relation between binary opposites was present in the Turner thesis on frontier (for example, his *Frontier in America History*, [1920] 2010) as well. In the 20th century, historiography based on the Turner thesis also notes frontier as relation of the opposites, for example, between free land and settlement, between indeterminacy and the determined. It has been referred to as the dialectical understanding of frontier (Klein 1997: 78–87). However, my contention differs from this historical approach. The fundamental difference is that this tradition of historiography sees frontier as a process which from a state/stage of contradiction (thesis–anti thesis) changes or *evolves* into one of order (synthesis). In their case, it evolves into the synthesis of 'America', i.e., the USA. There is a contest between the opposites or contradictions, played out in the phenomenal expanse of land from the East to the West coasts of the North American continent. But it is also a contest which resolves in the coming into being of 'America', the continental expanse of land being one of the prime factors making it possible. It is notable that the historiography cannot conceptually distinguish crossroad and frontier as different formations. Given the fact that the Turner thesis was formulated in the 1890s, when the frontier had almost become a past rather than still being a 'concrete', living reality, the positivist approach in such retrospective history is evident.

I will try to show that in the case of the trans-Brahmaputra Valley, it is not due to being a process (of change) that moves towards a resolution which makes it a frontier. On the contrary, it is precisely the irresolvable nature of the *relation* among the contradictions that distinguishes it as frontier. The key to explain this irresolvable relation could be in its shift from crossroad to frontier, especially the erosion of the shared domains of socio-spatial mapping which mediated and reproduced differences. Further, the area became a frontier with its annexation to the British-Indian Empire in 1826. But unlike the argument of the Turner thesis, it perpetuated itself only as frontier without emerging as a 'region' of the nation. Sanjib Baruah's approach, as indicated earlier, can only be treated as a proposition to make it a region, i.e., make it another nationalised area of India. Therefore, it can be explored if there are factors, other than cartographic location, which perpetuate its existence as frontier. But such an approach also allows us to explore whether frontier too needs to be seen as a region in itself, rather than only being a process towards a region. And if frontier is treated as a region, other than its cartographic location, what reproduces it as frontier over a period of time could well be explored in the relations that constitute it. Though not articulated thus, there were perspectives even in the early post-independence period which expressed self-doubt and recognised the need to rethink what it meant to be part of the frontier. For example, in the editorial of the influential magazine *Ramdhenu* (Rainbow), Birendra Kumar Bhattacharjya wrote ('The Tribal Question and Cultural Unity') on the issue of various measures to address the tribal question (translation mine),

> But if we observe the growing consciousness among the tribal people, it appears as if all our initiatives have not been able to touch their lives. The growing consciousness of independence among Naga people and their separatist attitude towards the people of the valley, these and other such developments make us realize repeatedly that somewhere there exists a fundamental lack somewhere, a complexity, in our perspective which we are not able to comprehend (1952–53, 1 (5): 7; 2007: 22).

I will argue in my study that the trans-Brahmaputra Valley as a frontier is a specific type of region. The specificity is not due to its location per se, but because of the socio-spatial relations that have constituted it as a region since the 19th century. Further, it is equally plausible to pose here that if the characteristics of the trans-Brahmaputra Valley as frontier are the irresolvable relations of contradictions due to the erosion of the historical shared domains, what could be created if shared domains, though of a different nature from the past, are developed once again? Would that be a regenerative process which restores the area with its historical existence as a continental crossroad? One of the issues which most contemporary studies (on ethnic violence or 'insurgency') highlight is the lack of a common politics from within the region. This lack is generally located in the fact that any two given ethnic politics in the region could only stand as contradiction to one another. It is in this context that regeneration of shared domains could be the critical factor to make possible common politics from within the frontier. As I will show, it was precisely what some of the cultural figures from the Valley attempted to achieve.

This study is primarily based on culture. What can a study of culture and cultural forms contribute to our understanding of the relations that constitute a frontier? First, pre-colonial textual traditions such as the neo-Vaishnava literature or the Buranji chronicles display how mapping of shared socio-spatial relations was practised during the period. Second, the development of 'modern Assamese' literature since the last quarter of the 19th century show us how the question of 'order' or 'lack of order' could play a critical role in the nature of narrative practised in different kinds of literature. Third, 'modern Assamese' literature clearly exhibited the consciousness of how identity discourses situated different communities in relations of conflict and contradiction to one another. As a result, there were also attempts throughout the 20th century on how literature could redresss the problem through narratives which could accommodate diversity. In fact, in the case of writers like Bishnu Rabha (1909–69), it was made amply evident that literature cannot *represent* the diversity of its social base. It can only represent a relation that binds the diversity. Therefore, a given literature needs to conceptualise the relation that can bind the diverse into a common politics and practise it through narrative forms. These attempts at redress are discussed in this study as possible frontier narratives which have critical significance in developing a common politics from within.

Notably, in most contemporary studies on the region, such cultural practices have been almost entirely overlooked.

The book is divided into two parts. In Part I, two broad issues are taken up. They are (a) how to situate the Brahmaputra Valley in the historical geography of the region; and (b) the process of culture formation in the Valley vis-à-vis Assamese language and narratives. As regards the first issue, the discussion centres on the historical transformation that the Valley underwent from being a continental crossroad into a 'frontier'. It was a transformation of socio-spatial formations. Importantly, the transformation was also instituted into structures of 'order' and lack of order in the policies of the colonial state, but also internalised by the colonised. The second issue takes up the problem of development of modern Assamese language and narratives, especially how it was based on fundamental linguistic and narrative rearrangements vis-à-vis the pre-colonial period. Therefore, the major debates on what comprised 'Assamese' language and narratives in the late 19th to the middle of the 20th century is emphasised. It is argued that the historical and ethnographic debate on the issue was not merely a matter of identity politics (as is generally shown in different studies) but was deeply rooted in the transformation from continental crossroad to frontier. Therefore, writers of modern Assamese literature wrote not because they knew what it meant to be Assamese, but because they were struggling to identify what it actually meant to be Assamese. In Part II, two substantive issues are taken up. They are (a) how modern Assamese language and narratives have addressed the problem of literature accommodating or representing the social base which is comprised of multiple 'identities'; and (b) if the authors were conscious of the historical and ethnographic debate embedded in language and narrative, did they make any attempt to create narratives which could overcome the problem of accommodation or representation noted above. Towards the end, based on some recent trends in Assamese literature, it is explored whether it is possible to develop 'frontier literature' in modern Assamese fiction. Another point discussed in this section is the 'irony of breakdown' in the relation between language/narrative and its social base. A general contention in literary criticism has been that the nature of narrative and its social base share a relation of correspondences (i.e., the principle of homology). However, as will be seen in this study, one of the distinctive features of this relation in the case of modern Assamese fiction, especially between the 1950s and the 1980s, was that of breakdown of any such relationship. The wider the ethnographic contradiction of language/narrative representing or accommodating its social base, the greater became the emphasis on generating or applying a narrative wherein the contradiction increasingly receives less space. Therefore, could the recent initiatives of 'frontier literature' mentioned above be seen as an attempt at creating a new literature to address this problem?

1
The Valley, Frontier and the Question of 'Order'

The Brahmaputra Valley is the largest valley in the entire north-east frontier region.[1] The Valley is formed by the river Brahmaputra. The Brahmaputra comprises an extensive network of rivers (i.e., it is a river system). Most of the rivers of the lower Himalayas of the region and the Patkai ranges that lie to its south flow into the Brahmaputra. The Brahmaputra river system has been a major geographical and climatic influence in north-east India. The river passes through three major kinds of landscapes: the mountains and hills of Tibet and Arunachal Pradesh; the foothills of Arunachal and Assam as it moves towards the Assam Valley; and finally through the plains of the Assam Valley and the floodplains of Bangladesh till it discharges into the Bay of Bengal. Though the Brahmaputra Valley (also commonly called the Assam Valley) was frequently viewed in ancient Sanskrit writings of the Gangetic area as peripheral to Indo-Gangetic geography, it was only with British colonialism that it became part of any South Asian political formation. Therefore, the first question that is posed is how to situate the Brahmaputra Valley in the context of 'border'.

The creation of the 'north-east frontier' can be traced to the colonial period. But I will begin with how the Valley was mapped in the pre-colonial period. The *Katha Guru Charit* (biography of Sankardeb by Ramsaran Thakur, c. 16th/17th century),[2] considered one of the most established biographies of the saint, can throw

---

[1] The term 'north-east frontier region' is used as the closest appropriate term for the region. Prior to colonialism, the region was not 'north east frontier'.

[2] The text edited by H. N. Dutta Baruah and published by Dutta Baruah and Co., Nalbari, Assam, 1978 is used in this study.

important light on this. Though the terms Assam and Assam *desh* were used in the text (they could be found even in Sankardeb's writings of the 16th century), they were used indeterminately. For example, it is not clear whether 'Assam' was used as a generic term to refer to the Valley or only for places where Sankardeb went and resided as part of his mission. A list of the different connotations of Assam is placed here (paraphrased translation of the verses mine):

> (a) Jaganath Mishra, a Brahman from *Tirati desh* (?) comes on pilgrimage to the Brahmaputra (Valley), and leaving behind his *rajya*, arrives in Assam *rajya* (Part Four, verse 2164). (b) The people of Assam *rajya*, the Barabhuyans, all the people who live under Ahom raja and those who do not have any king, all take to bhakti (Part Four, verses 2391–2392). (c) The Barabhuyans capture elephants of the Assam raja's *rajya*. When the people inform the Assam raja of this, he becomes furious and orders a Bora to capture the Barabhuyans (Part Four, verses 2393–2394). It needs to be noted here that though *Assam rajya* is distinguished throughout the text from the *Ahom* raja's *rajya*, *bora* used to be an officer (the first post in an ascending hierarchy) appointed under the Ahom system. (d) Naranarayan (Koch king) becomes the ruler of Kamrup and the guardian of all the people of Assam. Therefore, Sankardeb decides to leave his place and go to Kamrup. (e) On his voyage along the Burhiluit (the Brahmaputra) downstream, Sankardeb and his disciples leave behind Assam *rajya* and reach Kamrup. When a passerby is asked what the name of the *desh* is, he replies that it is Darrang. Sankardeb does not like the name and moves on (Part Four, verses 2470–2471). (f) When the Kacharis attack, the Barabhuyans leave Assam *desh* and go to Gangamukh. But there the Koch attack, which forces the Barabhuyans to go further north. Finally a settlement is reached between the Koch and the Barabhuyans (Part Four, verses 2597–2599). (g) As a result of the constant expeditions of the Ahom raja, Sankardeb narrates before Narayana that he and his disciples were forced to leave their place and come to a 'foreign land' (*bidesh*), which was Barpeta (Part Four, verses 2610–2631).

It will be evident from this list that though all the places referred to were in the Valley, their spatial mapping as or within a single space was quite indeterminate. In other words, though the word Assam *desh* frequently occurred, what constituted Assam *desh* was left as extremely vague. This was in contrast to the nature of determinate spatial mapping to be found since the 19th century when 'Assam' vis-à-vis the Valley came to have a distinct spatial fixity.

Similar modes of pre-colonial mapping of space could also be found in the mapping of society and identity. We can take up other kinds of evidence such as textual sources, legends and material culture in this regard. The Buranjis — the chronicles produced by the Ahom royal and noble lineages recording events, lives of individuals and genealogies of important individuals as well as the tree of clans — were one such example of mapping. A large number of Buranjis were produced in Tai (language of the Ahoms) and Assamese languages. But scholars like Surjya Kumar Bhuyan ([1935] 2007) and Yasmin Saikia (2004) have pointed out that Buranjis were written not only in Assam or the Brahmaputra Valley but also in Burma (or Myanmar), mostly in the Shan language. The Ahoms had migrated to the Valley in the 13th century from the Shan area of (Upper) Burma and established themselves as a ruling lineage. They had earlier supposedly migrated to Burma from China. Therefore, Buranji writing was a tradition which the Ahoms had brought with them as part of their migration. In this shared textual tradition from the Valley to the northern highlands of Burma, the nature of mapping of communities and spaces is noteworthy.

As Saikia points out, the Buranjis from the Brahmaputra Valley up to the highlands of northern Burma not only recorded a shared genealogical past, but also, in the Buranjis, the defined distinction of 'us' and 'them', i.e., the self and other, was largely absent. Different communities and spaces existed within the broad framework of *kun-how*, a notional shared relation that linked different communities and spaces. Two examples in this regard can help illustrate the point. In both Dutiram Hazarika's and Bisheswar Bidyadhip's 19th-century Buranjis, the shared rela-tion between the Ahoms and the Burmese is widely accounted for. In fact, in Hazarika's Buranji, the river journey of the Ahom general Badan Barphukan from Guwahati (Assam) to Ava and the successful mediation of his request with the king of Ava for supporting him on his plan to overthrow some factions of the ruling Ahom lineage are possible due to this shared relation of communities and spaces. Bhuyan collected and published an oral Assamese ballad, *Barphukanar Geet* (Songs on Barpahukan), in 1924.

The ballad is based on the episode of Badan Barphukan narrated above. Even in this folk ballad, the main reason behind the Burmese support to Badan Barphukan was the shared relation of community and space as in the other two Buranjis noted above, rather than territorial expansion as indicated in British colonial records, a notion legitimised through the Treaty of Yandaboo (1826) signed after the Anglo-Burmese War. The other example is the period when the Ahom prince Gadapani from the Tungkhun clan was a fugitive, fleeing to escape being killed by the boy-king Sulikpha. His hideout was in the Patkai ranges, among the Naga communities. The Buranjis note that he lived as a Naga among the people and later, with the help of the generals in Guwahati, overthrew the ruler and became king, assuming the name Gadadhar Singha. Hazarika's Buranji notes how he lived as a Naga betel leaf seller, who descended from the hills into the Valley to sell betel leaf, and then returned to the hills. His disguise fooled even the soldiers whom he once met on the way. What is important is the way the Valley, foothills and hills formed a part of a mapping of communities and spaces which were different from one another, but also coexisted within a relation of difference.

A further example is the legend of Jaymati, an Ahom princess who was punished to death for not disclosing the whereabouts of her absconding prince-husband Gadapani. Bhuyan, who plays a leading role in trying to prove that Jaymati was a historical character and not a legend (as part of his search for national heroes) notes that though there are few Buranjis in Assam which actually mention the name 'Jaymati' though quite a few record the incident (for example, Hazarika's Buranji mentions the incident), the Shan Buranjis from Burma link 'Jaymati' to the incident, proving her as a historical character ([1935] 2007: 278). Interestingly, in Hazarika's Buranji, in which Gadapani lives disguised as a Naga betel leaf seller, when the prince comes to meet his wife who is being punished in public she recognises her husband and, fearing that the officials might identify and capture him, addresses him as *peha* (paternal uncle) to add a second layer to his disguise. Gadapani leaves unrecognised (verse 86–87 in Bhuyan's edited *Asamar Padya Buranji*). What is notable is that despite the difference of valley and hills and that of communities (Ahom and Naga), the two layers of disguise did not exist as a rupture in the social and spatial mapping.

Along with literary evidence, there can also be other kinds of evidence to indicate how this trans-spatial nature of relations operated within a relation of shared idea and practice of space. In Stuart Blackburn's detailed folklore and anthropological study of the 'memories of migration' among the central Arunachal 'tribes', i.e., a group of communities inhabiting the lower Himalayas north of the Brahmaputra Valley, there are detailed accounts of how, in their social memories of migration, community formation and shared ancestry in legends and rituals as well as in their material culture, namely, their use of beads and their involvement in its trade between Myanmar to Tibet and beyond into China, the evidence of such trans-spatiality within a relation of shared socio-spatial mapping could be found (2003–2004: 15–60). What Blackburn's study highlights is that the trans-spatiality was not nomadism or a state of constant spatial movement. It was a nature of relation between community and space in which memories, material culture and writing were shared across space, despite each community being distinct from the other. Blackburn brings to light three kinds of evidence. One is that of speech forms. He notes that while in the 19th century and through much of the 20th-century linguistic anthropology emphasised on the central Arunachal communities as belonging to the Burma/China language family, in recent times, oral historians emphasise their speech forms as being more plausibly traceable to Tibet. To Blackburn, what is notable is that their speech forms have elements which share affinity with both the 'families' of languages. Besides the shared history of speech forms, Blackburn also highlights the nature of migration legends. Taking the example of the Apatani community, he indicates how the migration legends were not merely about the act of migration, but also about shared ancestry among all the different communities in the region which, in course of time, became distinct. Therefore, in the legends, they were different, but nevertheless shared elements of each other. The third kind of evidence Blackburn investigates is the extensive bead trade that took place between South Asia (Bengal), China and Burma, and Tibet to Central Asia. North-east India, Blackburn shows, was the zone through which much of the trade took place. As a result, from the northern Burma highlands, across the Patkai ranges, through the Brahmaputra Valley and into the lower Himalayas, the culture of beads became widely prevalent. But each community developed a distinct pattern of bead culture.

Once again, the notable point here is how despite differences in specific bead cultures, a shared material culture of beads was to be found across the entire region.

In each point that Blackburn discusses, there is a simultaneity of distinctiveness as well as shared imagination and practice of community and space. When such studies are collated with other sources, such as the Buranji tradition or neo-Vaishnava textual tradition, it is clear that the trans-Brahmaputra Valley as continental crossroad was not necessarily or only transnational 'flux'. More plausibly, it was a shared pattern of mapping community and space, *despite each being distinct and different from the other*. This is a point that most studies on continental crossroad (i.e., the trans-Brahmaputra Valley) as flux generally overlook.

From modes of pre-colonial mapping of space and community, one can move into the colonial and postcolonial periods. During these periods, a general contention which came to be widely used was that north-east India is a misnomer. It is argued that 'north-east India' was a term used by the British in the 19th century because the region was north-east to Calcutta or Bengal, the seat of colonial power during the period. Therefore, there is a mismatch between its name and its specificity as region. Thus the question — What it is as a region?

The answer provided was that it is a trans-spatial zone comprising the eastern borderland of India. The point can be illustrated through U. A. Shimray's critique of the concept of north-east India (2004: 4637–4643). Shimray argues that the colonial state used the term 'north-east frontier' after it colonised the Brahmaputra Valley and the neighbouring Indo-Burma Hills for strategic advantages. Shimray's main critique can be highlighted through the following. First, it is argued, 'In Independent India, the eastern Himalaya and the Brahmaputra Valley of the Indo-Myanmar frontier comprising the states of Assam, Arunachal Pradesh, Manipur, Mizoram, Tripura, Nagaland and Meghalaya is identified as single geographic unit and socio-economic identity' (ibid.: 4637) Second, it is argued that,

> The concept of north east India and the regional reorganization of this multi ethnic setting has done colossal damage in social, political and economic parameters. The region was earlier reorganized for administrative convenience, without considering ethnicity. ... Thus, over the years, this geographical entity, the social setting, economy,

politics and aspirations of the ethnic groups of the region was bunched together into one unit (ibid.).

Shimray's position is not different from that of Waddell or Baruah discussed earlier. To return to the history of colonial coinage of the term 'north-east India', R. B. Pemberton, in his 1835 report, referred to the region as the 'Eastern Frontier of Bengal'. Thereafter, various military and political administrators referred to it as 'frontier'. For example, Alexander Mackenzie titled his 1884 report as 'The North East Frontier of India' and Robert Reid titled his 1942 account as 'A History of Frontier Areas Bordering on the Province of Assam', published by the Government Press. There were other examples as well in this regard and importantly, these reports were major colonial reports of the time. The central question is whether the word 'frontier' was a descriptive or a conceptual classification.

Either termed as the 'eastern frontier' (Pemberton [1835] 1979) or the 'north-east frontier' (Mitchell [1883] 1973), it was during the colonial period that the region was transformed into a frontier. Therefore, whereas in the pre-colonial period the region had formed the continental crossroad *connecting* South Asia, East Asia and South East Asia, since the 19th century it had become the frontier that *separated* the British Empire or South Asia from the other two larger geo-spaces. How was this change realised? The colonial regime followed a conscious policy of transforming the region into an effective frontier. In this regard, a two-pronged strategy was followed, viz., (a) transforming the nature of the Brahmaputra Valley; and (b) transforming the historical relation of the Valley with neighbouring hills or mountains. Vis-à-vis transforming the nature of the Valley, one set of changes had a general colonial South Asian character, such as changes in land relation, forest policy, educational reforms, class formation and the setting up of a colonial administrative structure (Guha 1977; Saikia 2001). However, there were certain changes which were typical of the Valley, such as the tea plantations and social order within and without the plantations (Guha 1977); ethnicity and class formation in the plantations (Baruah 2008); recognising ethnicity as distinct from caste or class as a political category in the Valley (Pathak 2010: 61–69); and demographic reordering of the Valley through massive peasant resettlement (peasants from East Bengal or present-day Bangladesh) (Saikia 2005). The transformation in the relation of the Valley with the neighbouring hills/mountains was primarily in terms of the severing of the historical, socio-economic and culturally shared relation between the two geographies of habitation. The critical role in this transformation was played by the tea plantations. The enormity of the spatial scale of the plantation can be gauged from the fact that the Valley, throughout the 20th century, comprised the largest tea-producing area in the world and by the first decade of the 20th century, the spatial limits of expansion of the plantations was largely achieved (Baruah 2008). More direct assessment of the critical role of the plantations can be found in the two reports of John Mitchell ([1883] 1973) and Reid (1942).

Mitchell's report, a military one, highlights that the tea plantations need not serve only an economic function (providing an investment destination for colonial capital) but also a crucial military function. The spatial change through the plantations would help the colonial government to create a geography which could be controlled. The point was important because lack of control over the terrain was one of persistent strain in almost all military or administrative reports of the period on the region (Robb 1997: 245–83). It was since the 1860s that major military efforts were carried out by the colonial government to control the frontier. The report also discusses the disruptive impact of the plantation space on the traditional migration patterns in the region. While Mitchell's report belonged to a period of expansion of plantations in the Valley (1860s–1900s), Reid's report belonged to a period of consolidation of the plantations' military–economic paradigm. Reid argues that plantations played a major role in negotiating the relation between the Valley and the hills and that they needed to continue playing that role. Endorsing the colonial policy wherein in the name of self-defence the spatial frontier of the plantations was constantly pushed further into the socio-economic habitats of the people of the neighbouring hills to strategically control them, Reid argues that the policy was crucial to the management of the frontier and needed to be continued (1942). For example, endorsing R. B. McCabe's (Deputy Commisioner of Tezpur) views on the border between the Valley and the Naga Hills, Reid quotes McCabe: 'I have always argued that no final settlement of our relations with the Ao tribe could be obtained without a permanent occupation of the country. The interests of the tea planters demand that the hill tribes immediately bordering on the north east frontier should be under direct British control' (ibid.: 119) But Reid then cites the government's views (William Ward's letter) on this very question,

> All this annexation means further expenditure. ... The annexation of Mukokchung subdivision was due to the theory, started I think, by Sir Dennis Fitzpatrick, and adopted by India in which I have never agreed, viz., that political control of an area implies protection by us of that area from attacks of the area beyond. That practically means that to protect properly, we must annex and establish additional police outposts and establish political control of an area next beyond the area annexed, and so on, *ad infinitum*. (ibid.: 126).

Ward was opposed to extension of British territorial control. Sir Henry Cotton, then Chief Commissioner of Assam, agreed to Ward's views, but, in his letter (8 January 1897), stated, 'But there is always the risk of our hands being tied at any time' (ibid.). The plantations came up in the foothills, and it was also in the foothills that the British military and economic interests converged in the making of the frontier. This was evident from the position of Chief Commissioner Fuller, who succeeded Cotton. Fuller argued (Reid 1942: 132–33) that there were two strategic options available to the (colonial) Government of India regarding how to determine a viable border vis-à-vis the hills. One option, according to him, was to opt for a tribal boundary, i.e., an entire tribe is brought under control and their area becomes the boundary vis-à-vis those beyond control. The other option was to go for a natural boundary, such as rivers, which would be comprehensible, he argued, even to the local people as a boundary. However, Fuller argued that the first option was untenable because a tribe did not live in a designated area, i.e., they were scattered over the geographical space. The second option was untenable because it limited the scope for the British to manoeuvre vis-à-vis their requirements. Therefore, Fuller argued that a balance between the two options would have to be continued, as had been the practice. What is notable is that the balance was the foothills, which also had the plantations. Fuller was only endorsing the practice followed, and not advocating any new policy in this regard. It is in this context that Reid's endorsing of McCabe's views on plantation, space and boundary assumes significance.

What also needs to be noted here is that the foothills, classified as *khat*s in the pre-colonial Ahom kingdom (1228–1826), were free territories (only loosely under nominal Ahom control) in which socio-economic exchange relations between the people of the Valley and the hills/mountains could take place (Baruah 2008; Guha 1982: 478–505). The people of the hills/mountains required the foothills to have access to resources (and vice versa for the people of the Valley) as well as for movement/migration. It is important to note that the initial Ahom policy was to directly control the strategic foothills. But by the 16th century, the policy of *khat*s was in place as a mechanism to avoid choking the hills/mountains and gaining in return an end to the persistent armed raids into the Valley (for resources and routes of movement/migration). Tea plantations since the 1860s came up in these very foothills. It is in this context that the strategic contentions of the two reports (out of many) noted above on frontier management needs to be historically situated.

The Brahmaputra Valley was a central piece in the colonial strategic planning of the north-east frontier. Colonialism transformed the Valley from a continental crossroad to a frontier (Baruah 2010). Becoming a frontier meant a new order of space in terms of forest and wasteland policy (Siddiqui 1990) as well as plantations as vast tracts of planned industrial spaces coming up in the foothills. As a result villages, village commons and migration routes along with the strategic foothills were appropriated into the new order of socio-spatial relations.

The introduction of 'order' was also to be seen at the social level, especially with the introduction of a new category of people, viz. the workers, who were imported from central India through the indenture system (1862–1926). In the second half of the 19th century and early 20th century, it comprised one of the largest forms of forced internal displacement within British India. At the level of social demography, another fundamental change was in the policy of settling peasants from east Bengal in the vast tracts of fertile land in the Valley. The colonial government argued that the settlement took place in the *char* areas (alluvial islands) of the Brahmaputra which were not used for agriculture by the local inhabitants. However, the growing numbers of popular protests over grazing space and contest over land in the Valley made it clear that as in the case of wasteland policy, the policy of peasant settlement also involved displacement of the local people from land. The Valley was historically sparsely populated. The colonial policy of peasant settlement argued that peasant settlement would help increase revenue from the trans-Brahmaputra Valley. The colonial view was later also adopted in historical studies on the issue. But what was overlooked was (a) the sheer quantum of settlement; and (b) the fact that violent conflict over common grazing and forest space had emerged as an issue even by the first decades of the 20th century. In fact, in recognition of the problem the line system was instituted in 1920 by which territories for the migrant peasants and the local people were demarcated and separated. The approach of positive land–man ratio does not explain such developments.

Tea plantation could be seen as one of the forms of land reclamation or appropriation into the colonial order. The reclaimed land was not 'wasteland' as most government reports tended to notify and as most early historiography on tea plantations (such as the classic studies of Antrobus 1957; Griffiths 1967) argued. Therefore, they were not 'wastelands' which were transformed into 'civilised' space. Rather, they were *reproduction* of space in the colonial order. Reproduction of space could be traced to the pre-colonial period as well. Returning once again to the *Katha Guru Charit*, especially Part Four, the accounts of Sankardeb's travels from the central to the western valley provide ample evidence of spatial reproduction. Among others, the case elaborated in detail in this regard was the reproduction of Barpeta as an institutional centre of Sankari culture (Barpeta continues to be one of the most important centres of Sankari culture even today). Sankardeb was immensely attracted to the natural beauty of Barpeta, which the text describes as a *beel*, i.e., a large lake created by river floods. Sankardeb and his group of followers cleared the forest in the area, built houses and created several village settlements (Part Four, 2494–2498). Besides Barpaeta, there were other accounts of reproduction of space in the text, for example, as in the case of the Barabhuyans (Sankardeb's forefathers) when they were forced to move from place to place creating settlements, attacked as they were by different communities (before the birth of Sankardeb). However, three points can be noted when such spatial reproductions in the Valley are compared to that practised during the colonial period. First, the scale of the reproduction of space was infinitely smaller compared to that of the colonial period, as seen in the case of the tea plantations. Second, whether or not reproduction of spaces in the Sankari culture was transformation of nature into settlements, it is not clear to what extent such transformations affected the social relations of people, especially as they grew into larger settlements in the course of time. Third, what was fundamentally lacking in the Sankari process was a consciousness that a large-scale reproduction of space into an order was being carried out. The constantly shifting or indeterminate articulation of the idea of Assam, outlined earlier, clearly indicates that the question of order was more a social than a spatial consciousness.

If the *Katha Guru Charit* is a text which gives evidence from the central to the western valley, then the practice of the Ahom *paik* system can be taken as evidence of the situation from the central to the eastern valley. The *paik* system, often traced to similar practices found widely throughout South East Asia (given that the Ahoms themselves came from there and settled in the Valley in the 13th century), was a practice of control over people. 20th-century historical studies gave the *paik* system an economic interpretation, viz. as a system of 'forced labour' when surplus appropriation (or its forms) was not sufficiently developed and institutionalised in the Valley (Guha 1982).[3] However, when the practice is seen vis-à-vis the Ahom *khat* policy or vis-à-vis the consciousness of space

---

[3] The *paik* system needs further study. First, the focus on fixed labour services under the Ahom *paik* system (and not unlimited or 'bonded' services) rather than revenue collection in the form of taxes needs to be contextualised in a political economy marked with indeterminate relation between community and space (or people and land). This socio-spatial indeterminacy (from the point of view of revenue collection) was premised on the historical and geographical nature of the region. As already noted, the *khat* system (or foothills as 'free' spaces) can also be seen as part of the nature of this region. One of the most authoritative interpretations of the system by Amalendu Guha has been that it was a militia system of labour extraction, similar to those in Thailand and Vietnam and in the Imphal Valley, and was necessitated by state formation in a largely tribal base in the Brahmaputra Valley (1982: 478–82). Guha highlights two other points in this regard, namely, in place of land measurement, under the Ahoms, there used to be head count (or rudimentary form of census) and that in the absence of a strong cash economy, militia labour service was the only form available for surplus appropriation to create and

in Sankari culture, it is quite possible to consider that in a context when space was not mapped as a distinct order of territory, terrain and people, as well as when the space overwhelmed the size of the population inhabiting it, control over people was far more effective a mechanism to govern than control over a delimited territory and terrain. What is notable in this regard is that the Ahoms practised a rudimentary form of census operation (head count) of its people rather than land measurement in its base area of the central to the eastern valley. The British abolished the *paik* system as a system of forced labour.[4] The fact that the Inner Line Regulation (1873) came up as an acknowledgement of the difficulty (improbability?) of a fixed order of territory, terrain and people in the trans-Brahmaputra Valley could also be taken as testimony to the proportion of its improbability in the pre-colonial period. The important point here, however, is that despite the difficulty, though not the neighbouring hills, but the Valley was certainly identified as the space which *needed* to be reproduced into a new socio-spatial order during the colonial period. Colonialism,

---

sustain a state. Guha characterises the Ahom political economy as 'quasi-feudal'. But it needs to be explored and researched that in the given context of relation between community and space, and in the context of shared mapping of this relation despite the consciousness of difference, whether classifications such as 'tribal' or 'quasi-feudal' sufficiently explain the distinctiveness of the region. It is evident that Guha's approach is firmly situated in the Marxist framework of state formation in which absolute sovereignty and process of surplus appropriation are key components. Thus, any deviation from this standard falls under classifications as 'tribal' or 'quasi-feudal'. In the case of the Valley, I have shown that neither absolute sovereignty of the state nor meaningful surplus appropriation were possible. This was so not because of the 'tribal' nature of social formation but due to the very nature of the region under discussion. As I will indicate towards the conclusion of this study, even in the present times, some these problems persist despite everything of a 'state' system being in place.

[4] Though the *paik* system was abolished as forced labour, the colonial state made extensive use of 'coolie' labour, a new form of forced labour, to clear roads, make new roads or to help in the transportation of goods and people. In fact, Geoffrey Evans and Antony Brett-James (1962) recounting of their World War II experience is a graphic portrayal of how the colonial state fought much of the World War II in the Patkai Hills (or Naga Hills) against the Japanese using coolie labour.

as a political economy, had the capacity to do it, which the pre-colonial political economies of the Valley simply lacked. The order of colonial spatial reproduction and spatial consciousness were, therefore, fundamentally different from the peculiar 'fluidities' of shared mapping of space and people of the pre-colonial period.

The question of the Inner Line Regulation had already been raised. A detailed discussion of the Regulation can be found in Alexander Mackenzie's administrative report ([1884] 1989). The Regulation demarcated the territories that were to be directly administered by the colonial government in the north-east frontier and those which were to be left beyond the pale of colonial territorial jurisdiction, but nominal control would be exercised for safeguarding the British Empire. An example of the policy in the latter case was National Highway 39 (NH 39), which the British developed to strategically connect the Brahmaputra Valley with Myanmar (or Burma). The Highway proved crucial for the British in World War II while fighting the Japanese army and Azad Hind Fauz (Evans and Brett-James 1962). It ran through the Naga Hills and the Imphal Valley before entering Myanmar. The territory required to be controlled directly for the security of the Highway was directly administered after waging bloody wars with the local Naga communities while the rest of the territories in the Naga Hills were left as un-administered territories (Kumar 2007: 218–32). The Imphal Valley was governed by a subordinate prince. The same can also be said of the making of the road from Rani via Nungklow to Sylhet. Despite resistance from the Khasi people, 'Troops were immediately called up from Sylhet and Kamrup, and vigorous reprisals were undertaken' (Gait [1905] [1926] 1994: 287).

Two points must be emphasised here. The Inner Line Regulation did not prevent the British from taking absolute control over territories which they deemed strategically important. Second, as part of the Regulation, the Brahmaputra Valley was to be completely controlled and directly administered. The control was not only for economic reasons (tea and petroleum) but also strategic. It was a unique military–economic colonial complex designed for the Valley. Therefore, the entire colonial administrative system was introduced in the Valley, which was in sharp contrast to the rest of the frontier.

One the most significant examples of the frontier transformed into an 'order' was the discourse of 'Assamese' identity that came into existence in the 19th century. Saikia (2004: 77–144) argues, based on the Buranjis, that in the pre-colonial period, the term of reference of the self in the eastern Brahmaputra Valley was *kunhow*, i.e., 'us', which was a vague conglomerate of various people with their specificities left indeterminate. The similarity of the 'us' to be found in neo-Vaishnava literature (Neog 1963), i.e., in the central and the western valley, and the lack of a defined concept of the other as in the Buranjis, highlighted the condition of identitarian overlapping that marked societal composition and formation in the Valley. Numerous Buranjis were written/commissioned by the Ahom nobility and the kings. As mentioned earlier, another important feature of socio-spatial mapping in the Buranjis was that the genealogical heroes that they traced were shared by several communities in the region as well as in Myanmar (ibid.), an example of the shared mapping across differences that characterised the region till the 19th century. It is in this context that Saikia's contention of the term 'Assamese' as a defined people in the 19th century being a colonial invention assumes importance. Saikia argues that the invention of the term to refer to a defined people in the Valley was a colonial device to create a uniform economic category of peasants out of the multitude of communities which could be calculated/counted and taxed.

The early colonialists frequently remarked on the high heterogeneity in social composition of the Valley and the region in general vis-à-vis the mainland of British India. The colonial tax regime in the Valley could be studied in this context too. For example Edward Gait, in his *History of Assam* ([1905] [1926] 1994), which could very well be treated as an authoritative government report on 'Assam', uses 'tribe' and 'caste' with a thin margin of difference. For example, whereas communities like the Rabhas or Kacharis were classified as 'tribe' (ibid.: 1), the Koch community, which is a part of the Bodo Kachari group, was classified as 'caste'. Gait writes, 'In the Brahmaputra Valley Koch, formerly the name of a tribe, has beome a caste which admits proselytes to Hinduism from the ranks of the Kacharis and other aboriginal tribes' (ibid.: 8). But he also adds that, 'And yet, in the Brahmaputra valley, large sections of the population are still outside the pale of Hinduism or in the lower stages of conversion, where their adopted religion still sits lightly on them' (ibid.: 9). This condition of social classification can be compared to the taxation policy and its problems (for the

British). Gait comments on David Scott, the first Commissioner of Assam, 'He was most persistent in his efforts to correct the worst abuses, ... but his energies, and those of his assistants, were in the main, directed to the assessment and collection, of revenues' (ibid.: 278). Tax was converted into the form of money by the British. Gait comments on its problems thus,

> The duty of collecting this tax was entrusted to the old staff of khel officials, but the paiks of the different khels have become so scattered that this method of realizing government dues was found most tedious and uncertain ... The method of collection was changed from personal to territorial basis' (ibid.: 279).

As a footnote, Gait shows how the colonial *mauza* or revenue unit in Assam was different in its meaning and practice from the colonial *mauza* in Bengal. The problem that the British faced till the middle of the 19th century was differential tax systems for communities inhabiting the same area. For example, after defeating the Bar Senapati, chief of the Matak people, in 1835, the Bar Senapati was to pay tribute in cash, and the arrangement allowed to him was, 'three rupees per head in case of Morans and Kacharis, two rupees eight annas for Bihis or gold washers, and two rupees for ordinary Assamese' (ibid.: 277).

Colonial records clearly indicate that colonial revenue collection was directly linked to establishing a fixed order of relation between community and space (or people and land), i.e., territorialising the people. This was especially with regard to the central and eastern parts of the Valley, which were also the core base of the plantation political economy, and to control which it took the longest for the colonial state. Reid ([1942] 1983) shows that territorialising the communities, whether in the Valley, foothills or hills, was of prime concern to the colonial state, and immediately after demarcating a fixed territory (of settlement and mobility) for a given community, tax was imposed on the people. In the Valley, where wet rice cultivation was practised, there was both land tax and house tax, besides tax on trade and commodities. In the hills only shifting agriculture was practised. Therefore, house tax and tax on trade and commodities was imposed.

This is what lends credence to Saikia's claim that the fact that the term 'Assamese' was made broader towards the close of the century was to bring about an order and uniformity in revenue measurement and collection. But by the last quarter of the 19th century it got entwined with the question of nationhood, and 'Assamese' came to be circulated by the local bourgeois leadership as a defined political identity. Two other points in this regard can also be taken into account when discussing the order that the Valley was being transformed into. First, unlike for the hills/mountains where the classification of people (or 'tribes' as they were called) were (colonial) anthropological categories, the classification of 'Assamese' was vaguely defined as the people inhabiting the Valley. It was located somewhere between 'tribe' and 'caste' or the degree of 'Hinduisation', which Gait himself, however, admitted had been of a thin margin. But importantly, the nuances were slowly withdrawn from revenue measurements. Second, vis-à-vis the order of 'Assamese' identity, the correlation between (modern) Assamese language and the space of the Valley could be traced to the latter half of the 19th century only, in which both the colonialists and the local bourgeoisie complemented each other, though based on their respective interests.

In recent times, James C. Scott has exercised considerable influence on scholarship on north-east India. The influence had been on the question of the historical relation of social spaces, i.e., between hills/mountains and valleys and the question of frontier. Sanjib Baruah, endorsing Scott's work, argues, 'James C. Scott's distinction between state spaces and non-state spaces gives us a comparative handle on the region's well known linguistic and ethnic diversity' (2009). One of the world's 'largest, if not the largest remaining non-state spaces,' writes Scott, is 'The vast expanse of uplands from northeastern India and eastern Bangladesh through Burma, northern Thailand, three provinces of southwestern China, most of Laos, and much of upland Vietnam all the way to the Central Highlands.' Historically, this vast region's ethnic landscape has had been a 'bewildering and intercalated 'gradients' of cultural traits' (Scott 2000: 21–22). In the case of the Nagas of north-east India and Burma, for instance, ethnographers and missionaries engaged in a struggle 'to make sense of the ethnographic chaos they perceived around them: hundreds, if not thousands, of small villages seemed to be somewhat similar to each other but also very different, by no means always sharing the same customs, political system, art or even language (Jacobs et al. 1990: 23)' (Baruah 2009: 7). Based on this foundation, Baruah then argues,

Contemporary North east India's linguistic and cultural diversity reflects the resilience of a historic non state space despite powerful odds. For pre-colonial states such as the valley states of Assam (the Ahom state), Manipur, and Tripura, the project of transforming non-state spaces into state spaces was, to borrow Scott's phrase, no more than 'a mere glint in the eye'. But the colonial state as well as the post colonial Indian state is able to mobilize unprecedented amount of resources to realise such a project' (ibid.: 8).

Thereafter, Baruah tries to understand migration in this context when he says,

> The expansion of agriculture has also meant massive immigration into the region from other parts of the subcontinent, and increases in the density of population, and along with it, the minoritization of many indigenous communities, and the fear of other such communities of becoming minorities. In that sense the Northeast Indian story is part of the larger story that Scott outlines: the 'world's last great enclosure movement' taking over the vast Asian transnational non-state space 'albeit clumsily and with setbacks' (Scott 2006: 4–5)' (ibid.: 9).

Scott forwards a framework to understand the relation between hills and valleys with reference to South East Asia (2009). He argues that valleys had been the core of state-making projects in terms of land, wet rice agriculture and concentration of population. The role of river routes added to the formation. In contrast, the hills had been the space of refuge for those who chose not to be governed. In modern nation-building projects, which are premised on absolute sovereignty of the state, this historical character in the relation between the hills and the valleys needs to be noted while addressing issues like national space and nation states. Nevertheless, when Scott's framework is applicable in the case of the north-east frontier and its processes of historical formations, some of the significant differences can be pointed out. Neither the pre-colonial sources (such as pre-Sankari or Sankari narratives or the Ahom Buranjis) nor the colonial sources (such as colonial military and administrative records or the Assamese travel writings) or even modern literary narratives show the hills as a refuge for those not being governed. This variety of sources highlight that the people or communities inhabiting the hills had their own systems of governance, whether or not characterised as 'state' systems. Further, they note that habitation in the hills had been as historical as it had been in the valleys. Unlike Scott's argument, those inhabiting the hills came to be characterised as barbarians or savages only from the colonial period onwards. Pre-colonial sources give no evidence that the Valley (i.e., the Brahmaputra Valley) characterised the inhabitants of the hills as barbarians. As discussed later, the relation between people and space was mapped in terms of shared socio-spatial relations among communities. Therefore, the vagueness or indeterminacy in the 'us' and 'them' of the Buranjis could be considered as characteristic of the larger socio-spatial relations of the period.

A significant historical component between the hills and the Valley in the region had been the foothills. Whether in the Ahom or in the colonial period, the role of the foothills remained crucial. In other words, the foothills functioned as the symbiotic link between the valleys and the hills rather than leaving the two as confronting opposites. Colonial strategic planning recognised and acted upon this critical role of the foothills in the making of the frontier. If state making of the Ahom period is seen in its strict definition of determinate institutionalised relation between territory, governance and people, then even the Valley would not successfully stand a scrutiny. The *khat* or the *paik* systems were only two examples of frameworks to accommodate the reality of the indeterminacy of the relation. In other words, not only the hills but even the valleys, in that case, would have to be characterised as in a condition of 'anarchy'. But what changed with colonialism (and thereafter) was that the indeterminacy was rearranged. The relation between the valleys, foothills and hills were altered and brought within a new framework, namely, a frontier. Transformation of this relation in turn affected the social and political processes within each of these spatial components as well. The trans-Brahmaputra Valley was especially carved into a determinate order of the frontier, which was to serve as a signifier of its lack in the neighbouring highlands. In the process, the historical shared domains of socio-spatial relations were systematically eroded, now replaced by 'orders' of differences. Therefore, if there is a relation of contradiction in contemporary socio-spatial mapping, it is embedded in the very order of the frontier brought about through colonialism and not in the incomplete process of historical state formation as Baruah would surprisingly argue. The problem of the contradiction is not that communities are trans-spatial in nature and yet struggling for defined spaces (ethnic space) or that they cannot be accommodated within national spaces. The problem could well be that they exist (or are made to exist) in a given form of relation which came about as a historical break to the shared socio-spatial mapping across differences practised in the region, a mediating space which had been systematically withdrawn by both the colonial and postcolonial states in the process of making and perpetuating it as a frontier. It can very well be that if the shared mapping is regenerated, it would no longer remain a frontier but what was proposed before Independence as a confederacy of peoples by those like Bishnu Rabha (Assam), Phizo (Naga Hills) or Irabot (Manipur).

In his desire to design north-east India on the lines of the Turner thesis, subtly mixed with Scott's views, Sanjib Baruah writes vis-à-vis the Indian Look East Policy (i.e., economic integration with East and South East Asia while political integration with India or South Asia),

> The Look East Policy, in the words of a former External Affairs ministry official, 'envisages the north east region not as the periphery of India, but as the centre of a thriving and integrated economic space linking two dynamic regions with a network of highways, railways, pipelines, transmission lines crisscrossing the region (2009: 1).

Thereafter, Baruah states, 'Yet the exceptional efforts on the part of India's foreign policy establishment to explain the benefits of the Look East Policy probably reflect the expectation that convincing the locals of those benefits would translate into reduced sympathy for the region's rebel groups' (ibid.: 2). But where does Baruah locate the gap between foreign policy expectation and local response in this regard? He argues,

> The restrictions on land and labour markets are the legacies of the boundaries drawn by British colonial rulers between the spaces of law and spaces of custom. Today, they serve multiple goals including national security and protective discrimination for scheduled tribes (STs). It is hard to imagine that these restrictions would end without the political resolution of key conflicts. Yet their incompatibility with the vision of a dynamic transnational economic space is rather obvious' (ibid.: 2).

As I showed earlier, Baruah locates these political problems of key conflicts which create the gap between foreign policy expectations and local response in Scott's transnational framework. In this light, the removal of these problems would entail nationalising the transnational space. But that itself has been the problematic now for more than half a century!

Though it is not a part of this study, I would still like to indicate another strategic silence in this emerging discourse of 'borderland' that seeks to undermine the concept of frontier for the region. The Indian State's claim to *legitimate* violence is in the Indian Constitution. Yet, to govern the region, since the 1950s the state has legislated extra-constitutional powers (or special powers), i.e., powers which the Constitution does not otherwise give the State; this provides an unprecedented handle to the Indian military to participate in governance. The State's claim of the 'rebels' being forces of illegitimate violence is based on the principle that their violence is not constitutional. Therefore, it is pertinent to ask what constitutes 'unconstitutional' violence in the region. The second silence in the discourse of 'borderland' is that if nationalising the borderland has been precisely a structural problem (due to colonial policies and their impact) despite the availability and use of the 'democratic' mechanism of elected governments, how plausible can be the expectation that economic 'benefits' from transnational trade are necessarily the solution to the structural problem? In other words, if nationalising the borderland has been a failed democratic political project, then what is the basis of conceiving its viability as an economic project? Last, Baruah is strangely silent on the question that if transnational social space is the problem (following Scott), then rather than further attempts at nationalising (despite the historical experience of its political failure), what prevents the possibility of exploring the framework of autonomy for the region, based on a common politics from within, through which it will more successfully participate in the transnational paradigm of economy as the Indian state envisages? As discussed later, there is a substantial body of evidence of attempts in the region at a common politics from within, with culture being a prime area of theory and practice in this regard, since the late 19th century.

Scott's main area of study is South East Asia in general. Yet, it is important to refer to his work because it forms a part of increasing body of knowledge on north-east India which seeks to interpret 'borderland' as merely a collection of transnational differences rather than as a concrete socio-political reality, with its different components historically–structurally related to one another. It is undoubtedly true that Scott differs here from the framework of 'connected histories' that Sanjay Subrahmanyam has been following for more than a decade now (Subrahmanyam 2005). Through 'connected histories', Subrahmanyam tries to show how from Eurasia to South Asia and to South East Asia, there have been major historical, social and spatial connections. These connections were in the terms of trade, travel, kinds of literature or exchanges of culture. There is an enormous body of textual sources that highlighted how histories of these different continental blocks have been rather interrelated. Scott argues for ruptures whereas Subrahmanyam argues for connections. The important point here is that the north-east region, especially the trans-Brahmaputra Valley, as a historical continental crossroad shared elements of both the approaches, namely, it was different from the adjoining continental blocks but it also connected these blocks. Becoming a frontier in the 19th century was, therefore, a historical watershed.

Boddhisattva Kar carried out a meticulous study of the above condition vis-à-vis the trans-Brahmaputra Valley (2009: 49–77). However, his study also highlights the problems that emerge when the relation between geography, politics and economy is not situated in the making of a specific region, namely, frontier. For example, Kar begins his argument by posing the question of whether the Inner Line Regulation, formulated to distinguish between colonial civilisation and the savagery of 'slavery, nomadism and headhunting' of the hills was one of colonial perspectives only, or was it a euphemism to rationalise colonial political necessities. His research led him to compile endless evidence that creating a 'boundary' between colonial territory and those beyond was far less a matter of anthropological perspectives as it was of having an *effective* frontier. In pursuit of a viable colonial frontier, the line of boundary (Inner Line) could be made to change. To quote Kar on this point,

> Too much attention to the rhetoric of fixity has blinded us to the plain fact that contrary to its claim to the givenness of the distinction between the hills and the plains, the Inner Line was in fact a revisable,

mobile, and plaint boundary on the ground. Well until the second decade of the twentieth century, the Line was repeatedly redrawn in order to variously accommodate the expansive compulsions of plantation capital, the recognition of the imperfection in survey maps, the security anxiety of the state, and the adaptive practices of internally differentiated local communities. If new tea or coal tracts were found or valuable forest areas were reported to exist beyond the Line, small insertions in the Government Gazette casually declared unblushing extensions of the Inner Line to include those areas (ibid.: 55).

The next significant issue that Kar raises is that of *posa*, or a 'tribute' that the colonial state paid to some of the hill communities in exchange for the surety that they would not attack the plains. The colonial regime was continuing with a tradition which the Ahom system had earlier followed. Once again, Kar begins with the question of perspective: Was *posa* a blackmail into which the colonial system had succumbed to and which, therefore, needed to be discontinued? However, he successfully shows that the perspective among some British officers (for example, John McCosh) might as much have been a euphemism to hide the skilful colonial logic behind making the payment. Kar shows that by continuing the practice of *posa* payment, the colonial system rationalised the complete occupation of the foothills (for the plantations), i.e., a space which historically did not belong to any polity, ensured that mobility of the hill communities could be effectively monitored as the routes of mobility lay through the plains and foothills and, finally, integrated the hills with the cash economy of the colonial regime that had been firmly established in the Brahmaputra Valley. All three rationales behind the colonial *posa* practice were a fundamental break from the Ahom practice of *posa*.

If there is one point that Kar's meticulous study emphatically establishes, it is that the relation between the Valley and the hills was fundamentally rearranged from what it was in the pre-colonial period. If the point is pursued further, it is quite evident that what was being created through this rearrangement was indeed a specific kind of region, namely, frontier. Yet, it is also the point that Kar refuses to acknowledge. In fact, he argues towards the conclusion of his own analysis,

> Nobody but the commissioned-to-be-ignorant believes today that the Indian nation-state is an eternal and organic verity. ... However, contrary to another common assumption, nothing additional is

to be gained by prioritizing the 'region' over the 'nation'. It will be naïve to think that the regions are somewhat more durable, more historical, and more authentic than the nations, precisely because the seemingly more homogenous space of the region is also an effect, and not the natural theatre, of the same historical practices through which the tempting forms of national internality and territorial coherence are generated, understood and performed (Kar 2009: 71).

What is ironic about the conclusion is the refusal to see the fact that a region need not be an eternal entity with intrinsic properties, but is a set of socio-spatial relations in any given area and changes in the nature of the relation also leads to a change in what 'region' that given area is. Therefore, the rearrangement in the relation between the hills and valleys since the 19th century left a definite praxis of relation, namely, frontier, in north-east India while it was a continental crossroad earlier. One of the failures in Kar's eventual conclusion is not to recognise that a frontier, and not a transnational 'borderland', does exist. Kar poses that selective or strategic use of violence by the Indian State, the reality of differences in the relation between the various communities and their failure to emerge with a common politics or the fact that the State provides the people with 'easy money' (i.e., like the earlier colonial *posa*) were all practised by the colonial state. But if the argument is pushed further, then one has to ask if there has never been a postcolonial (change) in that sense (which is indeed true), what does it then highlight? Kar never asked that question. The answer can only be that the 'problematics' (as Kar puts it vis-à-vis 'when was the postcolonial') has to be situated in the fact of frontier, in its making and perpetuation. If there has never been a change since the 19th century, it is necessary to ask whether it is because the praxis of the relation in geography and people continues to operate with the same principle of frontier as the British created.

Conclusion

The line of argument I have pursued in my understanding of region formation in the trans-Brahmaputra Valley has been one of regions as socio-spatial relations. I have tried to show that if region formation is seen in a longer historical perspective rather than as a collection of identities in constant conflict with one another, the trans-Brahmaputra Valley can be better explained as forms of relations among communities which inhabit the space. The other issue that I have tried to address is that a given historical geography need not be seen as an essential region throughout history. Change in socio-spatial relations can lead to change in the region that historical geography transforms into. The shift that the trans-Brahmaputra Valley experienced from a continental crossroad to a frontier demonstrates the point. In this regard, I would argue that frameworks such as trans-regional or transnational are premised on assumptions of rigid structures, and invariably on notions of modern nation states. Such frameworks generally fail to explain long-term shifts in region formation, as seen in the case of the trans-Brahmaputra Valley. Unlike in most major contemporary studies on the area, I have also tried to highlight that the socio-spatial relations that constitute a given region formation can be meaningfully understood through a dialectical approach. Thus, while the pre-colonial dialectics in this regard was shared mapping of relations across differences which perpetuates a continental crossroad, the dialectics of colonial frontier was in terms of binary opposites as 'order' or lack of it, valley and hills, 'civilised' and 'savage'. They were not merely discourses but also institutional practices practised by the colonial state and the colonised alike in the trans-Brahmaputra Valley. The dialectics could also hold the key to understanding why there was a constant pressure in the period to frame identity as orders of 'tribe' or 'ethnic', i.e., what could be defined as specific and different from the others. The development of 'modern Assamese' language and narrative forms is riddled with this dialectic as well. This dialectical approach, though, varies from the one associated with the Turner thesis. My approach is not focused on the eventual synthesis, which characterises what the nature of the region would be. It is a historical approach where the emphasis is on the dynamics of the socio-spatial relations. In other words, it discounts the teleology of the Turner thesis. Therefore, I disagree with the view that a frontier is the historical process of becoming a region. I argue that frontier too is a 'region' since it is the relations that distinguish a region and not what it becomes at some point of time. This approach also provides the opportunity to envisage political action based on the nature of the socio-spatial relations that constitute a region. Thus, while most studies focus on how a common politics from within is improbable in the trans-Brahmaputra Valley, I argue that if the mediating space of shared mapping of socio-spatial relations across differences could be regenerated, a common politics from within might indeed be possible. The nature of the shared mapping would certainly be different from what it was in the pre-colonial period. But if it is possible to identify the fact that relations of contradiction are not essential to the Valley, and that they are only characteristic to the Valley being part of a frontier, then it could indeed also be possible to devise political action which regenerates new forms of shared mapping across the differences. One of the attempts of this book is precisely to highlight the efforts made through literature on how to regenerate shared mapping across differences in the Valley. Such regeneration would once again transform the trans-Brahmaputra Valley from a frontier into something else as a region. It is time to begin conceiving that future.

2

Buranjis and Sankari Culture: Language and Narrative in Pre-colonial Textual Traditions

The Buranjis: Mapping Socio-Spatial Relations

In my study of cultural forms, the focus is on how textual traditions of the trans-Brahmaputra had mapped socio-spatial relations. It is in line with my argument that in the analysis of continental crossroad or frontier emphasis needs to be on the mapping of relations rather than mapping of the self or the other. It is in the historical shifts of mapping relations that the specificity of the frontier and its cultural forms can be identified. I had argued that while shared mapping of socio-spatial relations across differences characterised the area as continental crossroad, socio-spatial relations as relations of contradictions came to distinguish it as a frontier. The first textual tradition I take up in this chapter is the Buranji tradition. The Buranjis were chronicles written or commissioned by the different noble families or royal clans. Buranjis recorded the past and often, until the time that they were being written, were in prose. Some 19th century Buranjis were written in verse as well. They were written in Tai-Ahom language or Sibsagar Assamese language. Sibsagar Assamese was the variant of the language which was practised in the eastern part of the Valley. However, the verse Buranjis were written in Kamrupi Assamese of the western Brahmaputra Valley. By the close of the 19th century, this tradition of historical chronicling was replaced by 'modern' history writing. Quantitatively, Buranjis comprise a very large volume of texts or chronicles. Today, they are preserved in different museums and archives across Assam. However, a large number of Buranjis are still in private possession of families. In this chapter, I will try to highlight the interrelatedness of three issues vis-à-vis the Buranjis: (a) the nature of Buranji chronicling; (b) the worldview that they represent; and (c) Buranjis and forms of cultural appropriation.

The first Buranji I take up is the Purani AsomBuranji. One of the oldest of the Buranjis, the Purani Asom Buranji was recovered by the Baptist missionaries and serially published in the magazine *Orunudoi* between 1850 and 1852. It was written in Sibsagar Assamese. The Buranji begins with the Ahom origin myth. The myth is summarised in the Introduction to the Buranji (by the missionaries) quite aptly thus (translation mine):

> In some old Ahom manuscripts (*puthis*), it is said that human beings were created from gourd. In some other manuscripts, it is said that Indra and Sashi were roaming in sage Basistha's flower garden. Basistha's ashram was to the east of Sadiya (on the banks of the Brahmaputra and bordering on the lower Himalaya ranges). Baistha was furious and cursed Indra. But Indra transformed into a giant and, seeing a beautiful woman, copulated with her. She became pregnant, and finally gave birth to Thenkam. Khunlung and Khunlai were Thenkam's sons (*Orunudoi* 1850: 461).

The Buranjis generally narrate that the Ahoms were descendants of Indra's grandsons Khunlung and Khunlai. The Ahoms were therefore born out of the union of god and human. However, I will show that this origin myth does not stand as the Indo-Gangetic appropriation of the Tibet–Brahmaputra–Myanmar worldview; on the contrary, it was the reverse which was achieved through the origin myth. The Purani Asom Buranji narrates that Khunlung and Khunlai later left Mungri Mungram and entered Laidoi. The rulers of Laidoi had failed to rule and therefore had crossed the Brahmaputra along with their followers (i.e., into present-day Assam), trying to establish their rule in Praphrunpou. But the migrants had to wage battle with the people of Praphrunpou. Later, it was a Naga who became king of the kingdom. However, the people were dissatisfied with the new ruler, and invited the group of Khunlung and Khunlai to rule the kingdom. Khunlai's son was made king. In the meantime, both the brothers fell out and Khunlung, before departing for heaven, made his son the king of Mungri Mungram. The Buranji gives a detailed family tree thereafter and indicates the movement of clans across space to carve out their own political domains. These domains range from the northern Shan highlands of Myanmar, especially on the Myanmar side of the Patkai ranges as well as the Brahmaputra Valley across the Patkai. It was as part of these constant movements across space that Sukapha, credited to be the first Ahom ruler, decided to cross the Patkai and enter the Brahmaputra Valley. Two points are notable in this very introductory phase of the Buranji and they remain a constant feature of the Buranji throughout. First, the calendar followed was the Tai Lakli calendar. Yet, the word *saka* was appended to the chronological dating. For example, the Buranji began (translation mine), 'In Saka Lakli Taosinga, there was a great flood' (*Orunudoi* 1850: 461) or, 'In Saka Lakli Katrao, Sukhranpha became the king' (ibid.: 874) Towards the end of the Buranji, a detailed table of the dating method is provided. Second, the word *ahom* does not occur anywhere, and it does not occur throughout the Buranji either. The only criterion followed to distinguish communities or spaces is 'us' and 'them'. The idea of foreign is not a part of this distinguishing criterion. 'Us' and 'them' were more of groups competing for power over space and people which was part of a shared socio-spatial mapping. But importantly, as I will show later, people who came from the Indo-Gangetic area were clearly referred to as 'Bongal', i.e., foreigners. Though Bengal was the immediate western neighbour, it was used as a generic term for all foreigners.

The framework of 'us' and 'them' can be traced in the Buranji in different contexts. For example, on who controlled the Khamzang, Tipam and Aiton people (they can be found from the Valley to the Shan area of Myanmar), the Buranji said (translation mine),

> Ours and Nara's messengers have not been received in each other's court for eight years now. Also, Mung Khamzang, Mung Tipam and Mung Aiton have not paid their dues neither to us nor to the Nara king. Therefore, our king Sudangpha sent his message with mesenger Tapongmao on Saka Lakli Mungseo to the Nara king Surungpha that Khamzang, Tipam and Aiton are under my rule. They have not given their dues to you or me. Therefore, I have decided to attack them and take control of the situation ... When Nara king Surungpha received the message, he sent for his brother Tipam's views on why he hadn't paid his dues (*Orunudoi* 1850: 495).

The Nara kingdom was across the Patkai Mountains, on the side of present-day Myanmar. The same classification of 'us' and 'them' can be found in their conflict with the Nagas who inhabited the Patkai Mountains. For example, in the reign of Tyeopha Susen the Nagas attacked the 'us' of the Buranji. 'Many Nagas were hiding in the forest armed with spears and daos (i.e., hatchets). But later they came out of the forest and fought with our men. Our men were careless. Many of our men died in the battle' (ibid.: 495). The Patkai was an important factor in relations among communities in the entire region. For example, the Buranji stated (translation mine), 'In Lakli Katseo, the Nara people from Khamzang came to our king to complain that due to the Naga depredations, it has become impossible to live there' (*Orunudoi* 1851: 604). The king thereafter despatched his men to tame the Nagas. After a series of battles, the king's men reached Khamzang, where the Nara people welcomed them.

Unlike colonial records, the Buranjis did not make any cultural comment (civilised–savage) on the 'us' and 'them' dichotomy. This is despite the fact that the notion of difference was not absent from the Buranjis. In the previous chapter, I discussed how the shared mapping of space and society and the notion of difference were not contradictory to one another, as some contemporary research tends to argue. Not only in forms of imagination or ideas, this was to be found even in material cultures, such as that of beads. Similarly, even in the Purani Asom Buranji, different communities such as the Naras, Nagas, Cutiyas, Koch or Kacaris were widely mentioned. The numerous battles fought with them or which they fought among themselves was also mentioned along with the dates (in the Lakli calendar). But these conflicts were not placed in the framework of savage and civilised. Nowhere in the Buranji can one trace any cultural comment on the different communities vis-à-vis the 'us'. Another notable dimension is that the distinction between hills and valleys (another distinction that is sought to be historically justified in some contemporary approaches, as noted in the previous chapter) is mostly absent. The hills and plains existed more as descriptive geographical features and were not conceptually linked to the societies inhabiting these forms of geographical spaces (i.e., communities are not seen as essentially territorialised entities). For example, whether the Nagas, Naras, Khamptis, Aitons of the Patkai ranges, or the Kacaris spread across the Patkai ranges, as well as in the Brahmaputra and Barak valleys or the Koches of the western Brahmaputra Valley, they all inhabited different kinds of geographical spaces, and the nature of their spaces did not condition their nature of society. The Purani Asom Buranji also records the large number of marriage alliances among the different communities, and in each case, along with the bride, a large group of people also came over to the 'Ahom' society. In each such population exchange, the new group of people became part of the 'us'. Further, different clans within what comprised the 'us' also fought for power. In such cases, those who were opposed to the faction who had commissioned the Buranjis were not considered part of the 'us'. In other words, in the Purani Asom Buranji, just like the Nagas or the Kacaris, even those opposed to the ruling king but from within the 'Ahom' long settled in the Brahmaputra Valley, could be left out of the 'us'. The explanation to such an approach in the Buranji tradition can only be the one already outlined in the previous chapter, that relation of difference was mapped in the larger socio-spatial framework that stretched from Tibet, across the Brahmaputra Valley and the Patkai ranges into the northern highlands of Myanmar. In such forms of mapping, notions of identity and difference from one another were not absent or suppressed. Rather, such notions were contained within the larger relation of a shared socio-spatial world and worldview.

I have already noted two aspects of appropriation and reference to the Indo-Gangetic world. In the first case, I showed that the Ahoms traced their origin to Indra, an Indo-Gangetic god. In fact, the rulers, throughout their reign of 600 years in the Brahmaputra Valley, stuck to this origin myth. But I also showed that through the origin myth, it was the Indo-Gangetic world which was appropriated into the Tibet–Brahmaputra–Myanmar worldview. The same could be said of the use of the Lakli calendar as well. In the second case, people or society to the west of the valley, i.e., the Indo-Gangetic area of Bengal, was referred to as the land of the 'Bongal' or foreigners. The notion of foreigners was remarkably distinct vis-à-vis the vagueness in the 'us' and 'them' distinctions as practised otherwise in the Buranjis. But there is still another dimension to the study of these frameworks which can be further pursued. Subrahmanyam (2005) highlights that between the 14th century and 18th centuries (i.e., the period of the Buranjis), the Arakan court of Myanmar showed clear signs of adopting Persian motifs in its court culture and in certain forms of court literature, Bengal being the point of contact between the two worlds. To Subrahmanyam, this is evidence of the connected nature of historical processes and formations. The Shan highlands neighboured the Arakan area, and yet the shared tradition of chronicling (i.e., the Buranjis) found across the Shan belt across the Patkai ranges into the Brahmaputra Valley framed the relation with the Indo-Gangetic world through an unusually distinct notion of foreign and separate, rather than as part of its larger socio-spatial mapping. Even more notably, the presence of acculturated Indo-Gangetic elements in their worldview only substantiated this distinct notion of difference rather than bringing the two worlds together, as Subhrahmanyam argued had been the case between Bengal and Arakan. From the Purani Asom Buranji, I would only like to add one last example to exemplify this point. The Buranji states that in Saka Lakli Mungrao, the Koch king advanced towards the river Dikhow. But 'our' king stationed some his nobles at an advance post and prevented their further advance. In the meanwhile, exchange of peace messages began to take place between the two kings. The Koch king, in his message to 'our' king, said (translation mine),

> Neither we nor them are of today. We have been there for quite long. They are descendants of heavenly king Indra and we are descendants of Shiva. Therefore, conflict between you and us isn't fair. Even in the past, we have enjoyed peaceful relation. So that it continues even in the future, you may decide on your domain and also decide our domain (ibid.: 563).

Both the kings exchanged gifts thereafter and once the matter was resolved, the Koch king withdrew, and so did 'our' soldiers. The point that I would like to emphasise is that despite the use of Indo-Gangetic motifs to resolve conflict, the Indo-Gangetic world itself remained distinctly foreign to the Buranji tradition. In contrast, in Subrahmanyam's framework (2005: 45–79), the Arakan king used Indo-Persian motifs to aggravate conflict rather than resolve it. Then where can these these differences in the interconnectedness of regions using shared motifs to map relations differently be situated?

Among a host of Buranjis, I will take another two texts and their narratives, namely Dutiram Hazarika's and Biswesar Bidyadhip's 19th-century Buranjis, to highlight the issue of socio-spatial mapping and forms of appropriation in the Valley. The biographical details of Hazarika are discussed in the subsequent section of this chapter dealing with the Jaymati legend. In this section, I will continue with the issues already raised and explored in the preceding discussion of the chapter. Hazarika's and Bidyadhip's Buranjis are unique for two reasons. They are written in verse and their language is that of Kamrupi Assamese of the western part of the Valley. The influence of these two features is noticeable in the Buranjis. In the Purani Asom Buranji, the narrative is both stark and meticulous. For example, in case of exchange of gifts, nature and quantity of items or in case of documenting of places, names of villages, rivers, hills, or the names of ministers, family tree of kings, of communities, etc. are meticulously recorded. Events are also recorded against the Tai calendar. It is possible to believe that the prose narrative of the Buranjis enabled this textual nature. In verse Buranjis, such as those of Hazarika's or Bidyadhip's, this stark and meticulous nature is conspicuously absent. For example, in Hazarika's Buranji, there is no specific calendar reference to events. Similarly, though the nature of items in use or exchange are mentioned, their quantification is largely absent.

Kamrupi Assamese had been historically closer to the Indo-Gangetic culture. As a result, forms of literature such as the epic and *punana* traditions, or *carita* and *vamcavali* traditions were prominent in the writings available in Kamrupi Assamese. Hazarika's Buranji, and more so Bidyadhip's Buranji, is an example wherein the impact of the nature of language on the construction of the narrative world is evident. Compared to the Purani Asom Buranji, the two verse Buranjis are closer to Indo-Gangetic culture through the use of motifs. For example, the analogy used for the battles between the Burmese king and the British in the India during the late 18th and early 19th centuries is that of the battle between Karna and Arjuna, borrowed from the *Mahabharata*. Similarly, in Hazarika's Buranji, when Prince Gadapani (who later became King Gadadhar Singha) becomes a fugitive to escape being put to death by the boy-king Sulikpha, he happens to come across a Brahman. Gadapani is in disguise as a Naga betel leaf seller. The Brahman predicts that Gadapani will eventually become the king. The motifs used in the prediction are borrowed from the Indo-Gangetic tradition. For example (translation mine):

> The sage said I know you are high born
> I see that you are worthy to become the king
> Thus hearing, Gada (Gadapani) sat down
> And on this, the sage asked him to carefully consult his Vedas
> He declared that his prediction will come true

> Else his Vedas will go up in flames.
> Gada said that if he would become the king
> He would award him the office of doloi
> Thus said, Gada moved ahead on his way
> And the Brahmana too reached his house. (verses 117–19)

But it needs to be asked whether language and narrative form also made an impact on the socio-spatial mapping of the Buranji, i.e., was there any shift in the mapping of the Tibet–Brahmaputra–Myanmar belt. In Hazarika's Buranji, the socio-spatial mapping continues to identify the Tibet–Brahmaputra–Myanmar belt as an interrelated corridor. For example, the detailed documentation of the process by which Badan Barphukan, the general posted in Guwahati in the early 19th century, managed to secure assistance from the Ava court to overthrow the dominant faction in the Ahom court clearly indicates that the assistance was not perceived as given from a territorial desire harnessed by the Burmese king, a point that colonial records emphatically argue. Rather, it was provided as part of a common world that they inhabited, materialised through exchange of people and traditions. Further, an Ahom princess from the Siring community, then a royal Burmese wife, and a minister of Ahom descent are shown to have played a key role in making the assistance possible. The route by which the Burmese soldiers came was across the Patkai ranges.

Despite the verse Buranjis retaining elements of the socio-spatial mapping of the prose Buranjis, shifts nevertheless emerged between the two kinds of Buranjis. Therefore, as will be seen, there is a question of difference in the 'interconnectedness' of histories. If both the language and narrative form of the verse Buranjis were borrowed from Kamrupi language with its closer association with the Indo-Gangetic worldview, then its influence in the characterisation of the socio-spatial mapping in the Buranjis was also evident. It was also where a culturalist comment of civilised and savage entered the verse Buranji discourse. For example, Hazarika's Buranji describes the Burmese soldiers who were on their way to the Valley along with Badan Barphukan thus (translation mine):

> By nature they are *mleccha*, what to speak of their customs
> Even Bargohain and Phukan become like one of them.
> They neither bath nor worship the gods (*devata*)
> But they bother little, it worries them little. (verse 869)

In another ironical description, though the eastern Brahmaputra Valley was largely inhabited by 'Mongoloid' people, the Ahoms themselves being a part, the Buranji describes the mongoloid features of the Burmese soldiers as exotic ('their faces are without beard or moustache, like women' — verse 896).

The prose Buranji and the verse Buranji represented two different kinds of socio-spatial historical mapping, but within the same kind of chronicling. As Saikia (2004) points out, it was the first kind of Buranji which was predominantly practised in the Valley, and found across the Patkai in Myanmar as well. The verse Buranjis were more of an exception. The prose Buranji also represented an older tradition of chronicling compared to the verse Buranji. Unlike the verse Buranji, the prose Buranji was a more stark and meticulous practice of chronicling in the Valley. At the same time, it is equally important to note that prose Buranjis like the Purani Asom Buranji exhibited clear signs of how the Indo-Gangetic worldview could be appropriated into their own socio-spatial mapping. What made the appropriation notable was that it did not deny the presence of the Sanskritic Indo-Gangetic cultural forms and practices, whether Vedic or Shaiva or Sakta or neo-Vaishnava. But these Sanskritic forms were appropriated into a worldview which is markedly different from the Sanskritic Indo-Gangetic worldview. It is an area of research which needs further investigation, especially because the Valley has been generally studied in this regard as stages of Sanskritisation or Hinduisation, whether in the colonial or in the postcolonial period. Some of the oft-cited examples in this regard are the Sakti goddesses like Kamakhya or names of major rivers like the Brahmaputra, both shown as historical examples of Sanskritic appropriation of the indigenous. But the Buranjis, which quantitatively and qualitatively comprise a huge body of writing, can provide us with different forms of appropriations at work. In the debate on Sanskritisation of the Valley, the prose Buranjis are of critical importance in another regard. Though most of them claim to be old manuscripts, as Saikia (ibid.) noted, they can be generally traced to being written around the 17th century in the Brahmaputra Valley. It is also the period to which the Hinduisation of the Ahoms has been traced. Increasingly, it is argued, that thereafter, the royal or noble clans took to Hindu customs and rituals, besides Hindu names. The Hinduisation was nothing other than the adoption of Indo-Gangetic

Sanskritic cultural ideas and practices. Yet the prose Buranjis, which generally began to be written since then and continued to be written thereafter, were apparently evidence of a reverse form of appropriation.

This brings me once again to the central question that I have tried to pursue, namely, how to historically situate the Valley and its mapping by the inhabitants. My argument would be that the Valley was a crossroad, a highway of migration as well as a destination of migration. Therefore, any attempt to straitjacket the Valley into one or the other cultural worlds would fall short of a plausible assessment. The Valley can only be explained as a space in which both South Asia (i.e., Indo-Gangetic world) and East and South East Asia (i.e., both trans-lower Himalaya and trans-Patkai) interacted. Cultural formations in the Valley exhibited elements of this process of interaction. If in the western part of the Valley there was a greater cultural proximity to the Indo-Gangetic belt, in the eastern part of the Valley, the proximity was to the trans-lower Himalaya and trans-Patkai belt. The neo-Vaishnava literary tradition in the western valley and the Buranji tradition in the eastern valley, both establishing themselves as major forms of knowledge production since the 17th century, clearly indicate these dynamics of cultural processes within the Valley. But the proximity did not lead to a complete appropriation of these kinds of writing into cultural worlds that lay beyond the Valley itself. For example, what a closer study of these writings amply highlights was that despite differences in the framework of worldviews in which they were respectively situated, the specificity of the Valley as crossroad was nevertheless retained. Attempts to alter it created ruptures within their respective narratives. I will try to show this in the case of the *Uttara Kanda*, especially with regard to the character of Sita and attempts at its Sanskritisation, in the latter part of this chapter. The same can also be seen in the case of the verse Buranjis. In Hazarika's or Bidyadhip's Buranjis, one can trace the conscious attempt to situate the narrative in the Indo-Gangetic Sanskritic world as seen in the use of motifs. The choice of language (Kamrupi) and narrative form (verse) therefore only compounds the issue. But despite this conscious attempt, the socio-spatial world largely dealt with was far different from the Indo-Gangetic Sanskritic world. Unlike in the prose Buranjis, the Indo-Gangetic cultural motifs found in the verse Buranjis therefore appear not only as means to rationalise the facts into the worldview but also to bridge the ruptures created in this mismatch between the socio-spatial world dealt with and its mapping. The trope of civilised and savage, once again not found in the prose Buranjis, can also be treated as part of this attempt to hide the mismatch between the socio-spatial world and the worldview in which it is located. Therefore, 'civilised' and 'savage' in these verse Buranjis could be more plausibly treated as textual ruptures, quite unlike their use in colonial records. Further, the issue of conscious attempt is important because as seen both in the cases of Madhab Kandali's *Ramayana* or in that of the oral ballad *Barphukanar Geet* (compiled and published by Surjya Kumar Bhuyan in 1924), language and narrative form alone need not create narrative ruptures. For example, *Barphukanar Geet* dealt with Badan Barphukan and the support he received from the Burmese in a positive light, and at the same time, it was a ballad sung in the eastern valley but in Kamrupi language and in the verse form practised in Kamrupi Assamese. The oral ballad is an example of how the two seemingly separate worlds and worldviews of Sanskritic Indo-Gangetic and Tibet–Brahmaputra–Myanmar could coexist without narrative ruptures.

To return to the insufficiency of the theme of interconnected histories, such a problematic in narrative, when shifts are attempted (as in the verse Buranjis) in its structure and worldview, can be more meaningfully gauged when the ruptures are focused upon rather than only what is shared across space and society. Further, what is shared within the Valley from across its geographical limits also undergoes different kinds of appropriation as part of the process of sharing, as in Madhab Kandali's *Ramayana* or the prose Buranji tradition. Therefore, it is not enough to highlight what communities across space share. It is more important to highlight the relation through or in which the sharing takes place. It is that relation which shows how historical geography operates in the cultural forms that emerge from within it, as in the case of the Buranjis. In other words, if the Valley had been a historical receiver of socio-cultural elements from beyond its western or eastern geographical limits, as part of its historical formation it had also developed distinctive narrative frameworks (for example in oral ballads like *Barphukanar Geet*) which, when stretched, could develop ruptures, as exemplified by the verse Buranjis. It is this delicate balance of a crossroad which came to be subverted when the region transformed into a frontier in the 19th century and an order of culture came along with the transformation which violently broke down the historical balance. I try to pursue this transformation in the following section on the legend of Jaymati and its appropriation into the Indo-Gangetic worldview as part of Indian nationalism.

The Legend of Jaymati: Appropriation of Buranji Tradition into Indo-Gangetic Worldview

The legend of Jaymati is an important example of how since the late 19th century the Tibet–Brahmaputra–Myanmar worldview transformed into the Indo-Gangetic worldview in the Valley. In Chapter 1, I already indicated this transformation. In this section, I will focus on the Buranji tradition and its interpretations in the late 19th and the early 20th century vis-à-vis the legend. To elaborate on this point, I will take Hazarika's Buranji in verse and Bhuyan's extensive work on the Jaymati legend. Hazarika's Buranji was one of the last written in the Ahom tradition of chronicling. Though the exact date is generally not available, it is dated to the second half of the 19th century. Bhuyan's work discussed here dates to the 1920s and 1930s.

Hazarika's (1806–1901) forefather Chirang was raised to the rank of Baruah by then Ahom king Siva Singha and put in charge of the Dafla community on the north bank foothills of the Brahmaputra river (present-day Arunachal Pradesh). The family had since been a beneficiary of royal patronage (until 1858, when the Btitish abolished the monarchy), securing bureaucratic positions till the time of Dutiram Hazarika. Hazarika's Buranji is notable because despite being written after the 1857 revolt, the idea of 'nationalism' is mostly absent from his chronicling. This is where the question of Jaymati assumes significance. Hazarika's Buranji has no mention of the name Jaymati, though the incident associated with Jaymati is recorded. Hazarika records that Prince Gadapani of the Tungkhung clan came to know that the Ahom boy-king Sulikpha was plotting to capture him. Acting immediately on the information, he decided to leave his wife and daughter, and became a fugitive. His wife was unaware of his escape under cover of night. In fact, it is Gadapani who is shown to feel the pain of separation from his family (translation mine):

Thus Gadadhar leaves his house
Escaping in the cover of night.
His beloved daughter and wife now left behind,
His feet felt heavy on the road.
How will I go leaving them behind,
Thus thinking, his teardrops fall.
With thoughts filled in sorrow, Gadadhar goes,
Dressed in disguise, he finally hides. (27–28)

When the king sent his soldiers to capture Gadapani, they found that the mother and daughter were fast asleep. They woke them up and enquired about Gadapani. The wife replied that after cooking rice, they had fallen asleep and were totally unaware of where Gadapani was. The soldiers warned them of dire consequences if they did not reveal his whereabouts, and departed to inform the king. They did not take along the wife and daughter because the king's order was to bring back only Gadapani. In the meantime, Gadapani had disguised himself as a Naga betel leaf seller and was taken care of by a Naga woman named Ramani. She is referred to as *puhari*, i.e., a female petty trader. Gadapani's disguise was complete because even the Ahom soldiers, once when they met him, did not recognise him, mistaking him for a Naga betel leaf seller. When the king failed in his efforts to trace Gadapani, he ordered that the wife and daughter be brought before him. He then ordered that they should be released if they disclosed Gadapani's whereabouts, else they should be punished. The wife continued to plead that she was unaware of her husband's whereabouts as he had left without informing them. For example, while being punished, when she was asked again, she replied (translation mine), 'When I don't know where he is, how can I say that I know. If you have to kill, then kill both of us, the mother and daughter' (77). The daughter eventually died of the torture. Gadapani came to know of the fate of his wife and daughter and, still in Naga disguise, visited where his wife was being punished. In the course of their conversation, she recognised her husband and to save him, addressed him as *peha* or paternal uncle, and requested him to leave, and that she be left to her fate. It is only at this point that her act of sacrifice is indicated in Hazarika's Buranji. Despite her husband in front of him she kept him in disguise, or provided him with another layer of disguise (of Naga paternal uncle). She finally died from the punishment. The episode ends on a patriarchal note, Hazarika putting in five verses on an ideal wife as conclusion to the episode. He writes (verses 89–93) that there was a general degeneration of women in the period, especially when compared to the past. Women no longer seemed to acknowledge the supremacy of the husband. Harsh words or minor acts of violence were not taken as part of living life as a wife. On the contrary, they would return to their parents' home and complain of what they had gone through. There was no end to the revenge that they sought upon their husbands. For example, (translation mine), 'Husbands are no longer spared. They die in their wife's hands' (90). The conclusion preaches that wives need to consider their husbands as gods.

Hazarika's Buranji does not mention the name Jaymati. Second, the episode emerges from the action of Gadapani, the husband, while the wife and the daughter are mere victims of the circumstances. It is only towards the end that the wife comes across the husband and yet refuses to expose him, thereby sacrificing her life to maintain his disguise. Third, the entire episode is narrated in an extremely matter-of-fact tone. In this regard, it followed the tradition of Ahom Buranji writing, despite Hazarika's Buranji being in verse which was not the general practice in Buranji writing. The episode, however, is only a small portion of the entire Buranji. I have already discussed, in the earlier section of this chapter, how Buranjis formed part of the worldview of Tibet–Brahmaputra–Myanmar spatial and social mapping. Thus, the Gadadhar episode in Hazarika's Buranji mentioned above was also a part of this spatial and social mapping. The consciousness of identity and its politics is largely absent in the Buranji. The fact was that the Valley, foothills and neighbouring hills all the way to Myanmar (when later the Burmese forces invade the valley to help Badan Barphukan) were part of the *kun-how*, in which there was no place for politics of identitarian consciousness.

Buranjis not only recorded the present but also its past as part of the narrative. But Hazarika's Buranji is an example of a long history of Buranji writing or chronicling which was slowly coming to an end by the end of the 19th century. By the early 20th century, this vast, major form of historical writing in the Valley was replaced by 'modern' historical works, one of the most famous exponents of the period being Surjya Kumar Bhuyan. Bhuyan relied majorly on the Buranjis to interpret the past. But his works are important in our discussion because they marked a fundamental shift in interpreting the past vis-à-vis the approach of the Buranji tradition. In other words, though Bhuyan used the Buranjis as source materials, his interpretation transformed the spatial and social mapping completely into the Indo-Gangetic worldview. On the legend of Jaymati, I will take up two of Bhuyan's works, namely his commentaries on the legend and his *Jaymati Akhyan* (or the Jayamti Episode), a ballad in verse on Jaymati, written and published by him in ([1920] 1958).

Bhuyan begins his ballad *Jaymati Akhyan* with the following Introduction (translation mine):

> Jaymati is generally well known in the educated circles in Assam. But she is little known in the rural society of Assam, which is the very backbone of Assamese society. The episode of sati Jaymati is also little known among the women of Assam. This is an attempt to place in their hands the episode of Jaymati composed in *dulari* and *lesari* meters so that it is convenient for them to sing and perform the ballad (1920: Introduction).

On the language used in *Jaymati Akhyan*, he writes (translation mine),

> The language of Jaymati Akhyan is old Assamese, in other words, it is the same language in which kirtan and other ever revered and well received texts in Assamese were written. The language is known to all in Assam.... Through Assamese marriage songs, kirtan, naamghosa, the language has enthroned itself in the hearts of every Assamese (ibid.).

In another essay titled 'Jaymati', Bhuyan provides an elaborate justification and explanation behind emphasising the historical significance of Jaymati. The following excerpts are helpful in highlighting his objectives in this regard. Bhuyan argues (translation mine),

> After coming to know of Jaymati, I was curious to know more about Jaymati. But this episode is not available in Kashinath's buranji, Gunabhiram's historical writing or Gait's historical writing. I even checked the palm leaf Buranji manuscripts, but they too do not contain any direct reference to Jaymati episode. Why was old literature in Assam silent like this on Jaymati? In the olden days, the death of a woman was not considered to be sufficiently important

or unusual a matter. The wave of nationalism that has swept the world today is a contemporary phenomenon. It is by being enriched from this wave of nationalism that we, the Assamese today, have acquired the rejuvenating mantra of Jaymati. In the olden days, people did not know to perceive such incidents through nationalism. Therefore, the Buranji writers of the past considered the death of Jaymati as an inconsequential matter. Because Kashinath, Gunabhiram or Gait wrote their histories using Buranjis which did not have the Jaymati episode, it got left out in their histories. But to think that because the episode is not mentioned in their histories, Jaymati did not exist would be an outrageous thought. I had a conviction that there certainly will be some Buranji in which reference to Jaymati will be found ([1935] 2007: 265).

Bhuyan then recounts how he found a reference to the incident in two Buranji manuscripts which were collected by Hemchandra Goswami. He writes (translation mine),

> There is no doubt any more that prince Gadapani's wife lost her life in the punishment. In one of these Buranjis it is said, 'At that time, Gadapani hid his two sons in the Naga hills in fear of Laluksula Burhaphukan. Pregnant princess died in the punishment.' In the other Buranji it is written, 'At that time, Barphkan captured and killed all the princes whom he could trace. But he could not trace Gadapani. So his wife was punished to death.' (ibid.).

But Bhuyan also had to establish that the princess who was punished to death and Jaymati of the legend were the same persons. Though he does not dwell on the issue at length, towards the end of his essay, he does take it up. He cites the newspaper article in *Batori* (8 April 1931) in which there was a reference that Kripanath Phukan had a Buranji in his possession which had details of the Jaymati episode. Bhuyan pursued the matter and met Phukan, who told him that the Buranji, called the Lailik Buranji, written in Tai Ahom language, was not in his possession anymore. Phukan also informed him that the Lailik Buranji was a copy made from another Buranji written in Shan language, which he had come across during one of his visits to the Shan province of Burma. I have already noted that the Ahoms had migrated to Brahmaputra Valley from the Shan area of Myanmar in the 13th century. Phukan nevertheless provided Bhuyan with details on Jaymati as narrated in the Buranji. Based on Phukan's notes, Bhuyan tried to create the family tree of Jaymati, probably one of the first attempts in Assam in this regard. Two further points can be mentioned here. First, like the other two Buranjis collected by Hemchandra Goswami, in this Buranji as well Gadapani is shown to have had two sons. This is in contrast to Hazarika's Buranji in which Gadapani is supposed to have had one daughter who was tortured and killed along with her mother. Second, the portions of Phukan's note that Bhuyan cites as songs that were sung at Jaymati's death do mention the incident but do not use the name 'Jaymati' along with the incident anywhere. In this, it is similar to Hazarika's Buranji.

If Bhuyan's use of Phukan's notes to develop a text-based (Buranji) narrative of Jaymati as a historical character appears ahistorical, given that the text in question is not traceable, then Bhuyan's attempt needs to be studied vis-à-vis the question of orality and its historical treatment as well. The question can be approached from how the historical value of ballads can be ascertained. In 1924 Bhuyan collected, i.e., wrote down, an oral ballad from the Lakhimpur area (eastern part of the Brahmaputra Valley bordering the lower Himalayan ranges) called *Barphukanar Geet*. The ballad is an account of Badan Barphukan, the Ahom general posted in Guwahati, who had approached the Ava court to overthrow the Ahom prime minister. It was a help which he also managed to secure. I have already discussed the details of the event in the first section of this chapter. *Barphukanar Geet*, despite being an oral ballad, is almost the same in terms of narration of events when compared to the other textual Buranjis. The only aspect missing is the use of calendar dates, whether the Saka calendar or Tai Ahom calendar. There are different versions of *Barphakunar Geet*, but Bhuyan shows how these different versions are similar in their narrative content. Thus, historical memory can indeed be found rather intact even in oral narrative traditions. But unlike *Barphukanar Geet*, the legend of Jaymati neither emerged as a strong textual Buranji tradition nor as a popular oral tradition (which Bhuyan himself admits to in his Introduction to *Jaymati Akhyan*). Therefore, it is this mismatch which makes Phukan's notes and Bhuyan's reliance on these notes suspect.

Until now, I have discussed the question of historicity of the Jaymati legend. The other dimension that I would like to pursue is what change Bhuyan introduced in the interpretation of the legend for the colonial and postcolonial periods. The point is important because the Jaymati legend entered state school textbooks in the postcolonial period portraying Jaymati as a historical character, aiming to inspire Assamese nationalism among children.

Bhuyan spends substantial space in his various Jaymati studies in trying to prove that the 'heinous crime' of putting a woman to death was carried out only on the personal orders of the king and in no way reflected the general nature of the Assamese people or the collective will of the court. This is in line with his approach to use the Jaymati episode to inspire a positive spirit of nationalism among the Assamese people. The transformation of the Jaymati episode from the Tibet–Brahmaputra–Myanmar spatial and social mapping into that of Indo-Gangetic spatial and social mapping could also be traced in this ideological orientation. Bhuyan's *Jaymati Akhyan* is a fictional account (on his own admission), but it proved extremely influential both in the colonial and postcolonial periods. The character of Jaymati in the ballad is based on the different pieces of information on the Gadapani incident in different Buranjis put together, but now cast as part of Indo-Gangetic mapping.

The Buranjis do not refer to Assam as a spatial formation. They mostly refer to Soumar, as the Ahoms used to term their kingdom, as the social and spatial formation. I have also shown that 'Assam desh' (or country of Assam) in neo-Vaishnava literature (such as the *Katha Guru Charit*) is not specific in their meaning of what constituted Assam. But in sharp contrast to this tradition of mapping, Bhuyan begins his ballad by first identifying Assam as a specific historical spatial entity and then firmly situating Assam as part of the Indo-Gangetic formation. He introduces Assam as a unique land not comparable to any other in the three worlds (the motif used was *bhuvan*). Then he borrows extensively from the epic (*Mahabharata*) and Purana traditions through characters and narratives such as those of Bhagadatta, Baan, Usha, Rukmini or Beula to highlight the significance of the land. Into this context of Hindu 'Bharat' (or India) he introduces the Ahoms migrating from Shan area of Myanmar. For example, he writes (translation mine):

> After the end of Hindu rule, there came from the Shan country (*desh*)
> The descendants of Indra (Hindu god), the Tai
> They took the name of Ahom and ruled over Assam
> Sukapha being the first to rule ([1920] 1958: 4)

The conflict between the Ahoms and the Mughals, in which the Mughals were finally defeated and forced to vacate Guwahati forever, becomes the motif to identify Assam as a definite historical formation. For example (translation mine):

> The lord of the empire in Delhi, sent his general
> To win Assam
> Therefore, the ruler of Assam, the brave Chakradhvaj
> Sent his army to the battle.
> The general of Assam, was the best in war
> Lachit Phukan was his name
> Near Pandu, he led Assam to the Mughals
> And waged a fierce battle (ibid.: 4–5)

Therefore, Bhuyan notably opens his ballad with two points. Unlike the Buranjis or the Mughal Persian texts (for example, see Guha's discussion in his study of economy in *Cambridge Economic History of India*, Volume 1) or the neo-Vaishnava textual tradition, Bhuyan creates 'Assam' as a historical entity and situated it firmly in Indo-Gangetic spatial and social mapping. They together form his nationalism. Thereafter, he moves to the character of Jaymati and her husband Gadapani. In his characterisation of Jaymati, along with the above two features, a third feature, that of patriarchy, also becomes part of the character. For example, Bhuyan writes (translation mine):

> In a house such as that, was a woman like Lakshmi
> A help for the helpless, epitome of compassion
> Her beauty unparalleled in the three worlds (*tribhuvan*) (ibid.: 9)

Further, as part of character illustration, he writes (translation mine):

> She had heard, of the troubles of the country
> That the kingdom shakes in turmoil
> But a woman that she is, she lacked the strength
> To understand what causes the turmoil.
> Yet, despite being a woman, she thinks of the country (*rajya*)
> It is indeed an unusual feat
> An Ahom princess, intelligent and wise
> She thinks therefore of the country. (ibid.)

Despite the ballad being culled out of the Buranjis, Bhuyan's motifs are not from the Buranjis, evident in his repeated use of frameworks such as '*tribhuvan*' or 'Laxmi' (as in the two excerpts above). There are numerous other examples as well, indicated subsequently in this section. But also contrary to Buranji tradition where women were not projected as meek, weak or incapable of thinking, Bhuyan already situates his Jaymati in the opposite framework. He establishes this characterisation even more strongly through Jaymati's own words spoken at the time Gadapani decides to escape. Unlike in the Buranjis, it was Jaymati who convinced Gadapani in this ballad that he should escape under cover of night before being captured by the soldiers. And then she lamented (translation mine):

> We are woman, what strength we have
> To do any worldly deeds
> Our lives are spent, merely waiting
> For death to pass.
> If you stay alive, our two sons
> They will gain fame
> If not you, who else
> Will look after our sons? (Bhuyan [1920] 1958: 13)

A more emphatic proof of the point can be found in Jaymati's prayer to the goddess (possibly Goddess Durga) after Gadapani had left for the Naga Hills in these words (translation mine):

> Falling at the feat of the goddess, she prayed and pleaded —
> Take care of my beloved husband.
> A prince today roams as a Naga
> How can I stay in peace ...
> I plead you, O *thakurani* (i.e., goddess)
> I am a mere weak woman
> I know not how to please you, forgive my failings
> Save my heart's beloved (ibid.: 17)

In the following part of the ballad, Bhuyan heavily borrows the motifs of Sita in the court of Rama (*Uttara Kanda*) or Draupadi in the Kuru court when Jaymati was ordered to be brought to the court by the king. The king's ministers express dismay at the order thus (translation mine):

> What are you doing O king
> Your order is immoral
> A daughter-in-law stays only inside home
> How can you bring her to the court?
> Whom the sun and the moon too cannot see
> How can she then be brought by the road? (ibid.: 23)

Jaymati repeats the same when the soldiers arrive to take her to the court. Nevertheless, she relents and prepares to go to the court in a palanquin, the common people and her servants pouring out their grief and dismay all along the road until she reached the court. It is quite evident that Bhuyan not only borrowed the old Assamese language prevalent in western Assam in which the Ramayana or the other Puranas were written between the 14th and 18th centuries, but also borrowed the motifs from those texts to recreate the scene of Jaymati going to court and her trial before the king and the ministers in the court. It is important to remember that the Buranjis were rarely written in Kamrupi Assamese. They were either written in Tai or in the Sibsagar form of Assamese of eastern Assam. Another example of how Bhuyan borrowed information from different Buranjis is evident here from the fact that Jaymati is shown to have had two sons (and not a daughter as in Hazarika's Buranji) and at the time of the incident, she is also pregnant. In fact, her pregnancy becomes another example of the pathetic treatment meted out to her by the king (translation mine):

> At the time, Jaymati was pregnant
> What troubles has the cruel king's order brought to her. (ibid.: 28)

Once in court, Bhuyan presents Jaymati and her thoughts with reference to Sita of Ramayana ('In the middle of the court stood sati, looked at by all like mother earth [*basumati*]' [ibid.: 30, translation mine] and then Draupadi of the Mahabharata while preparing for the trial ('Jaya remembered how Draupadi was humiliated in the court' [ibid.: 31, translation mine]).

The remaining two excerpts aim to show how the appropriation of the legend into nationalism and the Indo-Gangetic worldview was complete towards the end of the ballad. The first example is of the king himself who repents, having punished Jaymati to death, thus (translation mine):

> I punished a woman like her, in mad rage,
> My deed is unpardonable
> A supreme sati (*mahasati*) that Jaya was
> She lives as the meaning of life
> Duryodhan that I am, I killed a Pandu
> I have put my own house in flame. (Bhuyan [1920] 1958: 41)

The second excerpt is from the conclusion of the ballad in which the narrator (i.e., Bhuyan himself in the disguise of the poet-narrator Bhanunandan of the ballad) brings together the three features that I pointed out vis-à-vis Bhuyan's objective behind writing the ballad, namely, addressing the issue of Assamese identity; appropriating the identity within the larger Indo-Gangetic framework of Indian nationalism; and situating women clearly within a patriarchal framework, a phenomenon which cannot be directly traced to either the Indo-Gangetic-influenced textual tradition of western Brahmaputra Valley or to the textual and oral traditions of the eastern part of the Valley in the pre-colonial period. Bhuyan begins the conclusion by creating a pantheon of women figures from the Indo-Gangetic cultural world and thereafter situating Jaymati in it (translation mine):

> Prayers to sati Damayanti, to the beautiful Subhadra
> Rukmini Beula Usha and prayers be to Mandodari
> Sabitri, Draupadi Sita and the blessed Ahalya
> Pramila Urmila Satyabhama Bhanumati
> Kaushalya Sumitra Kunti Indumati Tara
> Their names are spread all over
> Hindu women survive chanting their names everyday
> Their names can be found in the ancient times
> In the Indian Puranas, you will find their names.
> But Jaymati's name isn't in the Puranas
> It isn't the imagination, the verse of poets ... (Bhuyan [1920] 1958: 52)

Bhuyan then addresses Assamese identity through the Jaymati episode (translation mine):

> Jaya's story is not an imagination
> Her name has now spread across the world
> When there are examples of sati in your own land
> Why look for them in other lands? (ibid.: 53)

Finally, Bhuyan wraps the entire ballad in the principle of femininity when he preaches the message of Jaymati to the audience (translation mine):

> Women are like innocent creepers without their husbands
> Where can they go without the protection of their husbands?
> You remain busy in your domestic chores
> Your husband goes out to do his work ...
> To take care of wife and children
> He labours immensely day and night ...
> To worship his feet is the duty of the wife
> He's her heaven, her dharma, her pilgrimage. (ibid.: 54)

I will show, in subsequent chapters, that in the 19th and early 20th centuries language and content in Assamese underwent a fundamental shift. Content which was based on Indo-Gangetic culture written in the Kamrupi Assamese of the western valley was now shifted to the Sibsagar Assamese of the eastern valley, and at the same time, the content and worldview of Tibet–Brahmaputra–Myanmar social and spatial mapping was transformed into the historical past. In this regard, Bhuyan's *Jaymati Akhyan* can appear its opposite. In his ballad, the matter of the Buranjis is placed in or framed through the language of the western valley. But on closer observation, it is clear that his ballad stands as the most complete appropriation of the latter mapping into the former. Bhuyan created the ballad by appropriating elements of different Buranjis into a single form, which though they comprised the content of the Buranjis, were cast entirely in Indo-Gangetic mapping. Through the ballad, he not only obliterates the Tibet–Brahmaputra–Myanmar worldview of the Buranji tradition which is embedded in the incident, but also recasts it in a socio-ideologically different form of language. The contrast with the Buranji tradition is notable also at another level. While in the Buranjis elements of the Indo-Gangetic culture were incorporated but recast into the Tibet–Brahmaputra–Myanmar worldview (as already discussed in the first section of this chapter), Bhuyan's ballad achieved its reverse. But what made this change important was that it became part of the larger transformation of the region into a frontier and its incorporation into a single continental block, i.e., Indian South Asia. The narrative successfully obliterated the shared mapping of relations in the most complete method.

If Bhuyan's *Jaymati Akhyan* was a major attempt at 'Assamese' nationalist identity and appropriating it into the Indo-Gangetic worldview, there were also critiques of such processes during the very period. P. L. Choudhury was Bhuyan's contemporary and one of the foremost scholar-writers of the time. In his comments on the relation between Bharat or India and Assamese people in his How We became Friends of India (collection of narratives meant for children), he narrates Puranic and epic characters such as Baan, Bhismak, Bhagadatta, Babrubahan and others which bore reference to Assam or Manipur and concludes for the children,

> From these stories, it appears that when initially we entered into the wide heart of Bharat (or India), there were indeed some conflicts. It took a lot of time for our non Aryan traits to be included in the Aryan culture. Yet, otherwise we were as advanced as the Aryans. (Choudhury 2007: 630).

Though he narrates stories for children on the conflictual process of appropriation of the region in the Indo-Gangetic worldview (which is entirely absent in Bhuyan's ballad), he also writes (translation mine):

> So what if we are not Aryans
> And never had the luxuries
> So what if others did not call us civilized
> Was there anything wrong in that?
> We would have lived in the forests
> In the hills, in caves, in lonely fields
> In mountain sheds, dangerous and precipitous
> Would have climbed peaks after peaks
> Wandering from place to place
>
> ****
>
> Living with sheer abandon
> That wild spirit of freedom
> Wish it was still there! (ibid.: 860)

In the first section of this chapter, I took up the approach of 'connected histories' and how it cannot conceptually explain the political shifts in processes of cultural relation. The example of the legend of Jaymati and the cultural and political shifts that it highlights, and the political positions vis-à-vis such shifts (or attempts at such shifts) once again emphasises the necessity of area studies, especially with regard to frontier formation. To take the example by Subrahmanyam (2005), the influence of the Indo-Persian worldview could be traced even in the Arakan court of Thirithudhamma in Myanmar in the 17th century. Not only was Indo-Persian medicine practised in the court, even the discourse of correspondence and court literature (from the 14th–17th century) bore Indo-Persian elements. It was because the Arakan court was filled with people from Bengal (ibid.: 71–72). In the same way, it is possible to argue that the legend of Jaymati proves the interconnectedness of history across space and society, from the Shan highlands of Myanmar, through the Brahmaputra Valley to the Indo-Gangetic plains. However, what this continental sweep does not tell us is that the legend also underwent major political and cultural shifts in becoming part of such continental sweep.

What is equally important is that these shifts were not universally adhered to, i.e., a framework which is agreed to by all involved in these shifts. In contrast to Bhuyan's approach to facilitate cultural appropriation of the region into the Indo-Gangetic worldview, Choudhury's approach is a clear reminder that such appropriation can also be problematic and problematised. Further, when such legends are contextualised as part of the churning taking place in language and discourse in the making of 'modern' Assamese, the problems in the very question of nationalism also come alive. Nationalism in the Valley was embedded with diverse discourses, *Jaymati Akhyan* clearly indicating one attempt, among others, not necessarily to resolve but more to negotiate with this diversity. In fact, Saikia's insightful ethnographic study (2004) shows how by the 1970s, there emerged a strong critique from among the Ahoms in the eastern valley against such appropriations into the Indo-Gangetic worldview. Significantly, this critique was an important part of their self-consciousness as 'Indian'. To be Indians, their difference as Ahoms needed to be restored. Thus, once again the issue is no longer of 'connected histories', but of how these connections are also entwined with political and cultural shifts. It is these shifts which more plausibly explain the cultural negotiations than the connections (a mistake already committed all too much in the name of pan-Indian commonalities).

Last, there is another issue which certainly requires further research, i.e., the issue of gender. I will show in the case of the

Ramayana tradition in Assamese and have already shown in the *Jaymati Akhyan* that every attempt at acculturation with the Indo-Gangetic culture/worldview in the Valley had been marked with attempts to introduce stricter norms of patriarchy, whether practised or not. Whether it is Sankardeb's *Uttara Kanda* or Bhuyan's version of Jaymati, the evidence is quite stark. The point can be exemplified through an example of depiction of women in the Buranji tradition. In the Purani Asom Buranji, it is stated that when the 'Ahoms' (i.e., the 'us') lost to the Koch (during the time of Koch king Naranarayan), they were forced to send some of the noble's children as surety against any retaliation. But Nangbokl, the wife of the minister Borgohain (one of the three main ministers), was furious with the decision that her son be sent to the Koch capital as hostage. She went to the court and addressed the king and all the others present in the court thus (translation mine),

> Why should I send my son to the kingdom downstream? You have lost to the Koch. Then what for what are you the king? For what you all are ministers? She told her husband for what you are the Borgohain? Alright, you have lost the battle. Now let me fight the Koch. I will wear your cap, dress, *kunbi kunkha* and fight the Koch. Then you will know if I am a woman or man. You all should wear my dress. Thus saying, the princess took away her son. Thereafter, the Borgohain told the king, it is alright if for the sake of the kingdom, I have to lose my son. But the princess refused to give away her son. She said who can dare to take away my son. First change the course of the Dikhow river if you can. Only then you will earn the right to take him away (Purani Asom Buranji.: 654).

So strong was her determination that in the end, the king had to send his own brother in lieu of Nangbokl's son. Bhuyan's characterisation of Jaymati in his ballad is in stark contrast to the depiction of women in the Buranji tradition, from which Bhuyan ironically borrows his content.

But also important to note is that what is different between the two cases, i.e., Sankardeb and Bhuyan, is that whereas in the former, as part of a crossroad, it retained elements which could negotiate with such attempts (as in the case of the *Uttara Kanda*), in the latter, the very systematic erosion of the crossroad and its conversion into an order of frontier (with all the prejudices of British-Indological interpretation of 'Indian' laws vis-à-vis gender and its perpetuation in the postcolonial period), these possibilities of negotiation were structurally weakened.

Sanskritisation and Mapping Relations in Sankari Culture

The Buranjis show how shared socio-spatial relations were mapped across differences of communities in the eastern part of the trans-Brahmaputra Valley. The Buranjis were primarily text-based traditions in which texts (or chronicles) were written to record events and worldview. Neo-Vaishnava literature, also called Sankari literature after the saint-reformer Sankardeb, was performance-based textual tradition. The written texts were primarily meant to be performed in front of an audience. Neo-Vaishnava literature emerged in the western and central part of the Valley. In the Introduction, I have already referred to the *Katha Guru Carit* (*carit*s were not performance texts, though) and its mapping of socio-spatial relations. Taking the example of use of the term 'Assam' (or 'Asom'), I tried to show the overlapping notions of socio-spatial relations that the *Katha Guri Carit* highlighted. If on the one hand the Buranjis showed how shared domains of relations were part of inter-community mapping, on the other hand the *Katha Guru Carit* showed how notions of specific spatial orders (i.e., Assam) emerged improbable in their own attempts at delineating such spatial orders. In the remaining section of the chapter, I will focus on Madhab Kandali's 14th-century *Sat Kanda Ramayana* and the Sankari intervention in the *Ramayana*. My focus will be on the relation between Sanskritisation and the mapping of socio-spatial relations.

By the 16th century, the two books of *Adi Kanda* and *Uttara Kanda* of Kandali's *Ramayana* were reportedly lost. Therefore, Sankardeb and his favourite disciple Madhabdeb added the *Adi Kanda* (Madhabdeb) and the *Uttara Kanda* (Sankardeb) to Madhab Kandali's text. Kandali's text was written under royal patronage. It was a tale of human relations. For example, he wrote (the *Sat Kanda Ramayana* used is the 2008 edition, edited by H. N. Dutta Baruah, published by Dutta Baruah and Co., Nalbari, Assam) (translation mine):

> The epic of Balmiki, I have considered and understood it my own way

> What I write then is the substance of it.
> Who can understand the entirety of *rasa* ...
> The way birds fly where their wings take them to
> Poets write the story of people according to where their writings take them to.
> My Ramayana is not a Divine tale; it is only people's tale
> Pardon, O listeners, wherever it fails. (*Kiskindhya Kanda*, pp. 3991–3993)

The change in the neo-Vaishnavite use of the *Ramayana* is evident from the following:

> Listen O people, of the character of Rama
> Your ears would feel a rain of nectar
> The sorrow of the world would disappear thus
> Recite His name, all happiness would be yours. (*Adi Kanda*, p. 1160)

Two notable features about Kandali's text are that it was aimed at/for royal clientele, i.e., the 'tribal' monarchy, and that the text has a social base which is 'tribal-peasant' in nature. Both were as much linked to the geographical location of the Valley. The 'reflection' of the social base in the text can be found, for example, in the nature of access that common people were shown to have to the royal palace as well as in the nature of gender relations that mediated social relations. The latter, for example, is evident not only in the uninhibited characterisation of the lead characters (whether sexual or social characterisation) but also in the uninhibited character that women assumed vis-à-vis the men and the 'tribal' monarchy throughout the text, including the common women. Sexual depiction of Sita was commonly found in descriptions such as 'Her ripe firm breasts' (*Aranya Kanda*: 2668) or 'Her sensuous thighs' (ibid.: 2670). When Sumantra, prime minister of Ayodhya, along with the other men of Ayodhya, returned without Rama, the women thronged the roads (the public space) and in sheer anger begin beating their husbands to avenge their mistake of leaving behind their prince Rama (*Lanka Kanda*, 2002–2003). It was the consistent independence of thought and action that the numerous female characters or women in general demonstrated which highlights the influence of context on the text. Women, in this capacity, remain central throughout to the social landscape of the text.

Despite these features, there is little evidence to study how Madhab Kandali's *Ramayana* not merely 'reflected' but also 'mediated' (Williams 1977) social relations. This difficulty in analysis may be overcome when one focuses on the re-use of the *Ramayana*, but for neo-Vaishnavism. The new dimension that gets incorporated into the text now is the mediating role that the neo-Vaishnava movement *needed* to play as an agent of change in the trans-Brahmaputra Valley. Yet, for the movement, the change also had to be situated in the everyday of the existing social base. This challenge or dilemma of the text can be clearly seen in the treatment of the gender dimension in Sankari intervention. Let me begin from the sexual vis-à-vis the divine. In neo-Vaishnavism, Sita became divine. Further, despite her divinity, though her sexual depiction was still practised through Sankari literature such as the *Adi Kanda* by Madhabdeb or in the *ankia nat* (staged play) *Ramabiyay* (16th century) written by Sankardeb, the difference from Kandali's *Ramayana* was that in Sankardeb's and Madhabdeb's writings, sexuality was no longer a human attribute but had become an attribute of divine perfection (Baruah 2007: 34–36). One of the explanations of Madhab Kandali's use of sexual depictions was as attempt or device at popular/populist consumption (Goswami 1991). However, different textual traditions repeatedly used sexual depiction and also depicted an uninhibited nature in women characters. For example, compared to Kandali's *Ramayana*, Sankardeb's *Siva-Parbati Akhyan* is a more robust and explicit case of sexual depictions between Siva and Parvati. Therefore, Hiren Gohain remarks that such use or depiction of the sexual in texts across time and cultural formations could only be explained by contextualising gender relations and sexuality in the 'tribal-peasant' social base which is different from any hierarchised and gendered society (1987). It can also be added that the significant historical influences of Sakti and tantric traditions (ethnographically documented in detail in *Devi* [Bordoloi 1986]) in the Valley could also be investigated as possible factors behind such common prevalence of the sexual in cultural forms.

Beyond the sexual, the challenge for Sankari culture in the use of Kandali's *Ramayana* was its reinterpretation (and appropriation) into the Bhakti framework (or Bhakti *rasa*). In other words, the challenge was to transform the human into divine. In the *Adi Kanda*, with which the text begins, the transformation of both Rama and

Sita into the divine are quite comprehensive. Rama and Sita were the incarnations of Vishnu and Lakshmi respectively. The battle between Rama and Ravana was also pre-ordained when Ravana had tried to kidnap Goddess Lakshmi, and she had cursed Ravana before disappearing from his chariot. Along with these commentarial changes, the characters also visibly shed their human behavioural and emotional attributes. For example, (in *Madhab Kandali*) when Rama comes and informs Sita that in place of becoming king, he will have to leave for exile, Sita reacts (translation mine):

> Hearing the tragic news from Rama
> Sita collapsed on the ground
> With an unbearable pain in her heart (*Ayodhya Kanda*, 1823)
> ...
> Gaining consciousness, Sita beseeched Rama
> What fault did I commit?
> I was under the earth before birth
> And yet it didn't kill me.
> For what crime, My Lord,
> You put me though this fire of ordeal?
> How come a dutiful wife
> Finds only punishment (*Ayodhya Kanda*, 1825)

But such attributes disappear in the *Adi Kanda*, replaced by omniscient and calm Sita, aware of being part of the divine mission to salvage the world with Rama from the demons. The same goes for the transformation of Rama. Attributes such as his anger and hatred towards Kaikeyi or jealousy towards Bharata (his brother, who now got the chance to become king) have no relevance in the *Adi Kanda*, since the past, present and the future was already known to him. The difficulty in this regard, nevertheless, could be found in the *Uttara Kanda*, which is the concluding book of the text. The *Adi Kanda* and *Uttara Kanda* were intervened by five older books or *kanda*s of Kandali. The *Uttara Kanda* (by Sankardeb) deals primarily with the relation between Rama and Sita as husband and wife, i.e., what they were in the previous five *kanda*s, and subsequently with the glorious rule of Rama in Ayodhya (i.e., Rama *rajya*). It is a shorter book. In the *Uttara Kanda*, the omniscience and divine calm and consciousness of Sita of the *Adi Kanda* is in the least to be found. On the contrary, despite the authorial commentary that Sita is divine, her actions or responses to the unfolding situation (of which she remains unaware) remain as human as they were in the previous five *kandas*. For example, when in the open court of Rama, she is once again asked to prove her purity through another ordeal of fire, she reacts to Rama and to everyone else present in the court (translation mine):

> If you had to abandon me, why did you marry me?
> You would have even got me killed before (*Uttara Kanda*, p. 7089)
> ...
> Your mind is worse than even demon's
> For there is no greater sin than killing of woman (ibid., p. 7092)
> ...
> For what else have you called me again now?
> It feels like rubbing grass on my wounds (ibid., p. 7094)
> ...
> And she started speaking again
> Never again will I see the face of Rama, this husband of mine (ibid., p. 7098)
> ...
> I served him like a Sudra
> No man other than my husband did I know of.
> Yet, see my fate!
> I will not see Rama's face again, O mother! Give me way.
> Rama have called me only to humiliate
> I will not live anymore in this world.
> Detachment now envelops my being
> Give way O mother for me to go (ibid., pp. 7102–7104)

A similar reaction is also to be found when Sita is requested by Hanumana and Rama's brothers to return to Ayodhya after the Laba–Kusha episode (Baruah 2007: 38). The characterisation of Sita exposes the dichotomy that existed between the message of Bhakti that was sought to be propagated through the narration and the given textual structure through which the propagation had to be carried out. The dichotomy becomes sharper if the characterisation of Sita is juxtaposed with that of Rama. The character of Rama in Madhab Kandali's *Ramayana* is brave and compassionate. But he could also be jealous, vindictive and could crave for material comforts or political power. In other words, one can locate a similarity in the characterisation of both human Rama and Sita. But Rama undergoes a more substantive transformation in the *Adi Kanda* and *Uttara Kanda*. The attributes of personality that make him human in Madhab Kandali's *Ramayana* are largely missing in the *Adi Kanda* and *Uttara Kanda*. There is only compassion and a sense of fulfillment of divine mission. In the *Adi Kanda*, his birth, battles with the demons and demonesses like Maris and Subahu (*Adi Kanda*, pp. 899–933), Taraka (ibid., pp.870–97), etc., salvation of Ahalya (ibid., pp. 1065–1160), marriage to Sita, confrontation with Parasurama over the divine bow (ibid., pp. 1394–1459) are all part of divine destiny. In the *Uttara Kanda*, his various victories and finally his death too are part of divine destiny. Very significantly, they do constitute a transformation of the plot and characterisation, i.e., reinterpretation or appropriation of the structure of the text. It is this divinity of Rama that also affected the attributes of his personality (already noted). Therefore, Bhakti, i.e., divinity and divine message, affected the textual structure through which the character of Rama was depicted in the neo-Vaishnavite movement. In other words, it could be taken as an example of textual structure corresponding to the concept and function of the text, which was Bhakti. But what prevented a similar transformation in the character of Sita?

In historical hindsight, it is possible to see that *Sat Kanda Ramayana* as it exists today consists of two narrations, pre- and neo-Vaishnavite. But what is indeterminate is whether they constitute two narratives or two narrations within a single narrative. Sita in the *Uttara Kanda* is an example of this aesthetic indeterminacy. On what caused this indeterminacy, one could locate in Sankardeb's own explanation on the nature of his contribution to Madhab Kandali's *Sat Kanda Ramayana*. When Ananta Kandali, a contemporary poet of Sankardeb and a Vaishnava devotee, expressed his reservation on the nature of Madhab Kandali's narrative which made Rama and Sita human beings rather than divine and said that Sankardeb could rewrite the entire tale transforming them into divinities, the latter declined the suggestion. Sankardeb reasoned that Madhab Kandali's *Ramayana* had served well the objective of spreading the message of the *Ramayana* among the common people.

Gohain's explanation (1987) is that aesthetic principles of Vaishnava art need to be seen in the context of the society in which that art was practised. Vaishnava art was motivated art. Therefore, it had to be conscious of and oriented towards the semi-tribal semi caste nature of the society. Propagation of neo-Vaishnavism could be possible only through a balance of accommodation of some of the existing societal structures and social norms and an attempt at the same time to change other such norms and societal structures. Therefore, the neo-Vaishnava movement whereas on the one hand could reflect republican spirit in institutions like the *naamghar* or an accommodative character in cultural productions in use of musical and dance genres, on the other hand could also practise a distance between god and devotees through the principle of Bhakti that it preached and in its various institutional symbolisms (ibid.: 90–107). He argues that the character of the Bhakti Movement differed in different parts of South Asia. For example, whereas with Kabir the principle of his teachings was to bring god closer to the masses, with Sankardeb it was to distance the two. This is despite the fact that through institutions like *naamghar*, there was a great levelling of the hierarchical differences among the people. The neo-Vaishnava movement in the trans-Brahmaputra Valley was an attempt at creating *a people* out of the existing semi-tribal, semi-caste social relations of the region. Therefore, the characterisation of men and women and of their relations, the nature of monarchy and the characterisation of divinity itself were all based upon the attempt at creating *a people*. The Moamaria revolt of the 18th century is an example that historically, however incomplete, such *a people* had come into existence as a result of the neo-Vaishnava movement.

The framework of correspondences has been significant in analysing the relation between cultural forms and their social or historical context (for example Williams 1977: 95–107). Added to the framework of homology has been that of mediation (for example Lefebvre 1961; Williams 1977;), i.e., cultural forms not only 'reflect' the historical context but also mediate the context. The aesthetic indeterminacy in the *Uttara Kanda* possibly exposes the contradictions between correspondence and mediation that Sankardeb faced regarding the use of Kandali's *Ramayana*. While Kandali's *Ramayana* could have established the correspondence between text and context (social base), it could not have mediated the context towards neo-Vaishnava objectives. The character of Sita could be considered as signifying the contradiction that Sankardeb was caught in.

I began with the point of Sanskritisation and mapping of socio-spatial relations in the neo-Vaishnava texts. In this section,

I focused only on the texts per se. In the next chapter, I will deal with how the larger socio-spatial mapping was carried out in the performance of these texts. Sanskritisation has been one of the major arguments vis-à-vis the spread of the epic traditions in South Asia, the argument being localisation of the Great Tradition (Iyengar [1983] 2003). In the process of localisation, changes were made in the texts. If the spread of epic traditions was a case of Sanskritisation of 'tribal' societies, then how did Sanskritisation try to map the socio-spatial relations of the 'tribal' societies? In this case, how did Sanskritisation map the socio-spatial relations of the crossroad? The neo-Vaishnava Movement was a more evident case of attempted Sanskritsation. The Bhakti *rasa* that it sought to introduce into Kandali's *Ramayana* was an example of the attempt. But the attempt faced serious challenges, namely, how to rationalise the Bhakti *rasa* in the existing *Ramayana*, for example, in the character of Sita. The limit that the challenge posed was also the limit to Sanskritisation mapping the socio-spatial relations of the trans-Brahmaputra Valley. When seen from this perspective, it can be explored whether similar to the Buranjis, Kandali's *Ramayana* can also be seen as appropriation of Indo-Gangetic worldview in the specificities of the Valley. Given the fact that the *Karbi Ramayana* (the Karbi Hills are located to the south of the Brahmaputra Valley) is a clear case of appropriating and transforming the Sanskritic into the specificities of their society, exploring Kandali's *Ramayana* can certainly be a step in this direction. The point of Sanskritisation and its inability to successfully map the socio-spatial relations is important because in the 19th century, the success of Sanskritisation in mapping the period was what came to be emphasised. It was precisely in the failure of Sanskritisation to map the socio-spatial relations wherein the critical role of performance of texts can be identified. If on the one hand Sankari texts (other than Kandali's *Ramayana*) did produce plays where the aesthetic indeterminacy was overcome (i.e., texts which were successfully Sanskritised), the performance of these texts were through musical genres, instruments and dance forms which were non-Sanskritic and remained non-Sanskritic in nature. It was in this balance that the Neo-Vaishnava Movement mapped the socio-spatial relations of the area and tried to communicate through the mapping.

Conclusion

In this chapter, I considered two cases of pre-colonial textual traditions — the Buranjis and the neo-Vaishnava. The Buranjis tradition clearly shows how socio-spatial relations were mapped. The distinctive feature of the mapping was the shared relations mapped across the differences of communities. The shared socio-spatial relations across differences were what distinguished it as a continental crossroad. In contrast to the Buranjis, the Neo-Vaishnava Movement aimed not only at mapping the socio-spatial relations but also transforming them. I tried to explore the problems involved in the twin process in terms of Sanskritisation and how it negotiated mapping these relations through texts (through performance is taken up in the next chapter). Vis-à-vis Sanskritisation, I tried to show that because it sought not only to map but also to change relations, it had ruptures within the narrative (as in the case of the *Ramayana*) and had to devise textual mechanisms to accommodate non-Sanskritic elements which continued to remain non-Sanskritic. I also explored possible research on whether the spread of epic traditions in examples of the *Kandali Ramayana* or the *Karbi Ramayana* could be studied as cases of appropriation of Sanskritic traditions within the socio-spatial relations of the Valley. Research in this direction would help in the comparison of such forms of appropriation with the Buranji tradition, which also practised appropriation of similar nature during the period. Such research is also relevant to study how since the 19th century, the Sanskritic paradigm became the most important criterion to study such epic traditions in Assam. To return to my point of situating textual traditions in the dialectics of socio-spatial relations, I would like to note that the line of enquiry as followed in this chapter highlights how textual traditions mapped these relations as well as the tensions that emerge in their narratives when these relations were sought to be changed. Mapping socio-spatial relations was part of narratives addressing and negotiating with the relations.

3
Language Shift and Narrative: Pre-colonial Continental Crossroad to Colonial Frontier

In the discussion so far, the attempt has been to show how one of the keys to understanding the pre-colonial textual traditions of the trans-Brahmaputra Valley is to focus on how these traditions mapped socio-spatial relations. This mapping highlighted not only the nature of the texts but also how historical geography made a powerful impact on the nature of these texts. Therefore, whether it was traditions of chronicling or traditions of performance texts, the peculiarities of continental crossroad were widely evident. In the earlier chapters, I argued that the shift from continental crossroad to frontier in the case of the Valley was in the qualitative change of the socio-spatial relations. One of the central forces driving socio-spatial relations since the 19th century was mapping of order and lack of order. The framework came to be shared by the colonial state and the colonised alike. The move towards delineating a defined and distinct order of identity (tribe, ethnicity, linguistic, etc.) that became widespread since the period could also be located in this shift. Did the textual traditions of the Valley exhibit the shift and the historical ruptures that it entailed? I will try to study the issue vis-à-vis the development of modern Assamese language and narrative in this chapter.

When the process of culture formation in the 19th and the 20th centuries is seen in a historical perspective, the significance of language modernisation and language shift becomes evident. Though language modernisation and language shift shared a cause–effect relation during the period, taking up the latter first may help in highlighting the historical process. Early analysis of Assamese language argued that it has two major variants, the eastern (valley) and the western (valley) variants, though each having its many sub-variants (Kakati [1941] 1995). However, later analysis listed the language as having four distinct variants.

They are the eastern or Sibsagar variant; central or Nagaon variant; western or Kamrupi variant; and the Goalparia variant (Moral 1992). In the previous chapter, I outlined how there were two important traditions of writing in the pre-colonial period, especially since the 14th–18th centuries. They were the Buranji tradition and the neo-Vaishnava tradition. The former was written in the Sibsagar variant of Assamese while the latter was written in the Kamrupi variant. Importantly, these traditions did not refer to the language in which texts were being written as 'Assamese' (i.e., Axomiya). As Saikia pointed out (discussed in Chapter 1), the word 'Assamese' or 'Axomiya' could only be of 19th-century coinage. Therefore, the idea of language variants can here be treated as retrospective markers used for convenience. In sharp contrast to the pre-colonial history of Assamese language use, the process of language modernisation since the second half of the 19th century was marked by a fundamental language shift, viz. the idea of 'Assamese' language and the Sibsagar or the eastern variant recognised as the 'standard' variant of the Assamese. I will focus on three factors as important in this regard, especially to explain the shift and its historical significance.

First, the Baptist missionaries played a major role in developing printed materials in the Sibsagar variant of the language for the propagation of Christianity. Since they were based in the eastern part of Brahmaputra Valley (in the Sibsagar area), they adopted the local variant for their activities. The fact that the variant already had a history of prose narrative, i.e., the Buranjis, helped the missionaries who published their texts in prose and not in verse. Further, the missionaries also extended their activities to the neighbouring Naga Hills, where the pidgin for inter-community interaction was largely influenced by the Sibsagar variant (Smith 2008: 253–267). Thus, adoption of the Sibsagar variant for missionary activities was beneficial for the Baptist missionaries in both the (eastern) valley and the neighbouring hills. Colonialism and the missionaries introduced modern mass printing technology (press) in the Valley. The result was the development of printing plates in the Sibsagar variant of the language as well as a significant rise in the use of the materials produced in the variant. Most of their literature was guided by the principle of propagating a moral order based on Christian doctrine, i.e., civilising the savage.

Second, the missionaries initiated the development of a grammar for the language which they used for their activities. Though early Assamese accounts attributed it to general missionary philanthropy (Baruah 1900: Introduction), a sociolinguistic approach can indicate otherwise. Between 1835 and 1873, the official language for 'vernacular' affairs in the Valley was Bangla. This was largely because the British extended the colonial system already in place in Calcutta into the Valley, which also brought its language for colonial convenience (Choudhury 2006: 13–18). However, the Baptist missionaries required local languages for the propagation of their message. In this regard, official recognition of the local language that they used was crucial for facilitating their programmes. Thus, the earliest modern dictionary of Assamese was written by the missionary Nathan Brown. Titled *Grammatical Notices of the Assamese Language* (1848), it was on the Sibsagar variant. It is generally recognised today that until the third quarter of the 19th century, the major voice in the Valley that argued for the cause of recognising the Assamese (Sibsagar) language as the official language (because the language was fundamentally different from Bangla which was opposite to the colonial position) was that of the Baptist missionaries. This clearly indicates how ideology of language use influenced language planning.

Third, it was not only a question of language planning and language use vis-à-vis the missionaries and the colonial establishment. Behind the language shift was also the question of the indigenous social base of/for the new process of language underway in the Valley. During the colonial period, the eastern valley emerged as the economic, political and cultural centre. In terms of recorded history (inscriptions and written sources), it was for the first time that a single area/zone emerged as the centre of socio-economic, political and cultural centre of the Valley. One of the major factors behind it was the role of the tea plantation economy. The bourgeoisie which emerged in the Valley comprised a few small local planters and a larger mass of people involved in the service sector related to the plantation economy, either directly or in its ancillary services. Most of the early educational initiatives, i.e., setting up of modern schools and colleges, also took place in the eastern part of the Valley, and in most cases, at the initiatives of the local planters. The first bourgeois political organisation, the Assam Association, also came up in the eastern valley in 1901. Behind the emergence of the above social base, it is important to note that a number of factors came together in the last quarter of the 19th and the early 20th centuries which made it possible. The significant expansion of the plantation economy in the eastern part of the Valley, the Inner Line Regulation which demarcated the Valley as a strategic locale within the frontier and which required it to be *ordered* into a manageable frontier, language planning and language shift with the Sibsagar variant at the centre, emergence of a bourgeoisie based largely on the plantation economy, growth of bourgeois politics (through the Assam Association) and educational initiatives by the bourgeoisie in the eastern valley, these various factors in conjunction contributed to the eastern valley emerging as the most significant *modern* social base in the region. It is worth mentioning that by the third decade of the 20th century, when peasant agitations under communist leadership began in the Valley, the social base of the movement was mostly in the central and western parts of the Valley. Further, peasant resettlement (from east Bengal) in the eastern valley was minimal when compared to the central and western valley, one of the major reasons being that most of the 'wasteland' was already appropriated into the plantation economy.

Language modernisation, however, was not only about language shift and the systematic listing of the linguistic features of the Sibsagar variant of the Assamese language to indicate its similarities and exchanges with both Indo-European languages (phonological, morphological and syntactic) and Tibeto-Burman languages (phonological and morphological). It was as much about changes in the mode of using language as a cultural resource in the valley. This became fundamentally connected to the question of order/civilised vis-à-vis the lack of order/savage in the valley.

One of the characteristic modes of doing literature in the pre-colonial period in most parts of South Asia (and South East Asia) was the multiple narrative system. In this system the manuscript, the oral rendition and its performance were intrinsically bound to one another (Ramanujan 2004: 532–52). The mode has also been termed as scripto-centric (manuscript), phono-centric (oral) and body-centric (performance), the three together comprising literature and the doing of literature (Satyanath 2008). In other words, the registers of literature were not only textual but also oral and performative. In South Asia, the mode was supposed to be typical of *bhasa* literature (as opposed to *marga* or Sanskrit literature) that developed between the 5th–6th centuries and 16th–17th centuries (Devy 1992). It is debatable, though, to what extent the *bhasa* vs *marga*, i.e., little vs great traditions, framework can be a successful one to analyse culture formation, as can be seen from the example of the Brahmaputra Valley below.

The Brahmaputra Valley was, on the one hand, the easternmost part of South Asia and on the other hand, was the space which connected East and South East Asia with South Asia. Though there is little direct evidence of how much cultural transaction and exchange took place through the Valley between the two geo-spaces at its two ends, there is a large body of evidence on how both the geo-spaces influenced culture formation within it. To reiterate a point made earlier, the Valley had served as both a highway of migration between South, East and South East Asia as well as the destination of settlement for communities from these socio-spaces. It was the historical uniqueness of the Valley. This role of the Valley can be attributed to two factors, namely, its location at the continental crossroads and geographically being a Valley in an otherwise mountainous region. It was this nature of the Valley that made it a receiver of influence from its neigbouring geo-spaces, creating in turn cultural processes unique to itself. The neo-Vaishnava performance literature in the Valley can be taken as one example which helps explain the phenomenon.

The texts of neo-Vaishnava literature (16th and 17th centuries) were indigenised trans-creations of the two epics of the *Mahabharata* and the *Ramayana*, the Puranas and the *Bhagavada Gita*. The neo-Vaishnava tradition did not, however, initiate this form of indigenised trans-creations in the Valley. It could be traced to the 14th and 15th centuries when the *Ramayana* and episodes of the *Mahabharata* were trans-created in Kamrupi Assamese, most often under the patronage of kings. While Madhab Kandali's *Ramayana* was patronised by the Kachari (Barahi) ruler, Mahamanikya, episodic trans-creations of the *Mahabharata* by Hem Saraswati or Harihar Bipra and others were patronised by the Koch rulers (western valley). Therefore, the general contention that the Bhakti Movement influenced the process of trans-creation in South Asia needs to be revisited. What is more plausible as a contention is that such literary practices became a part of the larger process of emergence of region-based polities during the period, and thus the political support that they received (Pollock 2006). Further, the general contention that the patronage provided was part of the process of Sanskritisation, given that none of the major royal establishments in the Valley during the period (neither the Ahoms in the eastern valley nor the Koch in the western valley) were part of the *varna/jati* order, also needs to be revisited. When the indigenised trans-created literature is not seen as mere production of specific texts but as a tradition and a mode of doing culture which continued till the 18th century in the Valley, the two arguments of (a) Sanskritisation and (b) Sanskritisation as a means of bridging the *bhasa* and *marga* literatures, can prove insufficient. Moreover, Sanskritisation through the Shakti sect is far more problematic an approach than otherwise, given its geography of influence in South Asia. The same can apply to Islam and Islamisation as well, as shown in the case of Kanu Fakir and his Sufi-tantric Islam in the Chittagong area in the 18th century (Ray 2008: 192–206).

The neo-Vaishnava movement of the 16th century incorporated this tradition of literature into its missionary corpus. It needs to be mentioned that the tradition of literature continued to exist even outside the neo-Vaishnava fold during the period, most significantly in the works of Durgabor (16th century) whose indigenised trans-creations were based on Shakti philosophy. As is shown in the case of most parts of South and South East Asia, literature included the manuscript, its oral rendition and its performance. Neo-Vaishnava literature in the Valley was no exception. The primary reason for it was that if literature had to be mass consumed, in the absence of textual mass production (i.e., printing press and a market), communication of literature had to rely on means beyond the textual. For a corpus of missionary literature, as in the case of the Neo-Vaishnava Movement in the Valley, mass communication was central to its objective of doing literature. Therefore, the means of arriving at or achieving mass communication of its literature was significant for the movement.

Whether in terms of music or of staged performances, indigenous resources were, therefore, widely used. These were both material such as musical instruments or masks, as well as non-material, i.e., genres. For example, the music of Borgeet (a form of devotional song), which was central to understand Sankardeb's (who initiated the movement in the Valley) cultural production, is traced to the musical forms of the Bodo community in which feeling of sorrow is paramount (Sharma 2009). Such use or form of music is widely found not only in north-east India but throughout South East Asia as well. Similarly, the Sali or Nati dance is traced to the prevalent forms of temple dance during the period in the Valley. These dance forms were not entirely based on Natyasastra models. Further, the dance movements of the *sutradhar* in Satriya dance is traced to the Bagroomba folk dance of the Bodo community. The *nagara* (drums) music (added to the Vaishnava cultural repertoire in the post-Sankardeb period) is traced to the Bodo Kherai dance-performance. The nature of use of the flute is traced to the Bodo Sifung. Vaishnava cultural production used existing cultural forms and musical instruments from different communities and transformed the context of their use. In the process, a greater Hindustani classical musical base was provided as part of the transformation. Further, the institution of *naamghar* or prayer hall, which became the focal centre of neo-Vaishnava practices and propagation, was the incorporation of the *morong ghar* or community hall of the youth, to be found in most indigenous communities in the Valley as well as the hills/mountains of the region (it was prevalent in South East Asia as well).[1]

Indigenised trans-creations in the Neo-Vaishnava Movement was more than the mere text. Based on available historical evidence, its similarities and difference from the indigenised trans-creations of the preceding period or by the contemporary Koch rulers can certainly be drawn. In both the cases, the language of the trans-creations was Kamrupi. But whereas in the neo-Vaishnava case, as trans-creations meant for mass communication, the text alone did not constitute the meta-text, in the latter case, for being texts primarily based on royal patronage and for a royal clientele the text or manuscript itself comprised the meta-text. The cultural

---

[1] *Naamghar*s continue to be one of the most ubiquitous institutions in the Valley, across communities and the rural–urban divide. The *naamghar* not only plays its role as community prayer hall, but also is a centre for economic and social decision making in the community or neighbourhood. Its role in the 18th-century popular Moamaria rebellion against the Ahom monarchy or during the anti-colonial agitation against British colonialism highlights its political role.

patronage of the Koch monarchy has been interpreted as part of the Sanskritisation process (Eaton 1994: 187–91). But was it truly Sanskritisation? I tried to indicate in the case of the Kandali *Ramayana* that the question of Sanskritsation vs appropriation of the Sanskritic in the indigenous needs further research. This fact of indigenisation of an otherwise Sanskritic source was more evident in the case of Sankari performance texts. Sankardeb claimed that he was opposed to popular (*loukik*) culture, based on which it was argued that he attempted Sanskritisation of the Brahmaputra Valley (Baruah 1995: 15–16). However, if the nature of his meta-text and its probable objective is considered, Sankardeb's claim appears more an ideological rhetoric to help distinguish his sect and facilitate its missionary goal. But if it was at all that the Sankari culture attempted to distinguish itself, it may also be studied what was its nature or extent or was it even the case. The Sankari cultural forms were not merely forms but were also practices (performance literature). The methods and institutions that were adopted (or appropriated from existing ones) towards the practise of these cultural forms were, however, not exceptions but part of the *everyday*. For example, institutions like *morong ghar* on which the most important *naamghar* was based were fundamentally part of the everyday. Thus, this line of enquiry can throw light on two issues, viz. (a) can the interpretative framework of Sanskritisation or localisation of culture explain such a cultural praxis (cultural forms and their practise); and (b) to what extent Sankari culture attempted to be the exceptional vis-à-vis the common or everyday, or is it that the very posing of the problem thus is a failure to conceptualise the cultural praxis in the given continental crossroad.

In the previous chapter, I discussed the problematic of Sanskritisation as a mode of mapping socio-spatial relations in the Valley. I took the neo-Vaishnava intervention in Kandalii's *Ramayana* as an example in this regard. My argument was that the neo-Vaishnava intervention (in the form of the *Adi Kanda* and *Uttara Kanda*) in Kandali's *Ramayana* was symptomatic of the problems faced when socio-spatial relations were attempted to be defined into specified orders of societies. As a result, characters such as Sita came to exist as ruptures within the overall narrative. It is worth noting that with regard to the neo-Vaishnava tradition, its success was in devising cultural forms which could accommodate within themselves the historically shared mapping of socio-spatial relations in the Valley. Attempts at transgressing the framework resulted in narrative ruptures (such as Sita). When such practices are collated with the Buranji tradition, it can certainly be explored further whether Sanskritisation is at all a suitable framework to study culture formation in the Valley (i.e., the Valley as a crossroad). Such an approach invariably puts attention on the socio-spatial relations which was at the core of pre-colonial textual traditions. It highlights how the presence of Sanskritic elements does not necessarily mean Sanskritsation. In this regard, the dialectic of shared mapping across differences could be treated as a more suitable framework than homogenising approaches such as Sanskrtitisation.

If the preceding discussion on the neo-Vaishnava tradition needs to be summed up in two points vis-à-vis the mode of doing literature, then I would state them as (a) its objective was mass communication; and (b) it was not only the indigenised texts but also the means adopted beyond the textual to achieve mass communication which were critical in production and reception of the literature (Baruah 2007). The literature thus produced was inclusive in nature. After the 17th century, the texts became largely canonical. But the means beyond the textual could vary and evolve and so did the nature of its propagation, especially as it moved further east in the Valley and into the neighboring foothills (Mahanta 2007: 20–27). In a geographical area which due to its location at the continental crossroad functioned as a highway of migration and also as the destination of settlement for communities, it was imperative for any form of culture, including literature, to be inclusive and 'indeterminate' in its framework. In reality, the indeterminacy was the presence of shared mapping of socio-spatial relations or attempts to engage with it. The Neo-Vaishnava Movement possibly did not necessarily produce a Sanskritised population. Colonial ethnographic (or anthropological) accounts of the 19th century are ample testimony to the fact that 'Hindu', 'tribal' and Sanskritisation in the Valley could be related to one another but (a) need not necessarily be so; and (b) were not the same processes. Further, there is no evidence from the 16th–18th centuries that a Sanskritised population was indeed produced in the Valley. In fact, what the Neo-Vaishnavite Movement did produce was a large-scale popular *ethnic* rebellion against the Ahom monarchy in the 18th century (Moamaria revolt), which eventually led to the entry of the British in the late 18th century (1792) with military help for the Ahom monarchy. The success of the Neo-Vaishnava Movement and its literature could be attributed to the way it contextualised itself into the peculiarity of socio-spatial relations of the Valley. This also once again highlights the need for further investigation on the relation of Sankari ideology (which attempted a new order) and practise (which adapted itself to the specificity of the historical and material condition of the Valley).

Language modernisation and language shift in the 19th century was a fundamental break from the past in terms of doing of inclusive literature. The transformation that literature underwent was connected to its larger transformation from being a continental crossroad to a (colonial) frontier. Language shift in creative literature from Kamrupi to Sibsagar in the latter part of the 19th century has already been discussed. The process of the Sibsagar variant becoming the 'official' language or language standard now entailed Kamrupi becoming a 'dialect'. Language modernisation was also characterised by two other changes in the nature of text and of communication of literature. Print technology, spread of colonial education and emergence of a market of readers introduced the phenomenon of 'books' as different from 'manuscript' of the pre-colonial period. Further, the mode of mass-produced books was also a fundamentally different mode of communication of literature as compared to the pre-colonial period. As a result of the change, language and books became the primary instruments of communicating literature. To be noted is that as the framework of narrative developed historically between the 14th and 18th centuries, language and manuscript were not the *primary* instruments of literature. The oral and performance dimensions were as central to the meaning and communication of the literary narrative. The specificity of the mode to the Valley was in its framework which could accommodate the diversity and shared mapping of relations of a continental crossroad. A notable historical fact in this regard is that though diversity of the social base continued to be a social reality even after colonialism, the Valley as a highway of migration or destination of settlement gradually came to a halt with colonialism. The Singpho and Khampti communities were the last recorded case of migration and settlement in the (eastern) valley. They came from Myanmar ('Upper Burma') and settled in the easternmost fringes of the Valley in between the late 18th and early 19th century.[2] The massive spatial transformations through tea plantations, the policy of settling peasants from east Bengal and the conscious colonial policy to achieve control over the space (territory and terrain of the Valley) were major factors that led to the change. Mitchell's report (Mitchell 1883) provides a detailed account of colonial planning over space and strategies of its control. Last, language and books becoming the primary instruments of literature introduced a critical contradiction in the relation between literature and the diversity of social base in the Valley. In the pre-colonial period, for example, during the Neo-Vaishnava Movement, there is no evidence to argue that language per se was assumed to be a sufficient communicator of its heterogeneous social base. Social heterogeneity was one of the basic characteristics of social formation in the Valley, thus, the given mode of doing literature during the period. Since the colonial period, a fundamental break from this assumption/practice became evident in the form of *books*.

The process of language shift during the colonial period was also marked by the phenomenon of language emerging as a marker of identity. The last quarter of the 19th century was significant in this regard. The establishment of Asomiya Bhasa Unnati Sadhini Sabha (Society for the Development of Assamese Language) in 1888 by a group of young Assamese students and their launch of the journal *Jonaki* (Moonlit or Moonlight) in 1889 became the early steps in language becoming a 'national' identity marker for the Valley. Among others, one of the major aims was creation of a written standard of Assamese which would be used all over the Valley. It was elaborated by S. S. Bordoloi, president of the society, in *Jonaki* ([1895] 2001, 5 (7): 661). He stated (translation mine), '… and to create only one written language in all our areas will continue to be the effort of the Sabha'. The rationale for the approach was traced to the European context

---

[2] The Singphos were the one of the first communities in the valley that the British waged war. The Bruce brothers, credited with discovering tea in the Valley, waged war against the Singphos in 1820s to recover the knowledge of tea production, which the Singphos had refused to part with (Baruah 2008).

wherein language was a fundamental marker of national identity. Standardisation of language and development of modern literature came to be seen as conjoined (Dutt 2004–2005). The two came to be seen as central to any *national* development. For example, Lakhminath Bezbaruah, arguably the most significant writer/intellectual of the period and member of the group, argued that colonialism had introduced modern thoughts in the Assamese social and intellectual environment, but the Assamese language was yet to be sufficiently modernised to be able to communicate these thoughts and ideas, which were fundamental to Assamese *national* development. Thus, Bezbaruah emphasised in the pages of *Jonaki* that standardisation and modernisation of language was crucial for modernisation of thought and self, and literature had always been a significant factor in such a process (Bezbaruah [1895] 2001a 5 (6): 642–44).

The approach was based on his notion that *progression* of language also marked the progression of its society from savagery to civilisation ([1895] 2001b, 5 (5): 627). For example, in a linguistic schema which would not find acceptance today, he argued (translation mine),

> The more we sail upwards the river of language, more we find it being narrow and poor. The languages of the Nagas, Miris, Misimis and their like are still savage because their thoughts are not yet developed. The developed languages of today were also at one time savage languages like them. It was because the thoughts of their forefathers were not developed. Less thought can be expressed in lesser words.

Colonialism was seen as aiding the process. Thus, in the articulations of the period, the shift from the pre-colonial mapping of socio-spatial relations was starkly evident. Also, the positive light in which colonialism was seen is evident, for example, in Hemchandra Goswami ([1891] 2001, 3 [9–10]: 367–68), one of the leading cultural figures of the period, when he argued on the British instituting Bangla as the official language in Assam in place of Assamese in 1834 (translation mine),

> ... we cannot blame the British administrative system for this ... It was due to the ignorance of its government in Assam that Assamese language faced such dire situation. Had they not listened to the

selfish Bangla subordinates and listened in turn to their own sense of reason, they would have never removed Assamese from our courts and educational institutions, replacing it with Bangla.

The process achieved its institutional peak with the establishment of the Asom Sahitya Sabha in 1917 (Padmanath Gohain Baruah was its first president), which aimed at *national* development of Assamese language and literature to facilitate Assamese language which had lesser linguistic resources to become modern and be able to communicate with a wider range of language resources.

But in a context of heterogeneous social base, the futility of language as a marker of identity was evident even by the 1920s, when the Bodo community registered its demand for separate and autonomous identity (before the Simon Commission, 1929, followed by the formation of Plain Tribal Council of Assam [PTCA] in 1935). To the Bodos, language became a critical marker of their difference from Assamese identity. By the 1930s, the Ahom Movement in the eastern valley had also gained considerable momentum. It had started with the formation of the Ahom Association in 1893. It distinguished itself as an identity based on its own set of language, religion, locale and history different from the caste-Hindu 'Assamese' identity.

Modern Assamese Language and Narrative: The Ethnographic Contradiction

If ethnographic characteristics are embedded in the nature of a language, then there would be limits to how much a given language can carry or communicate narratives which lie beyond its ethnographic paradigm. In this regard, language modernisation and language codification exists as problematic in or of the socio-historical contexts (Fishman 1989: 67–95). Existing research does not suggest that there were attempts at language codification of (Kamrupi or Sibsagar) Assamese in the pre-colonial period, as was the case in some other languages, such as the Dravidian languages (Sridhar 2008: 235–52). Interestingly, there are hardly any studies on the ethnographic limits that modern Assamese contains vis-à-vis the language groups that it claims to include or represent. Nevertheless, despite the lack of an ethno-linguistic study of the language, the debate itself arising from problematic of ethnography in modern Assamese can be traced to the late 19th century.

For example, in the pages of *Jonaki*, Lakhminath Bezbaruah forcefully argued that once now that a written standard had been accepted for modern Assamese, it should no longer be a matter of debate between eastern and western variants of the language ([1897] 2001, 7 (4): 817). The point was made in response to a complaint (hypothetical?) that examinees in the western valley found it difficult to comprehend the question papers (composed in the Sibsagar standard) of entrance examinations. Bezbaruah's argument is that every language has multiple variants, of which one is considered/taken as the standard.[3] Therefore, the Sibsagar variant as standard ought to be considered in that light. I have already discussed the process through which the Sibsagar variant came to be recognised as the linguistic standard.

However, this ethnographic debate over language continued, evident in the later magazine *Bahni*. In *Bahni*, Bezbaruah frontally addressed the question of language difference between the west and east of the Valley, with the latter occupying the position of the official language ([1910] 2001, 1 (2): 42–52). The essay is also reproduced in translation in the Appendix to this book. For example, he stated (translation mine), 'How do we see the Assamese language of today: as the celebration of the victory of the Ahom language or blowing the conch shell at the deathbed of Kamrupi language?' (ibid.: 42) He conceded that as a result of the Sibsagar variant becoming official language, ethnographic limits in communicating social and cultural life of the western valley were well in place. He stated, 'It might be that the language has more scope for expressing the eastern (dialect) and less scope for expressing the western (dialect), but there is no doubt that this language is real language of Assam' (ibid.) However, he justified the Sibsagar standard in terms of language of capital assuming the status of official as a natural and universal phenomenon ('There is no doubt that the language of the capital becomes the language standard' ibid). He argued that the shift of power from the west to the east of the Valley since colonialism had also caused the

---

[3] Interestingly, Gunabhiram Baruah published a letter (against colonial taxation policy) as a peasant from western valley titled *Kamrupir Patra* (A Letter from a Kamrupi) in the Kamrupi variant of the language in *Jonaki* ([1892] 2001, 4 (8): 518).

language shift. The severity of the debate became more evident in the subsequent issues of *Bahni*, especially over the poem '*Ha Mur Kapal!*' (My Luck!) by Umeshchandra Baruah ([1911] 2001, 2 (2) 41–43), which dealt with how people speaking Kamrupi were now left with little means of communicating themselves in writing. It was a long satirical poem which noted how in schools, in courts and even in general conversations, a new order of language had been imposed on the people of the western valley in the name of good and correct language. 'But how do we forgo the language of our forefathers?' was what came up repeatedly in the poem.

During the period, there was another dimension in the ethnographic debate over language which figured prominently. It was vis-à-vis the growing identity consciousness among the Ahom community. Padmanath Gohain Baruah, a contemporary of Bezbaruah and one of the leading popular intellectual figures of the Valley, contested in his letter to the editor, '*Purani Kathat Natun Rang*' (Old Wine in New Bottle; the letter is reproduced in translation in the Appendix to this book), that since there was little difference between Assamese used for writing pre-colonial Ahom chronicles Buranjis and the one now chosen as official language under colonialism, the credit needed to be given to the pre-colonial Ahom monarchy. However, he argued, the credit seemed to have been hijacked and appropriated by the upper-caste Hindus of the Valley, characterising the period of Ahom rule as a dark one (*Bahni*, [1911] 2001, 1 (7): 219–21). From the 1890s, it had become a commonplace to argue that though numerous communities with their respective languages inhabited the Valley, it was Assamese alone wherein the universe of the concept of 'Assam' was located. It had been the language which had tied different people together in the space called Assam (for example, Lakhminath Bezbaruah's numerous writings in *Jonaki* and *Bahni*). But what was new in Gohain Baruah's approach was that it attempted to create an Assamese universe and yet retained the particularity of Ahom identity. In his presidential address to the first congress of the Asom Sahitya Sabha in 1917, he argued that it was due to the political unification of the Valley achieved under Ahom rule and because from the very beginning Ahom rule had adopted the language of the people (i.e., Assamese) for the conduct of their rule that not only Assam could be imagined as a totality but also Assamese could be identified as the totality which constituted that universe. He argued that the term 'Assamese' ('Asomiya') itself was of modern origin. In the pre-colonial period, different communities had their respective identities. But Ahom rule, politically and culturally, created (or left behind?) conditions that made it possible to conceptualise the term 'Assamese' (Gohain Baruah [1971] 2008: 879–80). Based on the same grounds, he also argued in his address to the Ahom Association, 1941 that despite such fundamental Ahom contributions to the development of the framework of Assamese and Assam, the caste-Hindu Assamese in the modern period had relegated the Ahom community to the backwaters. Therefore, not only did the numerous Ahom groups (*khels*) need to come together but they together as a single group needed a separate electorate to achieve former glories once again and contribute to the larger national (Assamese) life (ibid.: 933–45). His argument was part of the larger attempts to *create* a category of Ahom people as a distinct ethnic identity in the Valley, different from caste-Hindu identity (Saikia 2004). What was unique about his argument was that it was historically situated. For example, in his address to the Ahom Association (ibid.), he made it clear that the various Ahom *khels* or groups (such as Mataks, etc.) in the past were indeed different people; but as part of the historical process of Ahoms indigenising themselves in the Valley through inter-marriage and other alliances, these communities became part of the larger Ahom family and therefore, rather than asking for separate electorates based on their respective ethnicity, should come together for a separate Ahom electorate only.

The ethnographic debate over language codification is one example of how attempts at order in the Valley did not lead to the homogenisation of social processes in the area. On the contrary, it exposed the problems in the very attempt vis-à-vis the context of socio-historical heterogeneity and the shift from the historical socio-spatial relations of a crossroad. But despite this above critique and contestation, it is also undeniable that an order of language and narrative was indeed institutionally put in place in the Valley. If codification and enforcing the codification are taken as the prime movers of the order, then the fissures it led to can also be clearly identified. In the striving towards ordering and differentiating the self from the other, the shared mapping of historical relations increasingly got sidelined. It became a process in which both the colonial state and the leading intellectuals from within the Valley participated.

Connected to the issue of modern Assamese language and pre-colonial Ahom past, there was another problem vis-à-vis language and narrative which can be indicated here. Though Gohain Baruah tried to reclaim modern Assamese for the pre-colonial Ahom past, he did not refer to another significant transformation that had taken place, which fundamentally distinguished modern Assamese from its Ahom past. The transformation was in the relation between language and narrative composed/written in that language. The modern language standard in Assamese was hardly different from the language used by the Ahom nobility to write their Buranjis. But the narrative of the Buranjis, other than recording of events, gave substantial space to Ahom genealogy. Importantly, one of the remarkable features of the genealogies was that the heroes and the spaces they (Ahoms) traced their ancestry to and regularised in their Buranjis were trans-spatial, i.e., trans-regional and trans-society, in nature, spreading from Myanmar up to the Brahmaputra Valley. I have already discussed this in the previous chapter. In contrast to this nature of narrative (in terms of the people and space that they premised on) the narratives that came up in the modern Assamese standard from the 19th century onwards primarily were with space and society which dealt with relation between the Valley and the Gangetic basin/culture. While in the Ahom Buranjis the people and space from Myanmar to the Valley was the present, in the latter case, this relation changed into the past or history of the Valley, while the present came to be located in the *historical* relation with Gangetic culture (for example, the emphatic writings of Kamalakanta Bhattacharjee's on Assamese culture in several issues of *Jonaki*).

At one level, the change could be considered as continuity of content. In pre-colonial neo-Vaishnava literature as well, the Gangetic connection was emphatic textually (though as performance literature, its meaning could sharply differ, as discussed earlier). Therefore, once the Kamrupi was overtaken by the Sibsagar variant as the predominant variant (in fact, it became the 'standard'), it was not a case of development of new content but of transference of old content, but into narratives written in a new language variant vis-à-vis the context. There is very little research on this process of exchanges between language and narrative in Assamese; nevertheless, it needs to highlighted that Kamrupi language and Buranji narrative became dialects and relics of the past respectively, while modern Assamese standard appropriated (or recreated?) a narrative which was new to itself, but had earlier been textually related to the Kamrupi language, now reduced to a 'dialect'. Though Gohain Baruah himself did not indicate it, when his critique of caste-Hindus appropriating the Assamese language in the 19th century is seen in the above light, new meanings to the process of language shift and narratives written/composed in the process of language shift can definitley be identified. Further, in the Buranjis, the framework which encompassed the people and space from the Valley to Myanmar was the trans-spatial *kunhow*. But in the narratives in the modern standard of the language, more fixed frameworks or order of identity, people and space were to be found.

It was a frequent nationalist contention that the Ahom monarchy and Sankari culture had created 'Assamese' as a category of people, both socio-culturally and politically (for example, Jogesh Das' presidential address, 51st Congress of Asom Sahitya Sabha, [1989] 2008: 279). Language and narrative or 'literature' as a marker of the identity was given crucial importance. It was argued that a common language and literature developed since the 16th century through the political unification of the Valley under the Ahoms. But seen in the light of these relations (or re-arrangements) between language and narrative, it is evident that not only the nature of the Ahom polity is overlooked in this regard (as discussed earlier) but also the re-arrangement that took place in the relations of language and narrative between the pre-colonial and colonial periods is as commonly overlooked in the Assamese nationalist political (ideological?) discourse.

It may be helpful to indicate the colonial position in this debate, given that colonialism played a key role in the entire process. I would try it through Gait's example. Gait remarked,

> So far as philology is concerned, it is, of course, admitted that language is no real test of race. The Ahoms have abandoned their tribal dialect in favour of Assamese, and Rabhas, Kacharis and other tribes are following their example. The reason in these cases is partly that Assamese is the language of the priests, who are gruadually bringing these rude tribes within the fold of Hinduism, and partly that it is the language of higher civilization. But there is another way in which one form of speech may supplant another, viz., by conquest. When one nation brings another under subjection,

it often imposes its own language on the conquered people. Thus within the last hundred years the Shan tribe of Turungs, while held in captivity amongst the Singphos, abandoned their native tongue and adopted that of the captors. It may safely be assumed that one or other, or both, of these processes has always been in operation, and that just as Assamese is now supplanting Kachari and other tribal languages, so these in their turn displaced those of an earlier generation (Gait [1905] 1994: 1–2). It is quite evident that both the discourses of Bezbaruah and of Gohain Baruah were influenced by the colonial discourse, though the emphasis in Gohain Baruah's was quite different from the colonial framework, or the respective positions of Bezbaruah and Gohain Baruah were different from one another.

In the debate on ethnographic contradiction in the making of modern Assamese language and literature, the analysis of text and context would be incomplete without taking into account the contribution of Bishnu Rabha, the cultural icon and communist leader who strode like a colossus (as a popular leader and popular cultural icon) in the middle of the 20th century in the Valley and its neighbouring hills. The intervention that Rabha made in the ethnographic debate through his cultural productions will be taken up in detail in Part II of this study. Here, only views which he applied in his cultural productions are highlighted. In contrast to the above approaches on the ethnographic debate over language and narrative, Rabha argued that both the roots and the body of not only the 'Assamese' language but also the various popular cultural forms of the Valley and its neighbouring hills needed to be traced to and located in the Bodo–Kachari community. One of the earliest settler communities in the region, he noted that whether it be language or musical genres or folk traditions, the influence of the Bodo–Kachari culture was palpable. Vis-à-vis the practice of Assamese language, he tried to show that whether at the lexical or syntactic levels Assamese could be more meaningfully traced to the Bodo–Kachari culture than any Aryan origin (Rabha [1989] 2008: 946–60). The same could be said for folk cultural forms such as Bihu or the various musical instruments and musical genres that were practised in the Valley and its neighbouring hills (ibid.: 960–69).

In an expression of irony, he said that the Bodo–Kachari community itself appeared to have lost sense of this reality. This he showed through an example of Bisoni and Katoha villages in the eastern valley (near Lakhimpur) where the Bodo–Kacharis of the eastern valley pejoratively addressed those who were resettled from western valley (by the Birtish) as *jharuwa* or from Jharkhand. The latter served in the British army, and when retired, were settled in these two villages (Rabha [1989] 2008 : 972–73). One of the major differences between Rabha and Bezbaruah or Gohain Baruah is that his fundamental emphasis vis-à-vis language or culture was not in terms of written 'standard' but practice, i.e., not what ought to be but what existed as a common practice as far as language was concerned. He consistently pointed out that irrespective of the cultural form one was talking about, such as language and narrative, songs, dance, plays and others, code mixing had been the predominant phenomenon in the Valley and its neighbouring hills. This is in contrast to the emphases in Bezbaruah or Gohain Baruah on the making of code (of 'Assamese') rather than mixing of codes. The location of the region (though Rabha did not use the term of crossroad, i.e., its Assamese equivalent, it is evident from his writings that he meant just the same) had played a crucial role in this (ibid.: 932–45). Therefore, to Rabha, such a historical experience could not be limited through the institution of a 'standard' in the modern period. In his cultural productions, he showed that if the objective of cultural form was to reach out to the masses, then such 'standards' were not relevant either. It was only through code mixing that the masses of the Valley and its neighbouring hills could be accessed and the masses would reciprocate and identify with the cultural form. Rabha's approach can be seen as cultural production from a practising communist leader wherein cultural form cannot be the markers of identity; rather cultural forms needs to identify the relation among people that it seeks to address, which in his case was the class relation of peasants and workers. For Rabha, only through such an approach could literature have political relevance. Between the 1930s and 1950s, the phenomenal popularity of Rabha among the peasants and 'tribal' people of the Valley and its neighbouring hills could be taken as a testimony of both the 'common sense' and 'historical sense' that Rabha showed towards the cultural question and the ethnographic debate on the issue.

Conclusion

In conclusion, I would argue that in the shift from continental crossroad to frontier, the issue that became most crucial with regard to language and textual traditions was that of code. Whether on the basis of the needs of the Baptist missionaries, or in terms of the methods that the colonial state employed to classify and understand the colonised at the level of language and its use, or even in terms of identity formation since the 19th century, the debate on language code, code switching or code mixing became extremely important. The debate on code, however, was in contrast to the nature of language use in pre-colonial textual traditions. The debate also highlights the shift in the nature of socio-spatial mapping between the two periods. This is evident in the discussions of Bezbaruah or Gohain Baruah (or even Gait in this regard) that shared mapping of socio-spatial relations could not have taken place when language gets instituted as a distinct code. As a direct result, it sparked off the debate on the ethnographic limits now embedded in the Assamese language vis-à-vis allowing different groups of people from within the Valley to communicate. Further, the discussions of Bezbaruah and Gohain Baruah, or even the colonial position on the matter, importantly highlights that the issue of code was primarily about means of conceptualising new forms of socio-spatial relations in the Valley. The idea of Assam lay at the very root of the debate. Conceptualising Assam as a concrete entity was corresponded by the attempts at devising a language code of Assam. Based on discussions in the previous chapters, it goes without saying that the idea of Assam in this regard was an invention of the colonial period, an invention closely associated with the making of a British-Indian frontier. It is in this context that Bishnu Rabha and his approach to the practice of literature and culture which assumes significance. Rabha was one of the earliest critics who articulated clearly the failure in conceptualising socio-spatial relations in the Valley in terms of language code, therefore his insistence on code mixing, whether at the level of language or at the level of practise. He was one of earliest to articulate the limits of literature based on notions of codes being able to represent the diversity which comprised the Brahmaputra Valley. His answer, as already indicated, was that literature cannot represent *a* people, the point that Bezbaruah or Gohain Baruah were trying to achieve. Rabha showed that literature needs to identify the relation among the different people that it seeks to represent, and to achieve it, there must be a break from the notion of code in the writing and performance of literature. Only such an approach to literature could be historically justified for the region. At the end of Part Two, I will show that these are precisely the issues which modern Assamese literature continues to struggle with.

Towards a Conclusion

In my conclusion to Part I let me pose the question: What was the impact of language codification on narratives in modern Assamese novels and short stories, the predominant Assamese literary forms of the 19th and 20th centuries? I will try to answer through the following example.

Birinchi Baruah's *Seuji Patar Kahini* (A Story of Green Leaves, 1958) is a classic ethnographic account on the Assamese tea plantation world. The novel revolves around the impossible love between Soniya, a female worker from the plantation community, who is an 'illegitimate' child born of a British colonial planter, and a local Assamese youth Nareshwar who works for a British plantation manager, Mr Miller. Soniya, a blonde but growing up as a plantation worker in the plantation community, despite her love for Nareshwar, is unable to live with the dichotomy of her racial and social existence, and finally leaves the plantation for good, wandering into the unknown world (for her) beyond the plantations. The critical point in the novel vis-à-vis the problem of the indigenous is the construct of the social world and the role of language in it. The social world of the novel is very inclusive. It comprises not only the world that was within the planned industrial space of tea plantation (i.e., a world inhabited by management, workers and clerical staff) but also the neighbouring local villages and their people outside the confines of the plantation space. The worlds within and without the plantation space share a close relation. As a novel written in the 1950s, the perspective was pioneering, predating the current emphasis that the world within and without the plantation spaces were not mutually exclusive, as it was argued for long, and argued especially in the colonial discourse of 'enclave economy'. Further, the novel also clearly indicates that what comprised the indigenous was not only the 'Assamese' as had come to be interpreted since the 19th century with language as a marker of that identity, but also the other social constituents such as the plantation workers, those from mixed parentage or other communities ('tribes'). In other words, the diversity together comprised the 'Assamese' universe.

What problematised the issue, however, was the choice of language which could communicate or bear in it the diversity that comprised the totality of the 'Assamese' universe. The language chosen as the marker of the universe of the 'Assamese' was the Sibsagar variant of Assamese language. There were three aspects to this choice of language. First, it was a phenomenon introduced by the language shift (Kamrupi to Sibsagar) and narrative shift from hybrid meta-text (text + oral + body) to mono-text (text) in the 19th century as a means and storage of information and communication in the different kinds of exchange relations among or within communities in the Valley. Second, language during the period (as in most parts of South Asia) emerged as a powerful marker of identity. The question of modern Assamese, therefore, also became a question of modern Assamese identity and the former assumed (or was provided) the role of marker and bearer of the latter. Third, as is already evident, language developed a dichotomy, a conflict, within itself, viz. it became exclusive but stood for the inclusive.

Seuji Patar Kahini was radical for its times in that unlike the common perception, it showed that the tea plantation world was not an exclusive enclave system. On the contrary, it was an inclusive world comprising a diversity of social groups and their habitation spaces within and without the plantations. However, it also needs to be added that by the 1950s, the construct of modern 'Assamese' had already come under sharp political critique from several social groups under the broad rubric of 'tribal' (Pathak 2010).[1] What made *Seuji Patar Kahini* historical (and most fiction since 19th century in that sense) was that it lacked or did not develop a linguistic mechanism which could be a marker and bearer of that diversity or heterogeneity, something that the term 'Assamese' claimed to represent. In the novel, one finds the diversity communicated only in one variant of the language, viz. Sibsagar Assamese. This was despite the fact that the languages of

---

[1] But it can be argued that modern Assamese literature, even in the late 19th century, did indicate that the larger Assamese universe was comprised of enormous ethnic diversity (for example, Rajanikanta Bordoloi's fictions). It was only that *Seuji Patar Kahini* was one of the first to make a case for it vis-à-vis the tea plantation world.

the communities which comprised the social world of the novel were comprehensible across the Valley irrespective of the community one belonged to. In other words, the constraint vis-à-vis the nature of language use was not related to reception of literature, i.e., whether the people reading the 'book' would understand the languages, if used. It was centrally connected to the very problems in language as code and the production of literature in the code. The problem could also be seen as a contradiction of the *order* of language and literature in a context of heterogeneity, viz. the exclusive claim to being inclusive and lacking the ethnographic means to be so.

The tension of this claim was amply present in the debates of the Asom Sahitya Sabha. There were three kinds of discourses (from within the Asom Sahitya Sabha) in this regard. First, the predominant discourse was that Assamese is the lingua franca of the Assamese people. The various other languages and their narratives in the Valley are sister/brother forms of Assamese. Assamese is the common historical thread among all the communities (and their cultural forms) which inhabit the Valley (for example, Mahendra Bora's presidential address to the 53rd Asom Sahitya Sabha congress, [1987] 2008: 298–327). The other discourse was to be found among those who belonged to the non-caste Hindu ethnic communities, such as the Bodos (for example, Sitanath Brahmachoudhury in his presidential addresses to the Asom Sahitya Sabha, 2008: 224–51). The discourse highlighted that the critique of the Assamese language-based nationalist discourse by the various ethnic communities and the emphasis the latter placed on their respective languages and narratives, even at the cost of the former, needed to be sympathetically seen. Any outright denial of their validity would only create further dissension within the category of Assamese. A third discourse too, though a minor one, was to be found in the proceedings of the Sahitya Sabha congresses (for example, Bhupen Hazarika's presidential address to the 59th congress of the Sabha, [1995] 2008: 403–20). The main argument was that the Asom Sahitya Sabha needs to move beyond the centrality of Assamese and it urgently requires to treat Assamese as only one of the many languages of Assam rather than centrally focusing on it. The discourse also emphasises the need for promoting not only greater cultural production in these many languages of the different communities but also an increased exchange and interaction among the languages and the narratives produced in them, i.e.m code mixing. In fact, Hazarika showed how his songs had found greater effect of communication when elements of different language variants were incorporated in a single piece of music (he gave the example of *Buku Ham Ham Kare*, i.e., 'fear grips my heart'; but the same can be said of his many other songs as well). In other words, the two distinct points in the discourse vis-à-vis the other two were (a) the absolute or universal connection between Assamese and Assam needs to be revisited; and (b) there needs to be greater emphasis on language convergence, which can facilitate new cultural forms. It needs to be added that Hazarika can claim to be a cultural figure with a following among all the different communities of the Valley in the postcolonial period. It is also notable that his mentor was Bishnu Rabha. Further, the issue of Rabha or Hazarika raises another question — Did people from performance backgrounds attempt (or attempt more successfully) a more accommodative narrative in the arts?

In this regard, Jyotiprasad Agarwalla, Rabha's contemporary and a pioneer cultural figure of the 1930s and 1940s (he died in 1951 at the age of 48) can be taken into account. He was a playwight, writer, essayist, film maker, poet-lyricist and music composer. He argued (translation mine), 'It can be seen that in our heritage of art, culture and music, more or less there is a noticeable impact of the various communities at different levels. It has made the Assamese civilization a confluence of East Asian and Indian civilizations' (Agarwalla 1996: 460). He further contended in the same essay (translation mine),

> Today, there are very few Assamese in Assam who carry with them an Assamese heritage. The plantation workers, those from Mymensing, the Nepalis, the Bengalis, the Marwaris and the others have come and settled in Assam and continue to live with their own respective specificities. Now if we are not able to incorporate the majority of these people within our heritage and language, then there is a definite danger. For the last 30 years, we have been surrounded by this problem. But we the Assamese have been ignoring it' (ibid.: 462).

What was Jyotiprasad's answer to the problem? He argued that through the spread of Sankari culture, they could be transformed into Assamese. But he also said (translation mine),

If today we ask these different people to give up their own culture and language and adopt Mahapurusia culture, it would go against the very principle of Sankardeb's own approach in this regard. Even if the Mahapurush used the cultural foundation of the valley to bring into the fold the Miri, Garo, Mikir and other people, he never allowed their own cultures and practices to be destroyed as part of the process. The process of accommodation and transformation was based on the cultural uniqueness of each community and using their respective uniqueness to create a larger society (ibid.: 469).

Agarwalla argued that whether in language or in cultural forms, Sankardeb extensively used the technique of code mixing and it is proof of the fact as to how the larger society was a confluence of the various specific components. It also opens up another area of further research, namely socialist intervention in the identity debate of Assam, an area of research almost unexplored. Rabha or Agarwalla or the early phase of Hazarika were part of the socialist intervention. It is evident, therefore, that to create a narrative form based on code mixing was a common quotient in Rabha, Hazarika or Agarwalla.

On closer observation of the first two discourses of the Asom Sahitya Sabha, as well as texts such as *Seuji Patar Kahini*, we find that two interrelated principles underlay their assumptions of the relation between language/narrative and social base. They were (a) Assamese (language) is the atom of the social and historical reality of the Valley and, thereby, it is present in all the various socio-cultural and historical manifestations in the Valley and constituted the universe of the larger Assamese reality; and (b) Assamese (language) is also the expansive paradigm within which is contained the variety or differences that dot the socio-cultural landscape of the Valley. Thus, either way, Assamese was no longer a language. Rather, it stood as the very 'Purusa', i.e., the atom and the expanse of the collective reality of the valley at the same time. The idea of Purusa (in Bhagavata) is philosophical mysticism. Similarly, the idea of Assamese in the above approach and putting it into practise was conceptual mysticism. The difference in the third perspective, especially its emphasis on language convergence in cultural forms of the Valley, was precisely in highlighting that each entity could be a universe in itself, but as a contradiction to one another, and that the conflict arising from it was only possible to overcome through a praxis which recognised the problematic and sought to accommodate it rather than attempting to *resolve* it.

The relation of contradiction cannot be resolved; it can only be accommodated in praxis. Therefore, to reiterate the line of the argument I have followed in my study, the tension of order in language or narrative and its relation to the social base can be more plausibly explained in terms of the dialectical relations that constitute the socio-spatial relations of frontier.

When the ethnographic contradiction in modern Assamese and narratives in fiction writing is seen in isolation, its peculiarity dissolves in the generality of the problem common to numerous languages and literatures in modern South Asia. Such approaches classify literatures that deviate or seek alternatives from the linguistic/narrative standard as 'regional' (*ansolik*) literature (Kakati 2000: 235–50). It is a framework (i.e., 'regional') widely practised for most languages and literatures in modern South Asia. However, and importantly, when the geographical area of the Valley is taken into consideration the paradigm of analysis can alter fundamentally, the paradigm being that of making of a frontier out of a continental crossroad. What the management of frontier since the latter half of the 19th century entailed was transformations at the levels of space, demography and of culture. These transformations in the Valley were not independent of its relation with the neighbouring hills/mountains, which together comprised the trans-Brahmaputra Valley. In the wider sense, the transformations were attempts at redrawing the nature of their relation. To that effect, the transformations were both historical and historic. If the entire northeast region was changed from a being a continental crossroad into a frontier (in both colonial and postcolonial periods), the mode and effect of that change varied between the Valley and the neighbouring hills/mountains. Yet the process of differential change was a conjoined one. In most contemporary research (for example Baruah 1999; Misra 2000) on the north-east frontier or the Valley in particular, it is this differential yet conjoined transformative process that is overlooked.[2] The frontier, in such research, is largely seen as a homogenous entity, thereby failing at the same

---

[2] Such contemporary research played a pioneering role in opening up the analysis of state and nation formation and its practice at the frontier. It emphasised that the frontier is not merely any other region of the Indian nation state. But herein also was the limitation of this researches. First, its analysis begins with the colonial period when the region becomes a 'frontier' for the first time. The historical existence of the region in the pre-colonial period as a continental

time to theoretically explain the possibility of different experiences of the process of identity formation but within the same frontier. It is at this juncture that recourse is taken to confusing categories like nationalism and sub-nationalism. For example, Naga identity struggle can be nationalist while Assamese identity struggle can be sub-nationalist, based on their respective distances or distancing from Indian nationalist identity. It is in this context that I argue that shifts in region formation studied in terms of changing socio-spatial relations could be a more historically plausible approach in explaining the trans-Brahmaputra Valley.

Does north-east India, and the Valley in particular, constitute a contested space? The answer is yes, and it is so at two levels. First, as a frontier, created during colonialism, it is an unresolved socio-space both territorially and in social demography. For example, there are large lower Himalayan areas which are claimed by China, a claim over which the Indo-China War was fought in 1962 and the Chinese forces came right up to the Valley while the Indian administration withdrew. It is claimed that socially and culturally, they historically belong to the Chinese sphere of influence. Similarly, in the south-east of the region, there are people from the Naga communities who are distributed historically in the hills of both modern-day India and Myanmar. The cluster of community which was historically neither a part of Indo-Gangetic culture nor the Buddhist Burmese culture, now finds itself torn between two countries in the 20th and 21st centuries. Second, the contested space is also internal, i.e., different communities within the frontier claiming their own ethnic spaces against the other. The problem is acute in the Valley as well, exemplified by the different autonomous

---

crossroad goes almost unaddressed. Second, this research is overwhelmingly preoccupied with the question of identity, whether national or ethnic and their conflictual interrelation. Sanjib Baruah (1999) even uses a confusing but a popular category of Indian mainland discourses, i.e. 'sub-national', as a framework of analysis (sub-national as is used by Baruah is smaller nation-within-a-larger nation, which is theoretically convoluted). As a result, the focus remains on the process of identity formation and the role of the state in the process. In most instances, the history of these developments begins with the colonial period. On the contrary, the historical specificity in the transformation of a continental crossroad into a frontier in which the identity formation is taking place gets overlooked.

councils already in existence or which are being claimed. The spatial base of modern Assamese literature is, therefore, a valley which *is* a contested space.

But as literature emerging from contested space, modern Assamese literature is fundamentally different, for example, from modern Palestinian literature, which too emerged based on contested space. In Edward Said's analysis (2001: 41–60), the indeterminacy of space in the latter case finds its literary parallel in narratives, prose or drama, which defy classical frameworks of narrative (i.e., with a beginning, middle and end). The overwhelming emphasis on scene or the episodic rather than the totality is related to the modern Palestinian experience of spatial dispossession and problems of identity, systematic and brutal that they have been. But in contrast, modern Assamese literature can be said to stand for its complete opposite, despite emerging from a context of contested space and identity, which has been quite a violent experience. Birinchi Baruah's text (*Seuji Patar Kahini*) is a testimony to the negating of any contestation of space and identity through the structure of the narrative. The difference, at one level, emphasises the necessity of region studies (and not *regional* studies), highlighting the particularity of given narrative practices. At another level more specific to the Valley, despite the indeterminacy of space and identity on which 'modern Assamese' literature has been historically based, it has lived with a remarkable claim of order of space and identity. Ironically, the very period in which the contest became both open and violent, i.e., the 1950s–1980s, was also the period in which narrative in modern Assamese fiction emphatically came to be structurally based on assumptions of order (*Seuji Patar Kahini* being only one example). This increasing conflict over space and identity in the Valley had to do with the protest of different communities that the growth of 'Assamese' as a code of identity marker meant the systematic erasure of their identity and collective memory of self, given the ethnographic limits of the term 'Assamese' to represent the heterogeneous social base. In other words, the conflict was over the recovery (and the invention that accompanies it) of their now 'fragmented memory' (Saikia 2004). This simultaneity of political breakdown of order of space and identity in inter-community relations in the Valley and the concretisation of narrative in modern Assamese literature based on the assumption of order highlights the ironical contradiction that can exist between literature and its social base, between *order* in cultural forms and the lack of it or its denegation at the social base.

The 1950s–1980s also was a period of acute linguistic politics in the Valley (best exemplified in Maheswar Neog's *The Language Question* [1961] written in the middle of the volatility). Thus, it could be argued that the acuteness of the linguistic politics (Assamese–Assam) found its absolute manifestation in the order of narrative and in the exclusive claiming to be inclusive through it. The correspondence was restored. But the correspondence was merely ideological. Whether taken as 'strategic' or 'tactical' (de Certeau 1984), one needs to situate such attempts on an awareness that the breakdown between the cultural form and its social base had indeed taken place, and therefore the attempt. Could this problem, i.e., breakdown of correspondence or the reality of contradiction between cultural form and its social base, be seen in the larger framework of the dialectics of frontier? The answer is yes. To repeat what had already been said earlier, textual traditions can be more meaningfully located in socio-spatial relations that comprised a region. Language or narrative was also symptomatic of the deeper issues of socio-spatial relations. Shifts in these relations affected language and narratives, while language and narratives also participated in these shifts in region formation. In the trans-Brahmaputra Valley, the socio-spatial relations were among different communities who were conscious of their difference from one another. It continues to be so. But what changed was the mapping of the relation among the different communities. The shift is evident in a comparison of the textual traditions of the past and the present. The key to understanding how or why textual traditions mapped these socio-spatial relations differently at different historical times is not in the language or the narrative per se, but in how textual traditions addressed and negotiated with these changing relations among the different communities. If in the 20th century language/literature and identity politics were closely related, it was the manifestation of the tensions that language and literature experienced in mapping the dialectics of these socio-spatial relations. The issue is discussed in greater detail along with case studies of language use and narratives in Part II.

Part II

Literature and Socio-spatial Relations

Introduction

In Part I, I discussed how textual traditions of the pre-colonial and those from the colonial period onwards mapped socio-spatial relations. I also showed how textual traditions have been part of the region formation, whether of pre-colonial continental crossroad or colonial frontier. I argued that region formation in the trans-Brahmaputra Valley needs to be seen in terms of the nature of socio-spatial relations. The issue I tried to explore, therefore, was where, in the mapping of such relations, could literature be situated. I also showed how texts could develop narrative tensions when negotiating these socio-spatial relations. In the pre-colonial period, such narrative tensions became evident in the neo-Vaishnava texts. In the colonial period, the very idea of modern Assamese language and literature came to be riddled with the tension. I tried to identify the moments when such narrative tensions develop in texts. My answer was that when textual traditions faced erosion of the shared domains of socio-spatial relations across differences among the communities, the narrative tensions became evident. Whereas neo-Vaishnava literature and its attempted Sanskritisation created narrative tensions in Sankari culture, the ethnographic contradictions in the making of modern Assamese language and literature created such tensions since the 19th century. On the other hand, I discussed that narrative tensions did not emerge in the Buranji tradition in the pre-colonial period or in texts such as those of Bishnu Rabha's in the 20th century. In both cases, texts tried to locate themselves in the shared mapping of socio-spatial relations that had historically characterised region formation in the trans-Brahmaputra Valley. The dialectics that I was trying to identify was the relation among the diverse and how it was mapped and negotiated in the pre-colonial and the colonial/postcolonial periods. In literature, I tried to identify how this dialectic operated and how texts tried to address or negotiate with this dialectic. I argued that for the Valley, the principle of correspondence between text and context needs to be situated in this paradigm.

If a shift in mapping of socio-spatial relations created an embedded ethnographic contradiction in modern Assamese language and narrative, Part II will focus on some of the specific cases of how the language and narrative addressed and negotiated with the question. Through the cases, I will try to show that the issue with modern Assamese language and narrative was not how codified language could become the identity marker, but how language and narratives struggled with the larger shift in the mapping of socio-spatial relations, when the crossroad became a frontier. The cases which have been taken up in the following chapters can be treated as representative examples from the point of view of this study. Notably, we have consciously considered only the popular and influential writers and their writings in three broad historical timeframes in the chapters. These timeframes are from the late 19th century to the 1950s; the 1950s to 1980s; and the 1980s to the present times. I try to show that these timeframes exhibit three distinct approaches to addressing the question of embedded ethnographic contradiction in modern Assamese language and literature as well as how to address and negotiate with the issue of mapping socio-spatial relations because of or despite the contradiction. For the period from late 19th century to the 1950s, the four main writers whose writings are studied are Lakhminath Bezbaruah, Padmanath Gohain Baruah, Banikanta Kakati and Bishnu Rabha. Among the four, Kakati's contribution was in critical writings. Bezbaruah was a champion of codifying the language and making it a modern Assamese language and a marker of Assamese identity. Gohain Baruah was one of the earliest to note the ethnographic contradiction which can emerge in such attempts. Kakati perceptively recognised the problem and explored the means of overcoming it, but without transcending the idea of language codification. Rabha dismissed the above debate entirely and argued that Assamese literature cannot become an identity marker of *a* people. It can only represent a relation among the diverse communities, and to achieve it, both language and narrative have to go for code mixing. It could be the only way to a true literature of the people in the trans-Brahmaputra Valley. For the period between the 1950s and 1980s, I mainly focus on Birendra Kumar Bhattacharjya, who strode like a colossus during the period. I argued in Part I that the peculiarity of the period from the 1950s to the 1980s was that the greater the ethnographic contradiction of modern Assamese language and narrative became exposed and came to be critiqued, the stronger became the discourse of Assamese identity that denied it. As a result, there was the irony of breakdown in the correspondence between modern Assamese literature and its social base. Bhattacharjya was possibly the biggest champion of denying this breakdown in his creative writing, despite recognising it in his critical writings. He was also a leading voice of the several movements of the period based on the discourse of Assamese identity. For the period between the 1980s and the present times, I discuss the writings of Mamoni Raisom Goswami (Indira Goswami), Rong Bong Terang, Anuradha Sarma Pujari and Anurag Mahanta. If in the preceding period the ethnographic contradiction embedded in modern Assamese language and literature led to a breakdown of correspondence between literature and its social base, each of these writers during this period emphasised on this breakdown and devised a narrative means of addressing the problem. If Goswami and Terang addressed the problem in terms of relation between 'language' and 'dialect', Pujari and Mahanta tried to show that when narratives are delinked from the question of specific space and identity and are used only as descriptive tools, the problem of modern Assamese language and narrative being unable to map the shared socio-spatial relations that constitute a frontier can be overcome. What is notable is that through the approach, I arrive once again at the fundamental feature of the Buranjis, namely, to chronicle and describe socio-spatial relations rather than conceptualise them!

4
Language and Narrative: Negotiating between Difference and Contradiction

I discussed Padmanath Gohain Baruah as one of the earliest to identify the ethnographic contradiction vis-à-vis modern Assamese language. Gohain Baruah was also a prolific writer himself, both fiction and non-fiction (for example, children's books). His plays, which are largely historical, could be taken as examples of how language/narrative could be used to negotiate the problematic of language 'standard'. In his presidential address to the first congress of the Asom Sahitya Sabha in 1917, he said (translation mine), 'Representatives from all over Assam have gathered here today to discuss initiatives for Assamese literature and to develop knowledge base through Assamese literature; therefore, to cover the entire dimension of Assamese literature, we are calling this a congress for entire Assam' (Gohain Baruah [1902] [1971] 2008: 874). In other words, despite the forum being for Assamese literature, any natural correlation between Assam and Assamese was consciously avoided. Gohain Baruah was not opposed to Assamese per se. In fact, he had championed throughout the cause of the language for and in the Valley. What he was opposed to was the history of the language that was being articulated during the period, and thereby the function of identity marker that the language and narratives written in it had come to stand for. Gohain Baruah's plays show not only how he attempted to make his language/narrative inclusive of ethnographic variety, but also to develop language and narrative structure which could accommodate the variety. In this regard, the following paraphrased translations of sections from his play *Jaymati* (1902) are provided below:

The (Ahom) soldiers in search of the fugitive Ahom prince Gadapani see someone rushing out from the backyard of Bogi's house. Bogi is an old woman. When they enquire who the person was, Bogi replies that he was just a Naga man who had come to give her betel leaves the day before. He had stayed behind to cut the grass of her field and, after lunch, was leaving. It was when the soldiers had spotted him, she said (Gohain Baruah: [1902] [1971] 2008: Part Two, Scene Three, 50). Though not specified, it is indicated that the search is taking place at the foothills between the Valley and the Naga Hills, inhabited by both Assamese and Naga people. (b) The fugitive prince Gadapani takes shelter in the house of an old Naga woman, Sinu. The place of refuge is located in the heights of the Naga Mountains. The woman understands that Gadapani is a fugitive, but agrees to give him shelter from the Ahom soldiers. The Naga woman communicates with Gadapani in 'Nagamese', pidgin Assamese. Despite difficulty, they manage to communicate and express their thoughts. Later, Gadapani ruminates, 'My goal is noble, but how do I achieve it? I don't need a large army. A group of able Naga men if I can gather around me, that should be enough to attack and defeat the Ahom ruler' (ibid.: 52). (c) In the Naga foothills, two Assamese traders of betel leaf discuss the case of the fugitive prince Gadapani, and how his wife Jaymati is being punished by the court in an open field for not disclosing the whereabouts of her husband. In the meantime, Gadapani, dressed like a Naga, arrives at the place, and enquires as to the subject of their discussion. Gadapani speaks in 'Nagamese'. From the traders, he learns of the arrest of his wife and punishment being given to her (ibid.: Part Four, Scene One, 65). (d) Gadapani, dressed like a Naga, approaches Jaymati, who is being punished in an open field for everyone to see. Jaymati recognises Gadapani, and becomes anxious that he would get exposed and arrested. Gadapani speaks to her in 'Nagamese', asking her why she refuses to reveal her husband's hideout. He says it is painful for him to see her being punished so. Jaymati replies that her husband, the prince, is the future, and she would never reveal his hideout. Gadapani leaves, and repeats the act everyday till she finally dies, tied to a tree (ibid.: Part Five, Scene One: 71). (e) Gadapani is still a fugitive, roaming the hills and valleys as a mendicant, singing Vaishnava or Sankari hymns. The hymns are in Kamrupi Assamese. The play ends with Gadapani finally deciding to attack the Ahom rulers (ibid.: Part Five, Scene Three: 75).

The first notable point about the play is the attempt to accommodate the ethnographic diversity of the Valley and the neighbouring hills as well as bring together the geography of the Valley and the hills into a common linkage. The ethnographic and geographic linkage, importantly, was part of the everyday, in fact, constituted the everyday (for example, Bogi and her Naga helper or the traders at the foothills, etc.) as well as the exception (for example, in the political vis-à-vis the fugitive prince). *Jaymati* was written in 1902, and it is to the credit of Gohain Baruah's historical sense that he could highlight the fact of shared mapping of socio-spatial relations in the historical past. Second, it is equally important that the variety of languages that together comprise the linguistic map of the area was woven into the very structure of the narrative. The fact that Gadapani could remain a fugitive by switching his language ('Nagamese') and adopting Naga dress, or the fact that Bogi could get Naga men to work in her field as an everyday practice, or even the fact that Gadapani could sing Sankari hymns in Kamrupi Assamese clearly indicates attempts to highlight the inter-linguistic and inter-ethnic basis of socio-spatial relations in the area. It was also a critical assessment of the historical and ethnographic contradictions that became embedded in the modern Assamese language 'standard' and its narratives. The play came at a time (1902) when there was a distinct approach to the concept of 'Assamese' language and 'Assamese' culture, viz. that its roots needed to be located in the Sanskrit or Aryan tradition. The writings of Kamalakanta Bhattacharjee and Hemchandra Goswami, widely published in periodicals such as *Jonaki* and later in *Bahni*, repeatedly emphasised this 'historical' root. Gohain Baruah's critique of that approach has already been noted in Part I. Vis-à-vis the play, it is evident that rather than focusing on the *concept* of language and culture, he had focused on the popular *practice* of language and culture. This nature of Gohain Baruah's approach can also be corroborated by his views on Assamese dictionaries and 'schools' of language. In his address to the first congress of the Asom Sahitya Sabha, 1917, he elaborated on the role of Hemchandra Baruah and Gunabiram Baruah and said (translation mine), 'In the field of Assamese literature, the two of them are like two distinct schools. While Hemchandra Baruah represents the school of indigenous Assamese, Gunabhiram Baruah represents the school of Sanskrit based Assamese' (Gohain Baruah [1902] [1971] 2008: 886). The indigeneity of Hemchandra Baruah being referred to was that of his dictionaries, which were grammatically founded on how Assamese is spoken and not on its morphological or syntactic roots. Therefore, both in his thoughts and his practise (of cultural forms), it is evident where Gohain Baruah's emphasis lay.

The play *Jaymati* (which is only one example among the numerous plays that Gohain Baruah wrote) also helps us expose two further issues in this regard. First, through the play, i.e., through the medium of literature, a conscious attempt was made to depict the 'concrete' historical reality of shared socio-spatial relations. But when seen in the context of his views of what constituted Assamese language and culture, it is evident that the play also performed or was designed to perform a mediating role in the historical and ethnographic debate on culture. Second, the play is primarily performance literature. This gives the text the scope to be inclusive of the social or historical base that it seeks to represent or seeks to mediate in. In other words, both as a means of culture and a form of culture, the text of a play is in an advantageous position vis-à-vis the text which is primarily literary or textual, such as fiction (for example, the short story or novel).

Therefore, a comparison with Lakhminath Bezbaruah's fictional narratives could be a revealing contrastive study in this regard. I broadly outlined Bezbaruah's political views on the role of language and on the question of language 'standard' in Part I. Therefore, could his fictional narratives be seen as generally application of the views in practise, i.e., both the practise of literature as well as literature as practice? It is noted that Bezbaruah popularised the colloquial as a literary form in modern Assamese fiction (Baruah 2010). It is amply evident that Bezbaruah borrowed the form from the tradition of tales in Assam. But the colloquial in his narratives is nothing other than the everyday practice of language, i.e., the way people speak or use language as a part of their everyday (everyday speech forms). However, the relation of the everyday and language code in a context of ethnographic variety cannot be a universal form. As a result, Bezbaruah's narratives are distinctly based on the locale of the eastern valley and the language of the Sibsagar 'standard'. It was only through this correlation that he could achieve a form of narrative wherein the everyday practice of language could appear a generic bearer of the linguistic universe of a people. In other words, Bezbaruah's colloquial was not the colloquial in the sense of 'dialect', as Sibsagar Assamese was already a 'standard'. Further, such use of the everyday practice of language helped him highlight how the everyday of the people could differ from the exceptional. For example, in the short story *Jagara Mandalar Premar Akhyan* (The Episode of Jagara Mandal in Love, 2003), Jagara, the rural revenue officer, visits Jorhat town and goes to meet the lawyer Saruram Sarma. He finds a gathering of lawyers and other professionals reading out from a novel, enjoying every bit of it. The following sequence of paraphrased translations from the short story will help highlight the use to which the everyday practice of language was put to:

(a) When Jagara enquires as to what they are reading, the lawyer Saruram says that they are reading a novel. Jagara asks what a novel is. Saruram replies, 'Novel is a kind of book. It talks about love.' An inspired Jagara asks whether it talks of Bhakti love for Krishna. Saruram replies, 'It talks of love between a young man and woman (ibid.: 35)

(b) Jagara continues to listen to the readings from the novel and decides that he should practise the love of the novel in his married life as well. His wife asked why they need to practise such love. He replies, 'Presence of love has much to do with our improved status now. It is important to be rich and powerful in a small place like this. So we'll have to change from the past. And love is an important sign of the change' (ibid.: 37).

(c) Jagara's wife is quite puzzled. She says, 'I can hardly understand you. Just tell me what I am supposed to do' (ibid.: 37–38). Jagara is impressed and begins his love. He comes closer to his wife and, lifting her chin with his fingers, says, 'Darling, do you see the moon? It's beautiful. But I also see the moon on the earth, your face. Tell me, which one is more beautiful for me' (ibid.: 38).

(d) Jagarani, Jagara's wife, gets angry. She replies, 'With these years of hard work, my face has become like a black cooking pot. And you call it a moon! Looks are only god's gift. Then why make fun of anyone?' Jagara continues, and compares her breath to divine scented air. Jagarani says that she is known to have a bitter tongue. How could anyone compare her words to scented air! Finally, she says, 'Quickly finish giving other metaphors too. I must leave to complete other household work now. I don't have your luxury of snoring away right after dinner (ibid.: 39).

In the story, the love of the novel is shown as an elite consciousness, distant from the practice of everyday life. But equally important is that while the former (love of the novel) is in the language 'standard', the latter is in its everyday form. In fact, the novel as a genre is located in the exceptional rather than in the everyday. But here, the important issue is that the given relation between language and narrative was possible (for Bezbaruah) because the everyday speech form and the locale or the cultural base of the narrative were same, i.e., the eastern valley. Bezbaruah's language use or his narrative can highlight the differences or contradictions at the level of class or hierarchy. But it cannot accommodate the ethnographic differences or contradictions of the entire valley. Bezbaruah's success was in developing a narrative wherein the practice of language could be accommodated into something quite new (modern) as a cultural form such as the novel or short story (he was writing in the late 19th and early 20th centuries in Assam). His success was also in developing a narrative, through everyday language, which could not only accommodate the common people into the text but also reach out to them more directly rather than through the author representing them. But it was also in such use of everyday language that the limits of the narrative could be identified. Everyday language being specific to cultural context, its meaning and scope differs based on the context. If the use of the everyday language created a narrative which could critique the exceptional, such a paradigm also came under criticism. For example, Birendra Kumar Bhattacharjya in his popular *Ramdhenu* editorials (1952–53) argued that Bezbaruah's technique of critique was a sign of his fascination for the past and its idealisation. The processes which Bezbaruah critiqued, Bhattacharjya argued, were precisely those which were the bearers of modern thought. He further argued that it was only through such thoughts that revolutionary change was possible. But given the fact that Bezbaruah could never be revolutionary (so much so that he always remained ambivalent on the question of the anti-colonial movement), Bezbaruah's narrative technique also revealed his political position which, Bhattacharjya argued, was not progressive (Bhattacharjya 2007, 1 (5): 5–6; (1952–53) 2007: 18–19). Jyotiprasad Agarwalla, a cultural icon and the younger brother of Bezbaruah's friend Chandra Kumar Agarwalla, had also remarked on this, but differently from Bhattacharjya. Agarwalla contended that Bezbaruah played a major role in bringing back Sankari literature into focus in the modern period. But the context of this was to make the Assamese people realise their own rich heritage, something that was forgotten in the face of the colonial influence. Then he remarked (translation mine), 'He re-inspired life and hope among the Assamese through the old literature and then through his own literature, tried to take them in the path of progress' (Agarwalla 1996: 524).

One of the important points that the debate raised (much earlier than the debate on Subaltern Studies came up) was the relation of the concept or practice of narrative and literature to politics of change. Another dimension was that while Bezbaruah used everyday language to critique the 'elite', which was represented by the 'standard', he also defended the 'standard' as the form of Assamese to be practised, as shown in Part I. One plausible way to explain this apparent contradiction is that Bezbaruah himself was struggling (rather than arriving at a solution) to devise a language and narrative which could indeed resolve the historical and ethnographic contradiction that had vitiated the cultural question.

Gohain Baruah and Bezbaruah are two examples of the engagement of language and narrative with the issue of historical and ethnographic diversity or mutiplicity. The problem in both their writings was how to create a common or universal language or narrative which could both accommodate *and* represent the diversity which comprised the Assamese identity. But that was also precisely the problem, viz. how to create language or narrative which despite being exclusive could yet be inclusive of its social base. Gohain Baruah's *Jaymati* is an example in which the diverse exists in the space of the text in their respective language (uses) and with their embedded ethnographic specificities. It was an expansive approach, i.e., an attempt to accommodate the diverse in the expanse of the textual space. The fact that it was performance literature added to its advantage. Bezbaruah's narrative, on the other hand, was not an expansive text. His narrative is a paradigmatic approach to the problem of situating ethnographic specificities in the space of the text. In this, everyday language, for him, was the paradigmatic element. But his narrative was also possible because it was based on the Sibsagar form of the Assamese language. Neither approach, however, could accommodate and represent, at the same time, the diversities with their peculiarities. At a deeper level, it is also evident that what both these narrative attempts were struggling with was to produce an order of a literary form which could stand for the diversity of culture and cultural practices of the area.

But if the texts showed signs of contradiction of which it was a part of or with which it engaged with, they also showed alertness on the need to achieve a common ground vis-à-vis the people. The latter point is especially important vis-à-vis different cultural attempts at a common politics from within the Valley.

The next distinct approach in this regard was to be found in the enormous range of cultural productions between the 1930s and the 1950s from the communist cultural figure Bishnu Rabha. But before that, it may be helpful to go through another perspective from the period on the question of how to create an order of language and narrative which can stand for the diverse. Banikanta Kakati, one of the most significant intellectual voices in the inter-War period in Assam, argued that the strength of national consciousness is founded on the strength of the language of the people. He said (translation mine), 'That is why people conscious of national pride strive hard to maintain language and its purity' (Kakati [written 1925] [1991] 2006: 277). He acknowledged that (translation mine), 'Of the numerous problems that the Assamese *jati* (nation or people?) faces, promoting national consciousness through language and literature is one' (ibid.). But pertaining to language and literature, what did Kakati identify as the fundamental problem that needed to be addressed? Kakati, in his different writings, forwarded three propositions which are listed below:

(a) In the *janajatiya* (tribal or ethnic?) areas of Assam, there are numerous institutions and traditions. If one tries to understand them in a systematic and sympathetic way, they can be the resources for future literature. Rajanikanta Bordoloi in his *Miri Jiori* and Lakhminath Bezbaruah in his *Jaymati* had tried something like this. ... However, the efforts of a few individuals are not enough. They should only be treated as paths being created for the future (ibid.: 280).

(b) The way to maintain relations among people having different language is to have a common script. In the case of Chinese pictographic script, it is said that it is precisely its pictographic nature that has helped different language groups of China to have a common language. If pictographic script is replaced by sound based script, there is a danger to their unity. Different languages can speak or write the same thing in different ways, but the common pictographic script expresses and communicates a common thought and ethos. These pictographic signs are known all across China, but in different parts of the country, they are spoken or written differently. Similarly, we need a common script to bring together our common past and present. Sanskrit based Devanagari script could be such a solution (ibid.: 281).

(c) When texts are being written for those who are not highly educated, what should be the nature of such texts? It is certainly a matter to be discussed. The importance of idioms and phrases indigenous to a given language is more important than erudite language to make text comprehensible to the readers. In our present day (Assamese) books and magazines, there is very little use of indigenous idioms and phrases. If texts are being written for the less literate, it is necessary to keep in mind the nature of their thoughts too to make the texts communicable. Tales, idioms and phrases, songs and verses, etc that are prevalent (or practiced?) in villages can help us know the rural mentality too (ibid.: 283).

Kakati situated language and narrative in the widest possible range of diversity. The diversity included not only the ethnic or the historical, but also the class, the educational, etc. Therefore, if language and narrative were to be inclusive, representative and relevant for the different people in that range of diversity, he argued, (a) there has to be generation of new content but from or incorporating the indigenous; and (b) there has to be a new script which can overcome the ethnographic specificity that remains embedded in any written as opposed to diagrammatic script. Kakati's propositions can be more meaningfully discussed when seen in the light of the cultural productions coming from Rabha. This will be taken up subsequently. However, what is already evident is that the basic issue that Kakati was struggling with was not different from the one that had troubled Bezbaruah or Gohain Baruah or their contemporaries. The issue was what could be that order or how to create that order in language and narrative which could accommodate and represent the diverse that together comprised the totality of the 'Assamese' universe. It was indeed recognised that 'Assamese' was not a homogeneous entity. That precisely was also the problem. Whether it was Bezbaruah, Gohain Baruah or Kakati, they were all grappling with the cultural question of that problem.

In most contemporary studies, the approach towards such an issue is that of language as part of the process of 'Assamese' identity formation. However, as shown, formation of identity was only the result of a deeper factor — the change of the continental crossroad into a frontier. What that change entailed was that notions of difference among the communities continued to exist, but the mapping of shared relations was eroded. As a result, difference came to be framed in a discourse of identity which, despite being structurally exclusive, claimed to be inclusive. Therefore, vis-à-vis the relation between identity formation on the one hand and language and narrative on the other, the context of the trans-Brahmaputra Valley is fundamentally peculiar to its own processes of shifts in region formation. The problem cannot be subsumed within the currently popular framework of Indian literature and politics of identity formation. In fact, it can be taken as an appeal for a greater focus on area studies than being content with India studies. In other words, it is necessary to make the transition from the study of the *regional* to the study of the *region*.

On language and narrative, each of the three interventions discussed above were attempts at engaging with the historical transformation discussed above, whether or not articulated thus. The fact that except for Ambikagiri Raichoudhury, there were very few during the period who argued for 'Assamese' as a primordial identity and recognised 'Assamese' as a modern construct (for example, Gohain Baruah; see Part I). If there is an active realisation on forming an identity as well as of the contradictions in that approach, then such cultural interventions cannot be located only in a politics of identity. They necessarily need to be located in processes deeper than that, politics of identity being only a form of articulation of the underlying processes. The point becomes clearer when one takes into account the intervention that Rabha made between the 1930s and the 1950s in this context.

Even though the people discussed so far were involved in the question of literature, Rabha, besides literature, was also involved in the question of mass politics. But whereas for the others mass politics meant electoral politics or anti-colonial agitation, for Rabha, it was to bring together the peasants and 'tribals' of the Valley and the entire north-east frontier region on the communist platform. In terms of affiliation to a political party, he was a member of the Revolutionary Communist Party of India (RCPI). But party membership per se explained little of his involvement in politics of or for the masses, as he understood it. Rabha's political or ideological background is important because his art did not merely espouse a cause but was also a device to bring about changes in socio-political relations in the Valley. The other difference between Rabha and the others discussed so far was that his art was not confined to only literature, but also encompassed music, dance, plays and cinema. Rabha's concept and practice of art can be found in the Introduction he wrote to his collection of short stories, *Sunpahi*. Though published in 1962, the stories were written much earlier, especially in the period from the late 1940s (after Independence) to the early 1950s. During the period, the Indian government had banned the communists, and Rabha became a fugitive. The Introduction is an account of his experiences of working with the people in the remotest interior of the area, of him going to meet them and them coming to meet him. Some excerpts from the Introduction (translation mine) are provided below:

(a) People crowded in hordes. The *sifung* flute plays out its soulful tunes. The *kham-madol* drums reverberate. The villagers start dancing, with the beats, in their joyous moves. In the silver moonlight, they appeared like silver statues, but alive. ... The next day, after having our food, both of us started early in the morning once again on our journey. We were the have-nots, aspiring for freedom, fellow travelers in the path of revolution (Rabha [1962] [1989] 2008: vol. 1, 566).

(b) This was the first sign of love that people showed me. On the one hand were the people and on the other was the government. The government is on my trail. They think I am their enemy. The people protect me. As if there is some contradiction in today's society. It is a people's government. Then why do the government and the people not think alike? (ibid.).

(c) In search of freedom, some take shelter in religion, some in different political parties, while some others become like vagabonds and dies in the pressure. There are still others who kill themselves in this search; but freedom ever eludes them. ... One ray of light. Its brightness can show the path. There is no need to keep stumbling in the search. Abject darkness disappears. It is the ray of ideology, the light of communism. ... In that light the path to freedom is illuminated, the path of revolution (Rabha [1962] [1989] 2008: vol. 1, 567).

(d) The privilege of travelling by vehicle or train or airplane never came my way. Come rain or sunshine, I walk and walk. And thus I have wandered from one corner of Assam to the other. In the east, the Burma frontier, in the west, the high mountains of Nepal, even the frontier of Tibet, I have thus travelled. The innumerable people I have met in my travels, the Abors, the Khamptis, the Ahoms, the Rabhas ... different people, different race, different religion, but their wish is same, economic emancipation. But why doesn't the government listen to them? (ibid.: 567–68).

(e) The people are the infinite source for art and culture. ... Like a honeybee, I gather honey from the flowers of the people and make my honey nest. That honey, I once again give away to the people. The honey doesn't belong to me. It doesn't become mine. It is the duty of an artist to do so. I try to carry out my duty (ibid.: 569).

Rabha wrote in both Bodo and Assamese. For example, stories like *Hiyar Pung* were first writen in Bodo as *Pung kha*, and later translated into Assamese, and vice versa. He also translated stories drawn from the communist movement from other languages into Assamese or Bodo. For example, the title story of the collection, *Sunpahi*, is translated from Jake Belden's *The Golden Flower* (from the book *China Shakes the World* [1949]) while he was a fugitive. In these activities, he takes the help of his comrade Kanaklata (Rabha [1989] 2008a: 570). Rabha's cultural productions were aimed at encouraging people to take the path of communist revolution. His story *Hiyar Pung* was an illuminating example. Rabha mentioned that the story was based on the life of a Bodo–Kachari woman, Sewari, in the north Goalpara area. The story is about the struggle that poor peasants have to wage everyday to eke out a living. Set in a Bodo village, the story begins with the abject poverty of Lakhra, his wife Sewari and their small baby. There is no food in the house to feed the baby, and an angry and frustrated Lakhra sits in the courtyard of his hut, awaiting the village moneylender to confiscate the hut. Religion or tradition is shown to be mere shackles that perpetuate the oppression of the oppressed. This is evident in Lakhra's angry outburst at the village priest (Oja), when he says (translation mine),

> I don't have any clothes to wear, no food to eat. The only hut that I have for shelter will no longer be there tomorrow. How much I had worshipped that Siju tree![1] Yet, look at my condition today. I have become that abject one who is left with nothing! Why doesn't all your gods come today to rescue me? (ibid.: 590).

The story, importantly, does not end with a resolution. Neither does it follow the classic framework of narrative, i.e., to have a beginning, middle and end. Lakhra indeed loses his hut, and is left homeless with a wife and a small baby. But the story is about his growing consciousness, an increasing realisation that class conflict is central to his condition, and that only a classless society could be the solution. The point towards which the story moves in conclusion can be reproduced from an excerpt from the conversation Lakhra has with an old man (translation mine):

> Lakhra asks himself — 'Will revolution indeed happen?' The old man consoles and encourages him — 'Inside an egg, there is both the yolk and the liquid. The liquid tries to destroy the yolk and the yolk tries to destroy the liquid. But in this process of conflict, there is neither yolk nor the liquid which remains. Something else happens, an offspring. Similarly, from the womb of capitalism emerge two classes, the rich and the poor. The rich try to oppress the poor while the poor try to overthrow the rich. But in this conflict, finally there is neither the rich nor the poor. A new class comes into existence. That is communism. That is revolution, from capitalism to communism. Revolution is not to kill or injure others. It is to transform into something new, something unprecedented. At first, the change is slow, and then later, it becomes rapid' (ibid.: 595).

Rabha's stories, as he himself remarked, were not meant to be merely read, but were meant to be of service to a political cause. Thus, they

---

[1] The Bodo people worship the Siju tree, a kind of Euphorbia, as a symbol of their Bathou god.

were stories based on the lives of common people, taken from the common people and, very importantly, meant to encourage them to realise the problem of class conflict and understand the role of revolution. It is interesting to note that Rabha was also a prolific writer on general issues (i.e., non-fiction), and he wrote extensively on what is Marxism, dialectics and revolution and the woman's question. The challenge for Rabha as a communist leader who spent most of his time with the people was how to communicate these thoughts to the people. The means to communicate these thoughts were the stories which were meant to be read and read out to the people in everyday village gatherings. In this, Rabha, like most others of his time, used a traditional platform of village gathering called *mel*. But he used it for communist ends. For example, it is quite evident that through the old man's explanation of yolk, liquid and offspring, Rabha was explaining to the people dialectics and revolution. Kakati had suggested that literature needed to come closer to the people, and for this to happen, the parameters of both content and language had to be widened. Further, Kakati emphasised the need for narratives wherein differences would not exist as relations of contradictions. Rabha can be considered the classic case of putting such a prescription into practise.

What was unique in the case of Rabha was that he was also a performer and spent long periods as a fugitive (and) revolutionary leader with and among the people. This provided him with the opportunity to gain not only a readership but also an audience for his stories. In Rabha's own accounts (for example, the introduction in *Sunpahi*), the basic aim of his cultural productions was to communicate with people ideologically, and to achieve it, stories not only required readers but also audience. Stories therefore become part of a larger paradigm of dance, drama and music, and it is in that totality that communicating with poor illiterate masses became possible for Rabha. It is open for further historical investigation why Rabha gained heights of popularity not only in the Valley but in the neighbouring hills as well, i.e., whether it was due to ideological support from the people or otherwise. But it is a historical fact that in the late 1940s and early 1950s, there were large-scale peasant protests in the Valley, and in the same period, Rabha played a pivotal revolutionary role in the peasant movements. Also notable is that many of his comrades remarked that the best of his cultural productions were produced during this very period of unrest (Choudhury 2006: 193–94). The observation throws up the interesting question of whether the core of Rabha's art was in people per se or in the revolutionary mass politics. In this regard, to return once again to Kakati's prescription, the framework of that prescription was the 'nation'. However, if in Rabha, the practice of culture came closest to that ideal, it nevertheless came closer in the framework of revolutionary class politics. An ironical close parallel on this can be found in the famous Italian communist writer Italo Calvino commenting on how his (now classic) post-War novel *The Paths to the Spiders' Nests* was written. In Preface to the novel, he wrote, 'The literary explosion of those years in Italy was not so much an artistic phenomenon, more a physical, existential, collective mood' (2009: 7). Calvino talked of how writing of such books was based on a conscious collective experience and an individual's urge to express and communicate it. For him, writing such a book again would be impossible, because the specificity of that collective experience no longer existed. The observation of Rabha's comrades, therefore, could be an acute observation on Rabha and his cultural output.

If the challenge in the field of culture throughout had been to create forms where differences do not become relations of contradiction, Rabha's stage, screen plays and dance dramas are of central significance. Three examples are discussed below.

In the dance drama *Na Prithivir Natun Jug* (New Age of the New World, written and staged in 1951; Rabha [1989] 2008c), Rabha directly addresses this question of differences among communities but shows that the differences were only illusions, the fact being that the poor or have-nots are all same despite differences. This is because they were all exploited in class relations. Rabha begins the play with the 19th century. Different communities from across the Valley and the hills (the Nagas, those from Manipur, from the Valley, etc.) appear one after another on the stage and represent the idyllic conditions of communal existence. The *sutradhar* or narrator narrates to the people what is seen on stage. Then appears the anti-colonial struggles that different communities in their own ways wage against the colonial system. The people and the leaders who lose their lives in the struggle are depicted sympathetically. The *sutradhar*, however, does not merely narrate; it is an ideological narration. For example, when the *sutradhar* narrates the case of Maniram Dewan, who the nationalists declared the martyr from the Valley during the revolt of 1857, the narrator says (translation mine), 'The first one to get the smell of capitalism, he was the first Assamese farmer to farm tea, he was the first Assamese capitalist, rich, who fought for his dignity and also to re-establish the Ahom rule, but the result, he was hanged to death!' (ibid.:: vol. 1, 258). Then finally there is independence from British colonialism, and the scenes change into the post-Independence period, i.e., the late 1940s. The people of the Valley and of the hills were surprised that independence has brought no change to their life. They continued to be oppressed. Thus begins their struggle against the new government, their *own* government. In the background, the *sutradhar* continues to narrate (translation mine), 'The fire of the revolution then spread everywhere' (ibid.: vol. 1, 294) Armed class struggle by the people commences toward the end of the dance drama. The *sutradhar* tells the audience,

> The police and the military will no longer fight for the five rich out of every hundred poor. They are marching to fight for the peasant, the worker, the poorest of the poor. They are not the children of the rich. They are the children of these rural poor peasants after all. They are on the side of the revolutionary peasants today. They are fighting for them to the last drop of their blood (ibid.: vol. 1: 295).

The police and the military did not fight for the poor, as the dance drama claimed. In fact, they were instrumental in crushing the widespread peasant protests of the period. However, the dance drama was part of the larger revolutionary politics, to explain to the audience (of peasants) that historical and ethnographic difference is not the real difference, and that they should come together to fight the real difference, viz. class difference. Most of Rabha's plays were dance dramas, which required minimal infrastructure to stage, and could be easily enacted by mobile groups even in the remotest parts of the Valley or the hills. Rabha himself was an expert in music and dance.

Importantly, Rabha, through his narratives, did not appeal to the people's 'identity'. The only way he could reach out across 'identities' was by using a framework which cut across identities, which for him was class *relation*. It was also the means for him to overcome the problem of devising a narrative which could accommodate and represent difference without becoming a contradiction at the same time. This constitutes a basic difference between Rabha's plays and *Jaymati* by Gohain Baruah which, despite its expansive paradigm, could not overcome the problematic of literature representing diversity.

The second short example from Rabha's repertoire is a narrative that engages with the problem of differences — the screenplay *'Simanta Soinik'* (Soldier of the Frontier, [1989] 2008d) — from the same period. It was, however, never made into a film. The relation between the young man Subimal and the young woman Lopong is the most important point for this discussion. The story is set on the Indo-China border of present-day Arunachal Pradesh. Subimal is from an Assamese family while Lopong is from a Monpa family. Subimal loses his father early, grows up amidst great hardships and, finally, as a young man, becomes a successful captain in the army. His father was also an army officer. Lopong, his child-hood friend, grows up to become a nurse. Amidst a dramatic turn of events, it turns out that Subimal and Lopong are blood relatives, brother and sister! This is because neither Subimal is Assamese nor Loping Monpa in origin; both are Nepali, born to an army officer, Sherbahadur Subedar. Due to health problems, the officer and his wife gave away their son to Subimal's father and Lopong to Sorgin, a Monpa from the area.

I would note two points about the story. First, if differences were a fact, there can be an ironical element to the fact of difference. For example, Lopong's parents caution her not to be too friendly with Subimal. 'They are Assamese and you are Monpa. We are very different' (Rabha [1989] 2008a: 443). Yet, the story ends on the ironical note that such differences, despite being so real, could be illusions. Second, the story emphasises how a relation of difference need not be an instrumental factor in social relations in a frontier. In a population- and resource-scarce area, society perpetuates itself only through bonding despite differences rather than through conflicts. For example, Sorgin, in the end, when describing how Subimal became Assamese and Lopong Monpa, says (translation mine),

> During the winter, we all come down to the valley. The movements are more in the Locra-Sariduar area. We come and meet Mohen Subedar (Subimal's father). We meet each other like brothers. We strengthen our relations. We are from the hills, they are from the valley. The relationship that we establish is also the relationship of the valley and hills (ibid.: 445).

Sorgin recalls that Sherbahadur Subedar, after retiring from the army, had settled in the Locra-Sariduar area with his wife. They had a newborn pair of twins, a boy and a girl. Once when he and Mohen Subedar went to visit the old couple, they were touched by their declining health. When the couple expressed their wish that Sorgin and Mohen Subedar take their children, they were both very happy as neither had a child. Rabha's take on social relations in the frontier was remarkably different from that of Waddell or Baruah, as discussed in the Introduction.

While in the first example it was an effort to create a narrative which cut across differences at the social base, in the second example, it was a storyline on how ironically illusionary could be the issue of difference in the area. In the third example, I will show how Rabha tried to create a narrative in which not only difference of people could be accommodated and represented in the space of a narrative (as in the first example), but also that difference of cultural forms could find a place in the narrative and could *represent* the diversity or multiplicity at the same time. This he achieved in his famous play *Mukti Deul* (Shrine of Freedom, written 1955; [1989] 2008d).

In *Mukti Deul* there is a reinterpretation of other cultural forms by situating them in a new narrative and a new politics. It was made evident in the Dedication of the play — 'revolutionaries fighting for the Shrine of Freedom' (Rabha [1989] 2008a: 270). The play begins with (statue of) Buddha sitting in meditation, the devotees chanting about non-violence as the absolute path of duty/religion (dharma). The playing of instruments and the chants are in the Sankari musical genres. As the statue is covered with a white cloth, the rich make their entry on the stage, carried in palanquins and followed by their servants. The *sutradhar* sings from his place (paraphrased translation of the verses throughout mine), 'Buddha today is imprisoned, his non violence is imprisoned in the prison of violence. The rich wear the mask of non-violence. But they perpetuate violence. Their capitalism perpetuates the violence' (ibid.: 271) As the light on the stage dims, from behind the white cloth, shadows of soldiers are seen fighting with each other. The *sutradhar* sings, 'War! The Second World War! The peasants and workers too became the soldiers in the hope of freedom. But once again, they became the prisoners of the rich. Their land not becoming theirs' (ibid.: 271). Behind the backdrop of the white cloth are seen shadows of the peasants and workers who suffer behind bars for fighting for their rights against the rich. Then suddenly the cloth is removed and in sight is the Shrine of Freedom. Peace chants are now sung in voiceover. Also heard at the same time are cries of pain of the peasants and workers. Then, both forms of sound subside, as the stage is filled with the worshippers of the Shrine, singing a song, which though structurally set in Sankari genre, is a mix of Sanakri *borgeet* (devotional song), *bongeet* (or folk song) and modern musical tunes. They sing (in fact, this song *Surar deulor re*, went on to become one of the legendary 20th-century songs in Assam), 'O priest of the shrine, you have broken open the silver shackles of the shrines for us, this shrine of blissful music, you are the priest of Beauty. O the Assamese people, sing your ancient *borgeet*s, your *bongeet*s, fill your hearts and minds with their music ... in this music is the form of freedom, the form of the gods, the forms of worship' (ibid.: 272). The song goes on, but towards the end, the revolutionary message enters, 'He (the priest) ignites the fire in the heart, the fire of revolution, makes the offerings of freedom to the shrine and sings in devotion ...' (ibid.: 273). Importantly, as the song is being sung, now as voiceover, the worshippers perform it in the *deodhani* folkdance of the Bodo people. The *deodhani* is a ritual dance which takes the possessed performer into a frenzy. The revolutionary message towards the end of the song is accompanied by the frenzied *deodhani* dance of the worshippers-performers. The play progresses, the *sutradhar* continues to narrate the rising revolutionary consciousness of the masses, and the priest is a figure of inspiration for the masses. Finally, the priest sings another revolutionary song (*Bischore chonde chonde*), but set in traditional *oja pali* (a form of community performance singing) musical genre, 'In this universal music, let us all dance in the blissful joy, lighting the divine fire which will burn down the darkness and enlighten our minds with knowledge, and then we will find around us the fragrant garden of flowers, the fragrant land ...' (ibid.: 273). The play ends with the priest rising from his seat and addressing the masses, pointing towards the horizon where a new sun is rising (performed through lighting). The masses start to sing that the people are the rulers, it is the people's rule from now on.

The notable aspect of the play, which is mainly a dance drama, on the question of narrative is that it became possible for Rabha to create one wherein different forms, whether performance or literary, could be brought together in the space of a single narrative, and at the same time, the narrative could stand as a representative of the diversity. Folk forms, Sankari forms as well as modern forms spread across the different communities of the Valley found a place in *Mukti Deul*. In the attempt at expansive text to accommodate the diverse, as found in the case of Gohain Baruah's *Jaymati*, and the attempt in Bezbaruah's texts to create a paradigmatic text which could *represent* diversity by assuming everyday language as the universal atom, it is possible to find the combination (if not the culmination) of the two forms in Rabha's *Mukti Deul*, often considered one of his best cultural productions. But what made it possible was not culture or people per se. It was the praxis of revolutionary politics vis-à-vis the play that made it possible. The nature of the play is rooted in its objective and function, which cannot be seen in isolation from revolutionary mass politics. Therefore, due to this context, it was necessary for Rabha to not only write short stories but also to communicate them to the masses. Thus, he did not rely on only one mode of communication, viz. textual or readership, but different modes such as gatherings, meetings, travels, leadership forums, etc. to communicate what was primarily a textual narrative form (as opposed to his plays and dance dramas). These modes of communication were his revolutionary necessity; but it was also this practice that helped even his textual narrative to overcome the limits of the given form and enter into everyday social life. Importantly, in such a practice, the distinctions between the everyday and the political (or exceptional) disintegrated and it became a social whole. Thus, such a narrative could seek to *represent* the social diversity, because what it sought to represent was not so much *a* people; rather it sought to represent a political relation that made them a people, viz. class. It also made possible a dynamic relation between form and practice in his revolutionary plays and dance dramas.

Another major difference between the narrative of Rabha on the hand and those of Gohain Baruah or Bezbaruah on the other is the role of language. I have already put the question earlier, viz. can a language communicate or carry content which is beyond its historical or ethnographic experience? Gohain Baruah and Bezbaruah attempted narratives wherein communication of content was through one form of language, viz. 'standard' Sibsagar

Assamese. In his *Jaymati*, Gohain Baruah put more than one form of language in use; but in his other plays, such as *Tetun Tamuli*, which are based on the locale of the entire Valley, Sibsagar Assamese functions as the communicator of the narrative. Even in the case of *Jaymati*, the two forms of language (Sibsagar Assamese and 'Nagamese') are closely related. 'Nagamese' borrows heavily as a pidgin from Sibsagar Assamese (since geographically, the Naga Hills neighbours the Sibsagar language belt). In the case of Bezbaruah too, the everyday practice of language which found space and added meaning to the narrative was the everyday practice of Sibsagar Assamese. Therefore, none of these texts stepped beyond the historical or ethnographic limits of the languages used in the texts. The centrality that language assumed as the communicator of the narrative also set the most fundamental of limits to claims for the narrative to linguistically *represent* the socio-cultural diversity. A single language form cannot represent the multiple. It was shown in Part I how the only explanation that Bezbaruah could offer (and it goes for most others as well) was that language of the capital area is always considered as the 'standard', and so would also apply, thus, for the Sibsagar 'standard'. Gohain Baruah, in his critique of caste Hindus appropriating Assamese, did not critique the issue of language 'standard'. He only argued that the credit for the language 'standard' needed to be given to the historical role of the Ahoms, which he found was not highlighted by the caste Hindus.

In contrast, Rabha made it possible to create narrative that did not rely on the language per se to communicate with the masses. His narrative was incomplete without being *practised* among the people. And practise allowed space for the mediation of numerous factors other than language to establish communication with the masses. Further, the narratives was not aimed at being listened to or being read by the people. The objective was to make them participate politically in a revolutionary praxis wherein culture and politics, the everyday and the exceptional constituted one social whole. In a praxis wherein form and its practice were dynamically related, more than language, it was communication and participation which assumed greater significance. Thus, whether it were Rabha's stories or his songs and dances or his plays and dance dramas, they all were part of gatherings, meetings, leadership platforms, or as a fugitive entertaining the masses who protected him. Therefore, even if a text was written in 'standard' Assamese or Bodo, the historical or ethnographic limits of the language did not chain the representative element of the narrative. In this regard, one morphological dimension, especially in his stories, is noteworthy. For example, if a story was written in Assamese but set in a Bodo village, there would be numerous Bodo words along with which the Assamese meaning would also be provided (and not as footnotes). Rabha (in his Introduction to *Sunpahi*) discussed this bilingual method, and argued that since the stories were meant for the masses and not for 'readers', indigenous words were retained in the text. Rabha does not give any further exact explanation to the method. But it is possible to see the method in two ways. First, given his focus on practice (of language and of form), such morphological features may be treated as part of the approach. Second, Rabha forcefully argued that when culture in the Valley is not seen in terms of traditional texts but in terms of practise, far more important than the Gangetic/Sanskrit connection are the imprints which different communities of the Valley have left on each other through their interrelations and exchanges. A double morphological method may be seen as an attempt to reflect that understanding textually. But in the process, the centrality of *a* language form in a narrative and thereby the contradiction of representation as discussed above was also overcome.

A small additional point can be made here. The case of Rabha's cultural intervention can also be understood through the interpretative framework of 'practical consciousness' provided by Raymond Williams (1977). Rabha's narrative practice can be explained only in its relation to revolutionary mass politics. But revolutionary mass politics alone may not be sufficient, without the role of the author, to bring about such an intervention. It can be best exemplified, for example, in a contrastive study with Syed Abdul Malik, another of the most significant Assamese writers in the second half of the 20th century. Though not a holder of the party card, Malik was known to be a sympathiser of the RCPI, for which he lost his job with the All India Radio. In the late 1940s and early 1950s, Malik's house was under surveillance from the police (Malik 2008). It was the time when communist parties were banned in most parts of India. But despite this similarity of context, what Malik produced as a writer was very different from what was produced by Rabha. For Malik, revolution was only in his content, and not in narrative practice as in the case of Rabha. For example, in his poem published in the Assamese magazine *Paigam* ([1945, 1 (2)] 2008), he wrote (paraphrased translation from verse mine), 'My identity is that of the soil, not the made up identity of this country, of Assamese, of Bengali' (Malik 2008: 247). The message was communicated in 'standard' Assamese. Thus, the role of Rabha, i.e., the individual, in creating the narrative practice should not be undermined. This is where the coming together, or the relation, of the individual and his/her context can be highlighted.

A reference can also be made here to one of the Rabha's contemporary Phani Sarma and his writings. Phani Sarma was one of the leading playwights and actors from the late 1930s to the 1960s. He was also Rabha's comrade. But unlike Rabha's plays or dance dramas, Sarma did not employ methods to create a possibility of common politics from within the narrative structure of a text. For example, in his acclaimed play *Siraj*, the fact of ethnographic contradiction vis-à-vis linguistic uses by the characters belonging to different socio-ethnic groups was not evident. The discourse of socio-economic equality existed in the Assamese 'standard'. In this, Sarma's narrative was similar to that of Malik's. But Sarma tried to resolve it in his fiction *Banariya Phul* (Wild Flower, [1976] 2003), a semi-autobiographical novel. For example, when the drunk author (an Assamese) appreciates the Nepali shopkeeper woman serving him local wine, the woman laughed and says (translation mine), '"What are you saying babu? Please tell it in our language," and giggled' (ibid.: 269). The author replies in his language, '"In my language, I am saying that it is good," and laughed, drunk' (ibid.). No one understood the words spoken, but the meaning was grasped. Similarly, in the case of the Haldar family in the same novel, when Haldar asks Satyamurthi in broken Hindi if he would like to drink wine, Satyamurthi, a Tamil, replies in broken Assamese that he would enjoy it but only in the evening (Sarma [1976] 2003: 286).

Conclusion

In the three examples of strategies of narrative (Gohain Baruah, Bezbaruah and Rabha) and one example of prescriptive intervention on narrative (Kakati), one common aspect in all the four cases was their recognition of how differences among communities could transform into contradictions when situated in a narrative. Each of the four cases was attempting to devise a strategy to overcome the challenge. However, as will seen in the next chapter, it was this very challenge or its recognition which apparently disappeared (not overcome) from strategies of narrative between the 1950s and the 1980s. But one of its earliest practitioners came not from this period but from the same period as the four examples noted above belonged to. He was the popular and influential poet-intellectual Ambikagiri Raichoudhury.

In an editorial (1920) in the magazine *Chetana* titled 'India's Self Rule and Assam's Self Rule', Raichoudhury argued that despite the Aryan influence in the shaping of Indian culture, as the influence spread into different geographical areas, the concrete result that emerged in each locale was unique and different from each other. The local elements mixed with the Aryan influence, so much so that they were no longer Aryan per se any more. These concrete results were the different nations that now dot the landscape of the subcontinent. This, according to him, constituted the bedrock of nation formation all over the subcontinent (Raichoudhury [1920] 2009: 533). He went on to argue (translation mine),

> The whole of India today is under British colonialism, and it is only due to this common experience that all the nations have come together in the name of *Indian* independence. None of these nations have independence, and therefore, to prevent weakening of the struggle, each nation is told to think along *Indian* lines and not along their own national lines. The latter is portrayed as negative. ... But when India gets its independence, these different nations will certainly struggle for their own independence. We can see this future right now. Every nation has its own proud history. It cannot forget its past (ibid.: 536).

Along similar lines, but on the question of control over one's own land, he argued in another editorial (1935) of the magazine *Deka Asom* (Young Assam) (translation mine), 'An individual and his nation has a natural right over his land. ... But when people neglect this relation, then the future of the nation becomes bleak (Raichoudhury [1935] 2009: 539). Raichoudhury considered the concept of India as only a pan-nation form, rather than a nation. It is along these lines that he related and naturalised Assamese–Assam nation. In another short commentary written in the early

1950s (exact date unavailable) titled '*Jatiya Jagaran*' (National Awakening,, 2009), he listed the numerous organisations and bodies that had come up in Assam for the many communities that inhabited the state, and said that each of the organisations needed to work for its respective community. However, he cautioned that the final culmination should be the national glory of Assam, for they all together comprised the Assamese nation (ibid.: 742).

Raichoudhury's intervention was important not only because it gained more prominence in the post-Independence period, but also because it gave a new approach to the question of language/narrative and people. First, Raichoudhury clearly demarcated Assam–Assamese as a nation. In the case of the others, i.e., his pre-Independence contemporaries, the word *jati* was used to refer to Assam–Assamese, which in terms of defining a people could either mean a nation or a community. Second, and more significantly, in Raichoudhury, the debate over the historical and ethnographic contradictions that can exist in the definition of Assamese (found in his pre-Independence contemporaries as discussed in Part I) simply disappeared, but was not overcome. The sum of all (the varieties) became the Assamese nation. Third, the issue of (Assamese) language and its forms and the problem of one being able to *represent* the other which had troubled his pre-Independence contemporaries also disappeared in his discourse. Modern Assamese became a natural bearer of the national elements of the nation of Assam. In that capacity, it could be the bearer not only of the socio-cultural elements (and their diversity) but also of a geographical locale.

These were some of the implications of Raichoudhury's discourse. However, there was another dimension to his discourse, equally important, viz. his universal humanism, dealing with the objective of his nationalist discourse. For example, Raichoudhury argues, in the editorial of the magazine *Deka Asom* ([1935] 2009), that the concept of India should become a universal idea of humanism in which different nations such as Assam from the subcontinent participate and prosper. But that universal idea of humanism cannot happen if India itself becomes a nation (Raichoudhury 2009: 541–44). The idea of Assamese nationalism has also been interpreted as bourgeois nationalism (for example, Gohain 1985). Nevertheless, it is open to debate if Raichoudhury's perspective can be considered a part of the paradigm of bourgeois nationalism.

In the post-Independence period (especially the 1950s to the 1980s), on the cultural question, the discursive line of Raichoudhury (without naming him though) gained pre-eminence, but without India as the universal idea of humanism. Further, it also became the period when several kinds of politics that distanced themselves from the Assamese language-based interpretation of Assamese 'nation' gained institutional strength and legitimacy. Thus, in this condition one can locate an ironical breakdown in the relation between narrative (or cultural form) and its social base. While the former increasingly assumed Assamese language as representative of the diversity/multiplicity and created narratives wherein the 'standard' form of the language represented the diverse/multiple, the social base from which such narratives emerged increasingly disintegrated on this very question. The irony was that the breakdown happened, and experiments and significant attempts as were to be found in the pre-Independence period on the nature of narrative to prevent this very breakdown, faded away. The issue is discussed in detail in the next chapter.

The four examples discussed earlier showed how differences transformed into a relation of contradiction within the space of the narrative. Each kind of narrative, in relation to the other, also highlights the point. This nature of narrative cannot be explained only in terms of *reflection* or *mediation* of text vis-à-vis the context. It is undeniable that the text was trying to both reflect and mediate the context. However, what was fundamental is that in the process, it itself underwent a transformation. Attempting to explain it in terms of politics of identity (which has become common) can be even more absurd. This dynamism can be plausibly explained only in terms of a praxis wherein the different factors (or actors) were related to one another in a dialectical relation. It is dialectical because for reflection and mediation to happen in the context of differences, a common ground, viz. a *representative* narrative in this case, was essential, which precisely was found improbable. Yet the struggle to create or practise that narrative possibility continued. The resultant tension within the narratives highlighted the mapping of socio-spatial relations of the Valley. The closest that came to the ideal was the work of Rabha, and the reason behind it was that he was not seeking to represent a totality; he was trying to represent a relation that made them a *kind* of people, viz. class. Rabha's narrative was neither textual or 'literary' nor performance-based, and neither was it performance literature as the term is generally understood. Compared to any other writer, it is also only in Rabha's narrative that one can see the extent to which a narrative had to keep transforming itself dynamically in different 'situations' in the attempt to reflect and mediate the masses across differences. If revolutionary politics in the Valley was a sudden flare that again died out, Rabha's narrative practise was also like a sudden flare that disappeared even before his death in 1967.

5

Narrative and Social Base: The Irony of Breakdown

In the period from the 1950s to the 1980s what was remarkable, as indicated earlier, was the disappearance of the historical and ethnographic debate over language and narrative, a debate that most practitioners of culture (and literature) had grappled with in the previous decades. What is found during the period is that the discourse that Raichoudhury most fiercely had advocated (Assam-Assamese nation) gained preeminence but without the other dimension of Raichoudhury's discourse, viz. India becoming a universal idea of humanism in which all nations (of the subcontinent) prosper. If Assamese language was naturalised as the bearer of the character of Assam, the question of contradictions was, or had to be, left unresolved. This was evident from the writings of one of the most significant intellectual and cultural/literary figures of the period, Birendra Kumar Bhattacharjya. His writings and editorials in the influential literary magazine of the period, *Ramdhenu*, were quite illustrative of his approach. I have shown that Bezbaruah, despite arguing in favour of the Sibsagar form of Assamese as the 'standard', did recognise the contradictions that such an approach or practice could entail. The only solution he could come up with was that despite the reality of multiple language forms in use, everyone needed to accept the language of the capital as the language 'standard'. With Bhattacharjya, the 'standard', rather than being a political choice, became almost a natural choice. In his review and analysis of Debananda Bharali's *Axomiya Bhaxar Moulik Bicar* (The Fundamentals of Assamese Language, 1912) and Bharali's later book in English, *A Study of Phonology and Vocabulary of the Assamese Language* (1959), Bhattacharjya tried to delineate the point that it was only in the 'standard', due to historical reasons, that one could find the indigenous form of Assamese language

(Bhattacharjya [1952-53] 2007: 50-54). He emphasised Bharali's argument that despite the fact that Sankari language became the 'standard' between the 17th and early 19th centuries due to the influence of Bangla, increase in trade exchanges and due to the political turmoil in the valley, the influence of foreign language on Assamese increased. He argued that due to political reasons, the spread of the influence was limited in the eastern valley, or the core of the Ahom ruled area. Therefore he said, (translation mine), 'In the areas neighbouring Ahom kingdom, the language which circulated as the language of the ruling class ... continued to survive as the indigenous Assamese language' (ibid.: 51) He also endorsed Bharali's contention (made in his 1912 monograph) on why or how the corruption of Assamese had taken place. Bharali had argued that in both officialdom as well as in trade, the non-indigenous people were dominant. As a result, the indigenous were forced to adopt the language uses of these social groups. From the market, these language forms enter the language use among the urban and then the rural people, and from there in the literature of the people. Thus, Bharali argued (translation mine), 'The future of the Assamese language depends on the overall socio-economic development of the Assamese people and not merely in promoting the language per se' (cited in ibid.: 52).

Bhattacharjya's position on the larger language question in Assam was based on this approach. In his *Ramdhenu* editorial titled 'Tower of Babel' (1958–59), he argued that in a democracy, language cannot be imposed on a people. Such attempts could only lead to discontent among the people. He said (translation mine),

> The government of India had imposed the Hindi language in the NEFA area despite the protests of the indigenous people of NEFA and Assamese people. It has led to serious discontent among these people. Another example is the All India Radio which now broadcast its programmes for the tea plantation community in Assam in the Hindi language. This too has created displeasure among the Assamese people. It is evident from the two examples that the central government is determined to promote Hindi even at the cost of Assamese. It can only create obstacles in national integration of the region (Bhattacharjya [1958–59] 2007, 7 (1): 183).

In his conclusion to the same editorial, he remarked (translation mine),

There are many in this country who think that the language is not the main problem, the main problem is economic. But even for economic development, we need a popular language, knowledge which is easily accessible, and cordial exchanges, which calls for a commonly accepted medium. Further, the development of language and culture is also a history in itself. ... In fact, making language a cause of discontent and disunity among the people is regrettable today (ibid.: 184).

If language and literature were important for national development, then what should be the nature of Assamese literature? Bhattacharjya argued that there was a great need for generation of new content in Assamese literature. The new content, according to him, could not be confined to issues that concerned only the bourgeoisie. It had to take into account problems of class and ethnicity, problems of irrationality, of a growing sense of alienation, etc. It was important, Bhattacharjya argued, that new literature should be scientific and progressive rather than looking back at an idealised past for inspiration (Bhattacharjya [1958–59] 2007: 275–77).

Notable in Bhattacharjya's approach and that of the influential magazine *Ramdhenu* was the relation established between language, narrative and the concept of people. But what was the context of the approach? The answer can be found in one of Bhattacharjya's editorials in the *Ramdhenu* titled 'Asomiya aru Bharatiyo' (Assamese and Indian). The first point the editorial made was the unique nature of the region and the people, viz. of being or comprising a frontier. Endorsing the views of O. H. K. Spate (*India and Pakistan*), Bhattacharjya cited Spate to articulate his point, 'The state of Assam possesses remarkable individuality. It is in a sense transitional towards High Asia and Indo China (in a broad sense) and even to China itself' (Bhattacharjya [1958–59] 2007: 273). The second point he made was that the Assamese language had not only been a key recipient but also a key builder of this 'remarkable individuality' that Spate noted. It had been that common element that made the people and the place unique. He then argued that not only was Assamese language prepared to take up the responsibility of the frontier, but also indicated that it could be the only language which could make possible what is most required in a frontier, viz. unifying the people through love and honour. The third point he made was that different communities (*janajatiya* — tribal?) on the frontier had come to critique Assamese as a language of domination, despite being the common language of the region throughout history. But Bhattacharjya argued that the critique had been misunderstood in Assam. What the communities wanted was that their own language and culture should find an opportunity for development, which did not mean that Assamese would be thrown out of their respective collective lives. On why the opinion was gaining ground among these communities, he placed the blame on the leadership of both Assam and of these indigenous communities. It was the leadership, according to him, which created the incorrect impression (for political benefit?) among the people that Assamese was the language of domination. He concluded (translation mine), 'Even the opposition parties have probably failed to explain the point to the people' (ibid.: 272).

From the position on language and indigeneity to that of language and frontier, Bhattacharjya drew a scheme in which the debate of the preceding period over the historical and ethnographic contradictions on language and narrative vis-à-vis the social base could disappear. It could disappear not because the issue was resolved but because the issue could cease to exist as an issue. On such a scheme, Bhattacharjya did not stand alone. It could be found among other articulations of the period as well, for example in Maheswar Neog, one of the most powerful voices of the period. In fact, *The Language Question* (1961) edited by Neog reached almost a canonical status. If during the period narrative was faced with a breakdown in terms of its relation with the social base, it was because the narratives came to be largely premised on the foundation of the above schema. It was also the reason why the range of experiments in language and narratives that were found in the preceding period tended to almost disappear in this period. What made possible for this schema to play the foundational role in the relation between language and narrative on the one hand, and socio-political relations on the other?

Politics of Identity

In Assam, the decade of the 1950s saw several agitations against the Indian 'nation' state. They were generally for creating infrastructure for human development, whether they were about physical infrastructure such as bridges or educational infrastructure such as universities. Such demands or politics based on such demands were/have been widespread in the rest of India as well. What distinguished the case in Assam was that the demands were part of a politics that protested against the idea (and seemingly its practice) of dispensable frontier, a territory being maintained only as a 'neo-colony' and buffer between China and Burma. Thus, the politics became not merely a protest against the government of India but also against the Indian 'nation' state system itself.

In addition to this politics, the decade of the 1960s witnessed the Language Agitation. When Assamese was made the official language for the state of Assam through a legislative act in 1960, violent protest broke in the southern Bengali-dominated districts of Assam (in Barak Valley) as well as in some of the hill districts (present-day state of Meghalaya). The Language Agitation brought out the politics of ethnicity in the region into sharp relief. Two hill districts (which formed Part A of the 6th Schedule of the Constitution) rose in protest against the language policy of the Government of Assam. The united Khasi and Jaintia Hills district and Garo Hills district (they later comprised the state of Meghalaya) opposed the policy on the ground that Assamese was not their language and therefore could not become their 'official' language. Further, the process that later led to the formation of the Bodoland Autonomous Council in 2001 for the Bodo people (for their economic and cultural protection from 'Assamese' people and culture and development of the Bodo people) became firmer and more institutionalised during this period as a response to the Language Agitation.

The opposition of the two hill districts can be seen in the larger context of *ethnic* politics of the period in the region as a whole. Both the Naga and Mizo politics (i.e., hills neighbouring the Brahmaputra Valley and the Barak Valley) of militant struggle for independence (from India) in the 1960s were premised upon ethnicity as a criterion of nationhood. What made the issue of ethnicity and nationhood a vexing problem was not whether ethnicity could be a basis of nationhood (which it theoretically can be, as well as in practise as shown by the case of Naga nationalism), but whether it was viable in the region. This is because in a primarily 'tribal' area, ethnicity could unite people horizontally across space but could also split loyalties (or divide people) vertically within the same area. A tribe may not be a homogeneous entity in itself. Therefore, subdivisions within a tribe could trigger the split. The problem was acutely linked to the relation of such politics to the question of ethnic/national territory.

The Language Agitation also brought the issue of Assamese 'nationhood' into focus. The role of the premier cultural body of the time, the Asom Sahitya Sabha, was central in and throughout the entire agitation. The Agitation spanned almost the whole of the 1960s. But it was accompanied by another major event of nationalist significance — the Chinese Aggression of 1962. With regard to the Indo-China War, that the Indian army was severely defeated by the Chinese forces was not of central importance to Assamese nationhood politics. Of significance was Nehru's radio address (read as the response of the India nation state to the War) to the nation in which, at the apparent defeat of the Indian army at the hands of the Chinese forces, he left the fate of the people of the region to the goodwill of China. On the evening of 19 November 1962, the Indian Army's 4 Corps began preparations to pull out from Tezpur (in Assam) in the face of the marching Chinese forces. This led to a panic that triggered the collapse of the local administration by the following day. Nehru's address to the 'people of Assam' came at this juncture. It became a most damaging scar on the relation between the nation and its frontier. It further strengthened the growing politics in the valley that Assam (and indeed the entire north-eastern frontier) constituted a dispensable frontier of the Indian nation state. The politics of nationhood during the anti-colonial struggle was only one of the kinds of politics operating in Assam (as shown in Raichoudhury's discourse). After independence as well, popular politics had other issues other than that of nationhood. However, if militant nationalist politics is kept out from the discussion, even the popular politics (with its diverse themes) came to operate from then on increasingly within the perspective of nationhood politics. The cause of all other problems was traced to the idea (and practice?) of dispensable frontiers. Events have significance both in their individual and collective capacities. Whether it was the partition debate (Cabinet Mission Plan), the Language Agitation, the development of nationhood politics or foreign aggression, the different events had their role in the individual and collective or cumulative capacities to contribute and sustain the resistance against nationalisation of the frontier, i.e., transforming it into like any other region of the country.

Herein, the question of whether the politics of Assam was a middle-class preserve is important. The other important point was the role of language in the political life of Assam. It is undeniable that since the turn of the 20th century language had been treated as a defining criterion of the Assamese people. The role of the Baptist missionaries, of the early and nationalist literary icons such as Bezbaruah and Padmanath Gohain Baruah and others and the formation of the Asom Sahitya Sabha in 1917 were landmark developments not only in the promotion of the language but also in the establishment of language as the fundamental cultural indicator of identity. But despite the realisation of the contradictions involved in such a politics or discourse, as was previously shown, what kept the effort alive? If on the one hand the colonial attempt at defining people (for economic reasons) employed the term 'Assamese', i.e., defining people from without, another attempt from within was also taking shape based on an emerging service-based middle class. Since the 1840s, the efforts of people (the intelligentsia/middle class) and of the missionaries in defining social identity had been through the Assamese language. This was a result of the British language policy in the region (of imposing/using Bangla as the 'official' language). Therefore, the justification of difference came about through the medium of language. Language became the means of constituting the 'other'. Herein lay a notable irony of identity formation. In the colonial administrative and military records the identity of the region was that of a frontier, and of the people as the 'wild' inhabitants of the frontier. For their convenience, people from Bengal were brought to govern the region. It also led to using Bangla as the official language. Yet, it was this very policy wherein lay the genesis of discourse in which language became the mode of constituting an identity and eventually a nationhood from within the region. The cultural 'rejuvenation' that came about at the turn of the 20th century was through the medium of literature. The fact that language and literature became the premier method of becoming *a people* could itself be taken as an evidence of the role of the middle class in the fashioning of an 'Assamese' identity and a politics based on it. I have shown, for example, that people like Bishnu Rabha critiqued this approach in making language and literature markers of identity and used them in turn as only tools of his revolutionary mass politics.

The Language Agitation (leaving aside the question of 'official' language) can be seen as the final consolidation of that discourse-in-making in which language and its literature were the markers of identity. In the process, the recognition of the contradictions that the lay embedded in the discourse was also disallowed. The presence of the recognition negated the very logic of the discourse. With such an approach, it becomes clearer why, for example, Bhattacharjya emphasised on indigenous nature of the 'standard', viz. that it carried the historical roots of a language that distinguished a nation from others. But if the Agitation established the language as a distinct discourse and practice of politics, it also highlighted the fact that ethnicity too could perform a similar role. In fact, the Agitation created an immediate space for ethnicity to become a powerful criterion of constituting a people (and eventually a nation). By the 1980s, ethnicity emerged as a competitive criterion against language on nationhood formation. The formation of the Bodoland Autonomous Council could very well be understood as a mechanism created to accommodate the ethnic within the (Assamese) linguistic in this regard.

The other movement that especially rocked the Brahmaputra Valley from the mid-1970s–mid-1980s was the Assam Movement. This was one of biggest mass civil disobedience movements in post-Independence Indian history. It was characterised by non-violent civil disobedience as well as violent protest. The movement was against the migrants from Bangladesh. It had both spontaneity and organisation. Peaceful protests in the form of boycott and civil disobedience and violent methods in the form of death/massacre highlighted the spontaneous and organised dimension to the politics of the movement. Sabita Goswami's autobiographical accounts on the movement in her *Man Gangar Tirat* (she was the BBC correspondent for the movement) provides a graphic analysis of both the spontaneity and the organization behind the movement (2009). Though led by Sodou Asom Catra Sanstha (All Assam Students Union [AASU]), as part of the boycott programme, not only teachers and students boycotted schools and colleges but also a very large number of government employees boycotted their offices, irrespective of urban or rural locale. On violence, the most dramatic and international events were the Nellie massacre and the police massacre. In the former, members of the Tiwa community massacred immigrants while in the latter villagers were killed by the police. At that time, the police chief in the state was K. P. S. Gill.

Hiren Gohain (1985) argued that the movement became possible due to an already existing politics of nationhood and the movement in turn facilitated the validation and establishment of that politics as an objective reality. Since then, for nearly two decades (till the 1990s), militant nationalism (ULFA) and popular politics (through political parties) remained merely the extremist and moderate varieties of the same politics of nationhood. The only difference was that the former wanted secession while the latter remained ambivalent about it. It was this character of politics that led to the imposition of governance through the army in 1990 in Assam. The major geographical target of this new governance was the Brahmaputra Valley, especially the eastern valley.

A fundamental contribution of the movement was to bring demography to the forefront of politics. If the Language Agitation had consolidated a politics in which language was naturalised as an identity marker of the Assamese 'nation' despite the debates of the preceding decades on the issue, through the Assam Movement, the question of demographic profile of such politics was articulated. However, the contradictions that lay embedded in the language question were also embedded in the demographic question. Therefore, the politics during the period showed two distinct trends. On the one hand there was the discourse in which language, indigeneity, people and territory formed a seamless structure of Assam–Assamese nation. On the other hand the discourse in turn made possible a politics of ethnicity which critiqued the above framework as hegemonic. The latter proved to be as popular as the former depending on their respective social bases.

Language, Narrative and Politics

If Bhattacharjya developed or worked with a scheme which extended from language and indigeneity to language and frontier and in which a form of Assamese language became the atom of the scheme, it was due to the political period in which he was operating. He was not only drawing on or articulating the politics. He was as much participating in it and defining it. It was visible in his narrative strategies as well, such as in his classic novel *Iaruingam* (People's Rule, 1960). I will discuss how language and narrative in *Iaruingam* engaged with the question of 'people's rule' and frontier.

Iaruingam focused on Gandhian nationalism as a viable method of politics in the frontier. Based on the Tankhul tribe (Naga Hills) and its relation with the Indian national movement and thereafter with the Indian nation state, *Iaruingam* explores the role of nationalism in a 'tribal' context. The novel could be considered one of the earliest literary attempts in India on engaging with the problematic of tribal nationalism as socio-anthropological concept. It shows how culture need not be a prerequisite for nation formation. Politics can mould culture into a national culture as well. It shows the politics of Naga nationalism as a conclusive example of such a process of nation formation.

In the case of Naga nationalism, World War II was a significant factor in the relation between tribal society and nationalism. The novel opens with the War and its impact on Naga society. The Japanese forces, through the help of Azad Hind Fauj, reached the Naga Hills in 1944. In the novel, three preliminary observations on the War are as follows: (a) the female body became a site of War effect (love and unwed motherhood of Naga women through Japanese soldiers and their separation with the subsequent Japanese retreat). The effect of war was temporary and permanent at the same time for the women due to its effect upon their body; (b) changes in Naga worldview due to contact with different people and ideas in the process of War were key to understanding the ideological changes that finally evolved into Naga nationhood; and (c) War played little role in the latter part of the plot.

Iaruingam is based on the author's personal experience and observation when he was working as a schoolteacher in the area. On ideology and text, it is possible to locate four distinct features in *Iaruingam*. First, the novel not only shows that tribal nationalism is possible, but also provides a detailed account of its mode of formation and operation. Second, the attempt of the novel at conceptualising the region (north-eastern frontier) as a distinct *region* and *people* within India is noteworthy. It is evident in the fact that the Assamese people are not (presented as) outsiders the way other Indians are to the Naga people in the novel. The people of the region share a commonality distinct from the Indian nation. This is made evident both in the experiences of the protagonist (Rishang) in Calcutta during the Quit India

Movement (1942) and also during his exchanges with Assamese people subsequently in Assam and in the Naga Hills. Though the novel does not conceptualise enough what that commonality could possibly be, it shows that the history and culture that they shared over centuries makes that bonding possible.

Third, in the context of the nationalist struggle of the Naga people against the Indian State (that is the prime mover of the plot in the latter half), the solution suggested is Gandhian nationalism. However, what is not made clear is whether Gandhian nationalism means allegiance to Indian nationhood or it is meant only as a peaceful mechanism towards achieving people's rule or democracy. Fourth, the text is ambivalent vis-à-vis defining 'people's rule'. This ideological ambivalence is evident in the characters/ characterisation of Rishang (who has faith in the Indian State system) and Phanitphang (who becomes a Naga extremist/ separatist). The ambivalence emerges from the fact that though the ideological context of 'Naga people' is emphasised, the ideological content of 'Naga people' is left less defined. Therefore, both Rishang and Phanitphang are nationalist. The text is undecided as to whether 'Naga people' is synonymous to the Naga nation or if they are two different ideological categories. As a result, the novel is balanced between both description of *a* people and attempts at defining *a* people.

What is the role of language in the narrative? In the cases of Padmanath Gohain Baruah, Lakhminath Bezbaruah and Bishnu Rabha, as well as in the prescriptive propositions of Banikanta Kakati, I showed that the attempt to engage with the problem of language is in two ways, viz. (a) if the social base of the novel is beyond the historical or ethnographic experience of a language per se, then language mixing or situating language use in a praxis of revolutionary mass politics (Rabha), or use of more than one language (Gohain Baruah), or the use of everyday language practised by people (Bezbaruah), or exploring the possibility of a common script whether or not based on experiences from within the region (Kakati); and (b) through the above devices, to make the language(s) *represent* the social base that the text deals with. It is only through either of these two approaches that a narrative acquires an identity of its own. In *Iaruingam*, no such use or conceptualising of language is to be seen. On the contrary the Assamese 'standard' becomes the bearer of the entire social diversity that forms the social base of the plot. It accommodates as well as represents the diversity. For example, whether it is the conversation between Ishiwara, the Japanese soldier, and Sarengla, the Naga woman who bears his child, or between the Naga people themselves, intra- and inter-tribe, or between Assamese and Naga people, the 'standard' form of Assamese is the only device in the text through which the communication occurs. Why is the point important? It is important because, as I have already shown in the cases of Gohain Baruah, Bezbaruah, Kakati or Rabha, such a textual mechanism was already found to be insufficient, and that knowledge was available to Bhattacharjya. The irony of *Iaruingam* is that while on the one hand it relies on realism to create its narrative (it is a *realist* novel), at the same time it relies on the symbolic role of language to create that very realist narrative.

Even if examples like Gohain Baruah's *Jaymati* are to be discounted, are there other examples which show that Bhattacharjya's realism was a political literary device in this regard? The autobiographical accounts of another of Bhattacharjya's contemporary writer, Syed Abdul Malik, provide us the answer. In his diary/autiobiography (published posthumously in 2008 in the collection *Syed Abdul Malikar Aprakaxita Rasanavali and Diary*), Malik wrote about his experiences as wartime (World War II) censor officer in the British Army between 1941 and 1944. When he was posted in the forward post town of Dimapur, he noted that there were numerous letters which were written in Naga Assamese (or 'Nagamese') in the Roman script, which he had to read and classify as per language and forward them to the other sections (Malik 2008: 208–13). What Malik's account highlights, possibly even more than Gohain Baruah's *Jaymati*, is that Bhattacharjya's narrative realism does not take into account one of the key factors of realism in terms of the role of language in narrative realism. It is equally ironical that in the preface to *Iaruingam* (first edn of 1960), the author says (translation mine),

> When living among the the Tangkhul Nagas, I tried to delve into the unique life of the Naga people. ... Nagas are also human beings. But they are unique human beings. There is something pristine about their life. In this book, I have tried to give an idea of it.

Yet the text also inflicts a violence of language form upon the very people whom he seeks to *present*. In Part I, I referred to Birinchi

Baruah's *Seuji Patar Kahini*, published in 1958. The close parallel in its narrative strategy with *Iaruingam* is evident.

Maheswar Neog, in his presidential address to the Asom Sahitya Sabha congress of 1973, made two important points. One point was (translation mine),

> Different communities inhabiting the hills and valley of Assam together has made Assam. But it is a frightening situation today that both the terms Assam and Assamese have become objects of critique for the people. It's true that these two terms, viz. Assam and Assamese, are not more than two hundred years old. In the time of Ahom king Rudra Singha, no one called one another Assamese. Sankardeb too did not hear of this term and never must have thought that the language in which he wrote was Assamese. 'Assam' and 'Assamese' are derived from the Ahom rulers. But the rulers themselves during that period referred to their kingdom in their copper plate inscriptions as Soumar. Some of them perhaps referred to it as Udoygiri. The name Ahom *rajya* was given by outsiders, and from that the names Assam and Assamese are derived. But even if given by outsiders, the terms have gelled well with the fact of the unity that was in place among the different communities of the region. ... The search today for who is indigenous and who isn't, etc has only created a great deal of confusion (Neog [1974] 2008: 88).

From this position, Neog moves to the question of language, identity and territory. Elaborating on the demand for a separate Bodo territory (called Udayachal) from Assam, he argues (translation mine),

> The demand does not stand as based on issues of language or ethnicity or territory when properly examined. All the *janajatis* (tribal or ethnic?) of Assam have no other language other than Assamese to communicate with each other. If ethnicity or territory is the criteria, then the territorial claim (of Udayachal) should have been also made into Nagaland, Mizoram, Meghalaya, etc. (ibid.: 91).

Neog then wonders if land could be the reason. He answers (translation mine),

> In 1888, the British government of Assam divided Assam into revenue circles and identified in the process 33 tribal belts and blocks. The British then settled non-tribal people in these blocks and belts with the aim of revenue increase. If these non tribal people

have dispossessed the indigenous tribal from their land, then the matter may be investigated. But what about the many from the tribal people themselves who may have dispossessed their own people from land? (ibid.)

Therefore, Neog traces the origin of the protests and politics to a conspiracy theory of certain sections of the tribal people to gain power from the turmoil. Therefore, he argues that Assamese language had a unique role in this context, viz. it could be the only meaningful vehicle to bring peace in the region. It not only represented the diversity but was also the medium in which the diversity participated as its common language (Neog [1973] 2008: 94–118). Neog's approach has a close parallel in Birinchi Baruah's or Bhattacharjya's literary strategies.

Conclusion

If during the period the issue of language and narrative being embedded with historical and ethnographic contradictions disappeared from the predominant discourse on language and literature, it was not because an ideology (of 'Assamese' identity) was being reproduced in language use and narrative strategies. In fact, the ideological discourse was also being consciously created at the same time. In that sense, both language use and narrative strategies were not reproductions of or by *ideological subjects*. In fact, on the question of literature and ideology, one of the most remarkable features throughout the 20th century in this regard was the conscious participation in the production of ideology. The fact that differences did not necessarily fall into a pattern and that literature, when faced with the challenge of engaging with the relation of differences, found itself wrapped in contradictions, was quite known to the producers of literature. What was ironical between the 1950s and the 1980s was that the knowledge was dropped from the textual space altogether. The irony was possibly most revealing in Neog's own comment on the demands for separate Bodo territory (translation mine),

> We have been *voicing at the top of our voice* (emphasis mine) that the Bodos are an inseparable part of the Assamese people, and even if recorded history does not show, our names of places amply prove how deep runs the imprint of the Bodos in the map of Assam."
> (Neog [1973] 2008: 90).

The discourse was trying to be increasingly and emphatically inclusive as well as exclusive at the same time. What caused the contradiction, which it nevertheless denied?

I argue that the contradiction manifested the deeper problems of engaging with socio-spatial relations in literary practices. It is undeniable that there was a breakdown in the principle of correspondence between Assamese literature and its social base during the period. As the literature became increasingly exclusive, the more strident grew its claims of being inclusive. I argue that this marked the breaking point up to which literature and its mapping socio-spatial relations could be stretched. While in the previous decades literature was marked by experiments to accommodate and represent the diverse/multiple as part of this mapping, during this period, such attempts were given up. The language 'standard' and all that it stood for came to be recognised as the cultural code or identity marker of Assamese. The order of the cultural code became supreme. It became the only method of mapping socio-spatial relations. Unlike in the previous decades, the inter-linguistic and inter-*ethnic* basis of mapping socio-spatial relations was no longer pursued. I argue that it did not mark the end of the struggle of modern Assamese literature mapping socio-spatial relations. It only marked the most acute point of the struggle lay at the heart of the breakdown in the correspondence between Assamese literature and its social base.

But the 1980s were also marked by a shift in literature and its mapping of socio-spatial relations. The fact of the breakdown did come to be recognised. New forms of literature were written wherein new methods of mapping socio-spatial relations were experimented with. The experiments identified the diverse as the starting point of their literatures. The period of the 1950s to the 1980s was critically viewed. Were efforts made to pick up the broken strings of the past?

6

Reinventing Frontier Narrative

In Part I, I argued that what distinguished the trans-Brahmaputra Valley as a frontier was the erosion of the shared mapping of socio-spatial relations of its historical past. Thus, it distinguished itself as a frontier from its own past as a continental crossroad. The critical mediating role of the shared mapping was in allowing differences across communities to coexist within a larger relation of shared mapping. In Assamese textual traditions, the erosion of shared mapping was accompanied by a drive towards cultural codification. Language and literature came to be seen as codes whose atom only lay within a given community. The heritage of inter-linguistic or inter-*ethnic* basis of culture formation was gradually sidelined. Despite attempts to define (or at least describe) the Assamese community, the problem still remained. It reached an acute point in the period between the 1950s and 1980s. But the contradictions of the three decades also introduced a shift in literary practice, a shift marked by a tendency to see literature beyond the confines of identity. Since the 1980s, one of the consistent features has been the giving up of attempts at defining 'Assamese' and increasingly moving towards describing 'Assamese'. In this chapter, I take up four examples. The first two are cases when attempts at defining Assamese' were critically assessed. The latter two are cases when the focus was on describing the north-east frontier, Assamese language being a descriptive tool in this regard. The latter two narratives are on the shared relation across communities in the trans-Brahmaputra Valley, and how any language or narrative can only describe the totality that they together comprise rather than represent. In this regard, it remarkably brought back the fundamentals of the historical Buranjis tradition, possibly the most successful textual tradition of the trans-Brahmaputra Valley. Also importantly, it raises the greatest possibility of once again picking up the broken threads of pursuing a common politics from within which Rabha had emphasised in the mid-20th century.

The first example I consider is Indira Goswami, more popularly known by her pen name of Mamoni Raisom Goswami. Mamoni Raisom had been writing since the late 1960s, and her first novel appeared in 1972 (*Chenabor Strot*, The Currents of Chenab). By the time her major novels based on locales in Assam appeared, she had already written two of her most celebrated novels — *Neelkanthi Braj* (The Blue Necked Braja, [1975] 2001) on the lives of the Hindu widows of Vrindavan, and *Mamore Dhara Taruwal* (The Rusted Sword, [1980] 2001) based on the lives of the Dalit industrial workers in Uttar Pradesh. But it is her novels based on locales in the Brahmaputra Valley that are significant for this study. Language use played a major role in the meaning of her texts. For example, in her novel *Datal Hantir Une Khowa Howdah* (The Moth Eaten Howdah, 1988), two language forms are used in the narrative. As in the case of Gohain Baruah's *Jaymati*, even in *Datal Hantir Une Khowa Howdah*, different socio-linguistic groups use different language variants of the Assamese language. But unlike in Gohain Baruah's *Jaymati*, the socio-linguistic groups in *Datal Hantir* are from the western part of the Valley. The narration by the author (in the third person) is in the 'standard' Assamese.

The novel is based on the turmoil that a Satradhikar family as well as the Satra village undergo on the eve of Independence. The Satras were set up as Vaishnava institutions and by the 18th century had emerged as landed family institutions. The novel is based on one such Satra institution, the Amranga Satra, in the southern part of the Kamrup area (western valley). The core of the novel is in the turmoil of change to 'modernise' that the traditional Amranga Satra faced as well as dealing with the politics of communism that the sharecroppers who worked on the Satra land posed to the Satras during the period. In the discussion on Bishnu Rabha, I had outlined that the peasant movement had reached widespread proportions between the late 1940s and early 1950s. In the novel, the turmoil is almost symbolised in the lives of two characters: the Satradhikar (or head of the Satra) Indranath, and his widowed younger sister who rebels against the traditional values for Brahman widows. She falls in love with an Englishman and finally gets burnt inside a house. In the novel, the people of the area speak the Kamrupi variant of Assamese.

Based on the nature of language use (use of both 'standard' and variants) in the novel, three points can be submitted. First, the Kamrupi language (or 'dialect') used in communication among the people (or characters) cannot be classified in terms of the everyday and the exceptional. Whether it is characters like Indranath or those from his family or the commoners, communication is in the same language form. In this regard, the remarks of the author also confirm the point. She states in the Preface (translation mine, 1988, 1st edn), 'The characters in the novel are provided with the speech which was prevalent in the Amranga Satra during the period. In this regard, Shri Dhaneswar Kalita advised me.' The organicity in language use becomes most evident towards the end of the novel. The multiple roles that same language can perform in the novel are indicated as follows:

(a) When Indranath goes riding on his elephant to meet the villagers/sharecroppers, his followers remark (translation mine), 'See for yourself Saru Gohei! Look at the greatness of your presence! Forget about them (the Communists) preventing villagers from harvesting, no one even comes to set foot here now' (p. 309); (b) The conversations among some of the villagers now become audible to Indranath. One of them says (translation mine), 'What on earth is happening (that Indranath himself has come to meet the villagers)! And seeing the Saru Gohei in his howdah, they (communists) have disappeared into their shelters like frightened cats. And why not, after all he is the Saru Gohei!' (p. 310); (c) The communists try to convince the people that the land does not belong to the Satra; it They say (translation mine), 'If the land would not have emerged from the river, from where would your Saru Gohei own it?' (p. 310); (d) Indranath gets down from the elephant and stands under the tree. There are some villagers at some distance. He shouts (translation mine), 'Who all are cultivating this piece of land. Bring them all to me now' (p. 311). The four excerpts cited above belong to different socio-economic classes and politics. Yet the same language variant is common to all. It is this linguistic organicity on which the novel is based. It is also this nature of language use that markedly differentiates it from earlier language uses found, for example, in Bezbaruah's narratives.

Second, use of language 'standard' in the novel plays a distinct role. The 'standard' is found in the third-person narration of the narrative, i.e., the author's voice. What was important and different from the experiments from the previous periods in this regard was that the 'standard' and the Kamrupi language variant were complementary to each other, and the two together constituted the universe of the novel. In other words, both the language variants together constituted the 'Assamese'. The significance of the method was in the fact that a narrative was attempted in which the different could coexist in a relation of differences. None of the language variants sought to *represent* the diverse or the multitude. They only reproduced (and represented) what was (assumed to be) organic to them. An expansive narrative was created in which differences were accommodated. The bearer of the relation among the differences was the 'standard'. The 'standard' did not represent the diverse or the multiple; it only bore the relation between them. Once again, it was a major intervention in providing the 'standard' only a symbolic value in narrative strategy and yet to be able to bind the diverse through it. It was different from the attempts of Gohain Baruah or Bezbaruah, and was closer to that of Rabha.

Third, language use in *Datal Hantir Une Khowa Howdah* can also be compared to Mamoni Raisom's other novel, *Bhikhar Patra Bhangi* (To Break the Begging Bowl, 1990). The fact that the 'standard' was only a vehicle of the relation of difference and did not (or could not) represent the relation of the diversity becomes amply clear in the novel. *Bhikhar Patra Bhangi* is also situated in the Kamrup area, and is based on the lives of a family of an ageing mother and her two grown-up daughters. As in *Datal Hantir Une Khowa Howdah*, in this novel too Kamrupi language and the Assamese 'standarad' are employed. For example, when members of the Mahila Samiti (women's organisation) from the (capital) city (Guwahati) came to address the problems of the family, the role of language use is critical. Vis-à-vis the Mahila Samiti (a) these members are from eastern valley; (b) their leadership role (in the women's organisation) symbolises the leadership role of the eastern valley in the modern period; (c) the members communicate in the 'standard', the language form of the eastern valley; and (d) they are unable to comprehend or communicate with the family whom they wish to help, because of the difference of language use among them and the family they came to help. Unlike in the discourse found in Birendra Kumar Bhattacharjya or Maheswar Neog who identify an intrinsic capacity in the 'standard' to represent or accommodate the multiple, Goswami's treatment of language and the social universe that comprised the 'Assamese' critiques such propositions. Therefore, if the narration (by the author) in her novels is in the 'standard', it is not with the assumption that the 'standard' possesses any intrinsic capacity to accommodate or represent the multiple; it is only in the capacity of the 'standard' as the bearer of a relation that together comprise the 'Assamese'. The 'standard' has only a functional role. Whereas for Bhattacharjya or Neog 'Assamese' is a concrete property in itself, for Goswami it is only a relation of concrete properties.

Mamoni Raisom's narrative is textual literature, as distinct from Rabha's performance narrative practice. But if Rabha's narrative practice was a major breakthrough in creating a language and narrative which could identify and address a relation (and not the concrete properties per se that comprise a relation), Goswami's narrative could also be considered a major breakthrough in this regard. Goswami's may not be the earliest user of the method, but she was the most significant practitioner of it in the period. What had created the problem for Gohain Baruah or Bezbaruah, or in the prescriptive propositions of Kakati was the assumption that 'Assamese' was (or ought to be) a concrete property in itself. Because they recognised the historical and ethnographic contradictions involved in the assumption, they grappled with language and narrative strategies which could address the issue. In the case of Bhattacharjya, because the issue of contradiction was not factored in, therefore there was no problem vis-à-vis language and narrative strategies in this regard. The commonality in both Rabha and Goswami is that their founding assumption was based on literature addressing the relation that constituted different communities into a people rather than directly addressing the people per se. But the nature of that relation was different for Rabha and Goswami. To Rabha, the relation was revolutionary class politics, while to Goswami, it was liberal humanism. For example, what drove her to write on the class antagonism in *Datal Hantir Une Khowa Howdah* was a humanist concern for the poor people. In her own words in the Preface (1988) (translation mine), 'The pain of human beings being unable to regard their fellow human beings as human runs through the novel.' Rabha's and Goswami's experiments in language and narratives, in other words, had different ideological foundations. But in their own divergent ways, they engaged with the question of developing a possible framework of a common politics from within the region. If Gohain Baruah, Bezbaruah and Kakati on the one hand and Bhattacharjya on the other seemed to indicate how relations of contradictions perpetuate (in the field of culture) by underlining and undermining other possibilities, the examples of Rabha or Goswami indicate how possibilities to address and redress such conflictual relation could be created as well. The fact that both Rabha and Goswami are iconic cultural figures in the Valley across the spectrum of social groups can be a message on the possibilities of a politics which has not only been ignored but is attempted to be defeated in certain intellectual discourses of today.

Therefore, the hallmark of Goswami's texts was that interlinguistic and inter-ethnic basis of socio-spatial relations that literature tried to map was duly recognised and practised in narrative strategies. Another example from the same period is Rong Bong Terang's classic novel *Rongmilir Hanhi* (The Smile of the Village Rongmili, [1981] 2010). The novel is based on the life of the Karbi people who inhabit the Karbi Hills to the south of the Brahmaputra Valley. Situated in the early part of the 20th century, the novel maps the problem of land alienation in the hills in which the indigenous people are being displaced by migrants from the Gangetic delta of present-day Bangladesh. The novel is considered an Assamese novel. But though the syntactic structure of language followed is that of modern Assamese, morphologically the entire novel is bilingual. Karbi language came to be considered a 'dialect' in modern times. One of the underlying questions that the novel poses is how does a 'dialect' communicate if communication (i.e., writing) is to be through a 'language'. Therefore, though the syntactic structure of modern Assamese is used, morphologically the entire novel is kept bilingual. Karbi terms, names, forms of address, etc. are used. These terms are explained in footnotes. The use of these terms was retained despite cases when availability of close equivalents in standard Assamese, such as for village head or wife, etc. were available. *Rongmilir Hanhi* was an emphatic statement on the question of 'Assamese', highlighting how even through written narratives, the relation between the dominant and the dominated (i.e., 'language' vs 'dialect') could be explored and commented upon. The novel was published at a time when the Assam Movement was at its peak.

Rongmilir Hanhi is not merely a text, but also a critique of the modern practice of 'language'. The novel is not a rejection of 'language' or vice versa, but a statement on the dialectic between practices of communication, and the problems of situating 'dialects' in such contemporary practices. Therefore, there is an active and critical communication between 'language' and 'dialect'. The method adopted to situate the critique within the text transforms the novel into a text-in-translation. Throughout the novel there is a constant interplay between 'dialect' and 'language' and how the only possible mode to create the Karbi everyday or social life in the narrative is in juxtaposing 'language' and 'dialect'.

Anuradha Sarma Pujari and Anurag Mahanta are the last two writers to be taken up in this study. How is Sarma Pujari's *No Man's Land* (2007) an example of narrative exercise in this regard? The locale of the short story *No Man's Land* is the town of Dawki, at the border between the state of Meghalaya in India and Bangladesh. Though inhabited predominantly by the Jayantia people, it has a shifting population of people involved in trade between either sides of the border. Trade ranges from the high-value movement of coal from India to Bangladesh (Meghalaya is a major coal-producing area of the north-east frontier) to other consumer items such as fish, confectionary etc. The story has Lily, a Jayantia woman who sells fish in the town, as one of the central characters. It revolves around how she negotiates her existence in the specific life of the town, amidst the heavy presence of the army, and how in the end she is shot on suspicion of aiding 'illegal' human movement across the border. The illegality is that she loves a man who happens to be from the other side of the border. If human movement is almost freely allowed in the town across the border, it has to remain confined to business and cannot spill over into any human relation. But despite the story revolving around the life of Lily, the author is not merely the narrator in it, but is also a character in the story (narrating the story in first person). For example, the story begins (translation mine),

> When I first set foot here, it felt as if I have come to some unknown place beyond India. Crossing through impossible mountain tracks, with peaks of hills high enough that they touch the clouds of the sky, and waterfalls that make the world appear watery, this is the town which I reached, and it is called Dawki. It lies at the border of Meghalaya and Bangladesh. It is the last Indian town here.

For the last two years, I have been here to make a demographic survey of the town. I have no idea whom such a survey might benefit. But I am quite enjoying it. I realize that people, after all, cannot be confined within national boundaries (Sarma Pujari 2007: 158).

Thereafter, throughout the rest of the text, the author remains a character of the narrative. Her understanding of the people, whether it be the residents of the town, the petty shopkeepers, the officers of the army or even those who come to sell things from across the border, are based on her experience. What her experience does not help her understand, she finds unable to define. For example, she is unable to comprehend how an officer who could be so sensitive to art could become thirsty for human blood in the name of the border. For the 'crime' of loving a man from across the border, he is furious enough to want to shoot Lily dead in the open field. He only manages to injure her (ibid.: 165).

If seen another way, the story is hardly different from any ethnographic fieldwork report. But the author as a character of the narrative adds other dimensions to the text. At one level, there is narration within narration in the narrative. The distinctive presence of the author is not only communicated through the fact that she is narrating an experience or a historical memory, but also through language use. For example, when she first meets Lily in the tea stall run by Robin, Lily asks her in Hindi (translation mine), 'To which side of the border do you belong?' (Sarma Pujari 2007: 160) Despite the fact that most of the communication the author had with the range of people in the town, from officers in the army to petty traders and local people from both sides of the border (and they all speak different languages) was in Assamese, through such linguistic interventions as noted above from time to time, the fact that Assamese ('standard') in the narrative only performs a descriptive function out of convenience is made amply evident. This approach was fundamentally different from the earlier approach of using Assamese ('standard') as representative because it possessed an intrinsic propensity to be so. The fact that the title of the story is *No Man's Land* signifies the point.

Therefore, for example, *No Man's Land* is qualitatively different as an 'Assamese' text from *Iaruingam*. This is despite the fact that both the texts are based on locales and people who lie beyond the parameters of 'Assamese', as acknowledged by the authors themselves in their respective texts. The given nature of language use and narrative allows *No Man's Land* to overcome the historical and ethnographic contradictions of language and narrative, and yet engage with the question of frontier. In the story, the author comments on the issue of frontier based on her own understanding. For example, when she stands on the official 'no man's land' between the two borders, she reflects on the issue of borders (translation mine), 'Since when has the land of this earth become subservient to human?' (Sarma Pujari 2007: 162). She expresses her idea on the issue by literally accepting the statement made in the border signpost on the side of Bangladesh, written in Bangla: 'Where you stand is your country' (ibid.: 163). She wishes this to become a universal concept, breaking down its political content.

Sarma Pujari is one of the widely-read authors in Assam today. On the question of appreciation of 'Assamese' writers by 'Assamese' people, Abdul Malik remarks in his autobiography (translation mine), 'Assamese people love Assamese language and literature from their heart. That's why they deeply love those who try to do something in Assamese language and literature. Can there be anything more valuable than that?' (Malik 2008: 306) But in its treatment of 'Assamese', Pujari's narrative is fundamentally different from that of Malik's. Yet what makes her literature popular? Maybe it is still early to answer the question. Nevertheless, it is possible to identify what distinguishes her narrative. As in the case of Goswami or Terang, Sarma Pujari also focuses on relations that constitute a people or a region rather than the people or the region per se. The ethnographic limits to any language defining a people are well recognised. Thus, language describes rather than defines a people or region. I would like to consider this new genre of literature as frontier literature or the narrative practice as frontier narrative. The literature or the narrative nowhere claims to be so. Yet, I would characterise it thus because its mapping of the socio-spatial relations through language use and narrative strategies most aptly highlights the region as frontier. The same could be said about Temsula Ao's *These Hills Called Home* (2006), though written in English. Anurag Mahanta's *Aulingar Zui* (The Fire of Spring, 2007) is also a part of this new genre which attempts to conceptualise socio-spatial relations rather than the people or the region per se.

Aulingar Zui is based on life lived in a 'no man's land' at the border between India and Myanmar. The social base in the novel is the Naga people, who had historically inhabited the area. Yet, due to the arbitrary drawing of boundary, their historical area got bifurcated between the two postcolonial countries, and a few villages ended up designated as 'no man's land' between the two countries. The role of space which the novel explores is important in this regard. A few questions can be posed on the novel and through the answers the role of space can be highlighted.

First, what constitutes the novel? The 'no man's land' at the border was a historically inhabited area for the Naga people. Yet decades of political and military violence resulted in a mix of communities inhabiting even a single village. There were three agents in the violence, viz. the Indian army, Myanmar army and NSCN (the overarching Naga militant outfit seeking independence from the Indian Union). The mode of violence was guerrilla warfare. As a result of the violence, displaced members of different communities came and settled in the villages, for example the Hanyat village. These different groups of displaced people comprise the social base in the novel. The people are far removed from any developed area, the small town of Mon being the only developed area situated nearby. There are no laid-out roads to reach Mon; one has to travel through mountains and forests to reach it. The people still live life based on foraging or *jhum* cultivation and on little quantities of food and clothing which come from the NSCN, the only agent which the people consider a part of their own. Through most of the year, there are only two activities for the people: (a) *jhum* cultivation; and (b) running for shelter to the forests in case of raids from either the Indian army or Myanmar army. Foodgrain and huts were often burnt down in such raids, and therefore the dependence on the NSCN for food and security is crucial for the people. But despite such a context, Aniam, one of the young men of the village, desires to start a small school for the children so that they may have a future beyond the confines of the 'no man's land'. He brings an Assamese teacher named Atanu to teach in the school. In the course of a year, Atanu also becomes one with the villagers, running for shelter to the forests in times of raid and helping the villagers rebuild the village in whatever little time of the year when there is relative peace. There is no life beyond this building and rebuilding of the village. These details comprise the plot of the story. As in the case of Sarma Pujari's *No Man's Land*, *Aulingar Zui* is also similar to an ethnographic report, describing the ironies of life in the locale. They are narratives without any 'conclusion'.

Second, what is the role of space in the novel? Space is central to the narrative of the novel. In Mahanta's own words in the Preface (translation mine), 'The pain and suffering of life here arises from this very space' (Mahanta 2007: 4) The space is situated in a frontier. But the space also has a character of its own, viz. it is a distinct guerrilla space. Whether as a theatre of war and ambush or as a mode of living and movement, whether it is for the agents of violence or for the people, the only character that the space possesses for all is that of guerrilla space (Baruah 2009). The space does not exist as a defined space. 'No man's land' is an official category; yet it also reflects the irony of such categories which are inhabited spaces but where fixed or defined categories cannot come into existence due to their very location in a 'no man's land'. The only character it is left with is that of guerrilla space. In the novel, the 'no man's land', a guerilla space, exists as a relation among its different constituents such as people, geography, actors of violence or the very experience of life. The narrative does not try to represent any of these components. It only seeks to map them descriptively as properties that share among them a socio-spatial relation.

One exemplification in this regard could be the case of the teacher Atanu. Mahanta, in his Preface where he introduces his characters and the novel, introduces Atanu as a disillusioned young man from the Brahmaputra Valley, who was trying to run away and escape from the reality of disillusionment. Mahanta uses the word 'escapist' for Atanu. But when he spends time in Hanyat village, Atanu realises how much the people of the village await help and sympathy from the larger world outside. Therefore, Mahanta wrote (translation mine), 'Taking a decisive decision one day, Atanu had left for this no man's land. But he hadn't ever imagined then that with so much of pain and surprise the land was waiting for him' (Mahanta 2007: 7). Towards the end of the novel, Atanu too is transformed by the very specificity of the guerrilla space. He enters into a relation with the space and its people. Just like the others who had come and settled in the village, Atanu too enters into a relation with the no man's land. *Aulingar Zui* highlights how fake the concept of no man's land could be. No man's land is a definition coined by orders of national spaces. It does not fit into such spatial orders. But when seen from within such spatial forms, these spatial forms are not indeterminate zones. They are as much an inhabited zone as any part of national space. Areas designated as no man's land signify the failure of modern nation states to conceptualise forms of human settlement patterns. *Aulingar Zui* attempts to map the socio-spatial relations constituting a no man's land. The novel points out that different individuals or groups of people who inhabit a no man's land have different histories of how they came to inhabit that space. But after having settled, they also develop a shared relation with the space. They would retain in their memory their different pasts and respective histories of arriving in the space. But once settled, their specific histories and memories would also develop the shared patterns of mapping collective existence. Thus, though Atanu becomes part of that space, he continues to retain his own individuality in the specificity of his personal memory and history.

When along with Wati, Amon and four others, Atanu has to take shelter in the mountain cave of the forest to escape the Myanmar army which has already destroyed the village, Atanu, in the course of hushed conversation with the others, realizes that he had never known all the while that Umli Appa (an elderly authority of the village who had now been killed in the raid) was an intelligence officer of the NSCN. He asks with hurt ego (translation mine), 'Couldn't you have told me about it before?' 'There was order not to do so,' Aniam replies. 'It means you never trusted me?' asks Atanu. 'It's not that. We trust you, but the underground has its own ways of functioning, you know,' Aniam replies (Mahanta 2007: 198). The entire conversation leaves Atanu hurt for a while. But it cannot dissuade him from his decision to stay back in the village, despite the advice from the others to return to the Valley than die there. Atanu replies (translation mine), 'I won't go, until you chase me away. I will stay here, for the sake of the school, for the sake of Sebang and Priam (children) ... for the sake of the memory of Umli Appa, Laipa, Taizat and Tempu (they were all killed), I will stay here' (ibid.: 199). Atanu can see in the eyes of the others a profound sense of gratitude. He also realises that life could, after all, have a mission too. The entire group is still inside the rock cave, and Amon begins to pray in Nagamese (translation mine), 'We who are here pray to Jesus for Teacher, and also for Appa, Laipa and for everyone who had died. The dead are no more with us. We pray

Jesus that the dead may rest in peace' (ibid.: 200). Everyone joins in, 'Amen!' 'When they opened their eyes after prayers, the rays of the afternoon sun had lit the mouth of the cave.' (ibid.). The sounds of the guns could still be heard outside. *Aulingar Zui*, despite being an Assamese novel, is in no way on the 'Assamese'. The novel acutely explores how fake the relation between territory and identity could be. It also highlights how literature need not be about defining a people. It could as much be about describing the socio-spatial relations that people share across their differences over a given space. It shows that language need not struggle to become an identity marker. It could very well be an instrument to map relations among people. The immensely popular recent novel *Makam* (2010) by Rita Choudhury on lives the Chinese people who lived in Assam but after the 1962 Indo-China War were shipped to China is another example in this regard. An explosive novel, *Makam* not only demolishes 'Assamese' as a political identity, but in the process also liberates the modern Assamese language from the need to perform any role of representing 'Assamese' identity. In this regard, narratives such as *No Man's Land*, *Aulingar Zui* or *Makam* were giant strides, taking modern Assamese literature away from the premises that guided it between the 1950s and the 1980s.

Conclusion

Between Mamoni Raisom Goswami and Rong Bong Terang on the one hand and Anuradha Sarma Pujari and Anurag Mahanta on the other, is it possible to identify a gradual maturing of a genre of literature set to redefine modern Assamese literature? Goswami or Terang marked a fundamental shift in language use and narrative strategy in the 1980s. It became possible to explore whether literature needed to struggle at all with defining an identity out of a heterogeneous social base or literature through language use and narrative strategies could very well focus on how socio-spatial relations could be mapped. In such mapping, the focus no longer remained on identity, but shifted to the elements that comprised a social universe and the interrelations within. As a result, it became possible to critique the discourses of identity as exclusivist in nature and their false premises of being inclusive. In the writings of Bezbaruah or Gohain Baruah, the struggle was how to devise language use and narrative strategies which could accommodate and represent the diverse that together comprised the Assamese universe. The tension in the struggle manifested in their expansive or paradigmatic approaches. With Goswami and Terang, literature was no longer about accommodating or representing the totality of the Assamese universe. Literature was now about showing how the diverse that existed in that universe were related to one another. As a result, the fact of difference among communities was no more a literary challenge. Literature now needed to identify the differences and map their interrelation. Along with Rabha's narrative strategy in the middle of the 20th century, it was possibly another major breakthrough towards the end of the century, one which survived. Within approximately two decades of the breakthrough, Assamese literature had further moved away from attempts at defining people or regions to exploring relations that comprised people or regions. For example, Sarma Pujari or Mahanta would no longer concern themselves with the 'Assamese'. Assamese was only a language to describe the components and their relations that comprised a region. For them, this region was the frontier. The frontier was seen as a set of socio-spatial relations in which different individuals or groups of people were related both socially and spatially. They understood and practised these relations differently. Yet, they had also developed shared relations across their differences over the given space. With such an approach to the understanding of region, language use in Assamese literature underwent an even more radical shift. For example, in *Aulingar Zui* or *Makam*, despite the use of 'standard' Assamese (as in *Iaruingam* or *Seuji Patar Kahini*), it was totally emptied of any representative quality, i.e., having any capacity to denote identity consciousness, whether visible or embedded. It is in this context that I argued that such literatures or narratives could be considered frontier literatures or frontier narratives, i.e., literatures or narratives which are able to identify the frontier as a distinct region without getting caught up in the ethnographic contradictions of language or literature as marker of identity. It manifests the long history of over a century struggling, failing and yet struggling to devise a framework of common politics from within the frontier, using language and literature as the resources. Can the present narrative shift help realise it?

Conclusion

This book began with the contention that existing research on the 'Assamese' question (and the identity debate in north-east India in general) is founded on identity as an essential category and explores how identities have shared a conflictual relation with one another. The cause of the conflict is either located in 'tribal' or 'ethnic' politics or in challenges faced when nationalising a historically transnational area. In either case, precisely because identity is an essential category, it is both the cause and the manifestation of the problem of identity. I argued that the 'Assamese' question needs to be studied in terms of mapping socio-spatial relations. In other words, there is a need to shift the focus from identity to the socio-spatial relations that bring different communities into a relation with one another, whether or not the relation makes possible *an* identity. In other words, politics of identity in the Valley needs to be located in these socio-spatial relations rather than on the construct of identity per se.

The focus on socio-spatial relations also enables one to explain processes of region formation. Research based on the discourse of identity has failed in conceptualising the trans-Brahmaputra Valley in particular and north-east India in general as a region. For example, it is not clear in such studies whether the trans-Brahmaputra Valley is a frontier or a continental crossroad or a transnational zone. In fact, what they struggle with is how to situate these spatial categories in the context of the Indian nation state. My contention is that region needs to be seen in terms of the socio-spatial relations that constitute it as an entity. Taking the case of the trans-Brahmaputra Valley, I tried to show that the same area was a continental crossroad in the pre-colonial period while since colonialism it has been a frontier. As a continental crossroad, its hallmark was the shared mapping of social and spatial relations across difference of communities, of which the communities were conscious. In becoming a frontier, the shift was in the erosion of the shared mapping, leaving only the differences to negotiate with one another. In the absence of the shared praxis to mediate, the differences became contradictions to one another. The inter-linguistic and inter-ethnic basis of socio-spatial relations of the past was replaced by mono-linguistic or mono-ethnic approaches to conceptualise the relations between land and people. This shift formed the basis of the discourses of identity since the 19th century. Therefore, I argued that from colonial anthropological accounts (for example, Waddell) to contemporary accounts (for example, Baruah) there was an inability to historicise the problem of conflict in the trans-Brahmaputra Valley. Inter-community conflict of the pre-colonial period was not identity conflict. They were to maintain the balance of shared socio-spatial relations across the differences of communities. Practices such as *khats* or *posa* were a part of maintaining this balance. But since the colonial period, the conflicts came to be articulated in terms of identity. In the absence of the mediating role of shared socio-spatial relations, communities were increasingly being conceptualised by both the colonial state and the colonised as specific ethno-territorial units. It was the basis of the conflictual politics of identity in the Valley. Therefore, the historical shift in the nature of inter-community conflict is a relevant premise to understand shifts in region formation in the trans-Brahmaputra Valley.

I argued that similar to nation, a region too need not be an essential phenomenon. Changes in the socio-spatial relations that constitute a region also change the nature of the region that a given geo-space is. It was the basis of the trans-Brahmaputra Valley transforming from a crossroad into a frontier in the colonial period. In other words, the dialectics of socio-spatial relations was at the centre of the changing nature of the trans-Brahmaputra Valley as a region.

The significance of textual traditions in this regard is that they highlight how these socio-spatial relations were central to the cultural imaginings of the self or political consciousness of identity. Pre-colonial textual traditions such as the Buranjis or the neo-Vaishnava performance literature, or modern Assamese literature were examples of how mapping socio-spatial relations was at the root in types of language use and narrative strategies in literature. What literature attempted at its core was not to map communities with their specific features, but to map the relations that communities shared with one another. The Buranji tradition as well as neo-Vaishanva performance literature were remarkably clear about it. It is true that modern Assamese literature had to repeatedly negotiate with the identity debate, i.e., the 'Assamese' question. In fact, it even articulated it in terms of identity. But I tried to show that modern Assamese literature throughout had only been struggling with how to conceptualise the socio-spatial relations among the diverse (communities) into a people. Identity consciousness or its politics was only the surface manifestation of this deeper struggle. From Bezbaruah and Gohain Baruah to Bhattacharjya, the struggle to define an improbability of 'Assamese' identity through language use and narrative as identity markers had always remained an underlying tension.

The early phase from the 19th century to the 1950s was marked by different experiments in language use and narrative strategies to map the dialectics of these relations in the making of Assam and Assamese. Rabha, during the period, went on to argue that literature cannot represent an identity. It can only represent a relation among different peoples. For him, that relation was class. Rabha was one of the most emphatic voices of the period who rejected the idea that language and literature can at all become an identity marker, especially given the historical past of the trans-Brahmaputra Valley. But between the 1950s and the 1980s, such approaches came to be entirely sidelined. The series of identity movements in those decades played a role in it. Thus, the thrust was on making language and literature markers of identity. But there was also the acute tension of being unable to devise narrative strategies which could legitimise the construct of 'Assamese'. The path taken, therefore, was to treat 'Assamese' as an essential category and devise narrative strategies based on the assumption.

However, since the 1980s, there was a visible shift when language use and narrative strategy was used to explore the relations that constitute 'Assamese' and critique the assumed notions of the preceding period. Literature was no more about the struggle to conceptualise identity. It was about mapping the inter-linguistic and inter-community exchanges that were at the heart of the relations between land and people in the trans-Brahmaputra Valley. By the first decade of the 21st century, a new genre of literature (in fiction) had come into existence in which narrative strategies, including the use of language, were to situate literature in the larger context of the north-east frontier and explore the socio-spatial relations that constituted it and perpetuated it as frontier. Thus, literature was no longer about cultural codes (which constitute an identity) and their practise. It was about mapping how the diverse respectively conceived of themselves differently and yet were related to one another over shared space, history and politics. I termed this 'frontier literature' because it most clearly located itself in frontier as a region rather than struggling to become an identity marker of a community. From the beginnings made by Mamoni Raisom Goswami to present-day writers like Sarma Pujari or Mahanta, from mapping dialectical relations among communities inhabiting the trans-Brahmaputra Valley to devising narratives which are conscious of being part of a frontier, there has been an undoubted shift in the way nature and function of literature is conceived today. The shift has taken literature out of its imprisonment within the identity debate. Rather than representing any essential character of an identity, it seeks to describe socio-spatial relations as they operate or that communities, despite their differences, share. Could the shift then be considered the realisation of the fallacy in framing literature within identity consciousness? And could it then be the stepping stone in using literature as a resource to generate a common politics across identities from within the frontier? If it is indeed possible that a common politics from within can emerge, would the trans-Brahmaputra Valley undergo another shift as a region?

Appendix

(a) An Outline on Text and Social Origin of Author in Assamese Fiction*

The social origin of writers makes an important intervention in texts that an author produces. With regard to Assamese fiction between 1940 and 1980, it can be seen at three levels, viz. (a) choice of theme; (b) nature of characterisation and the plot, i.e., treatment of theme; and (c) nature of engagement with the discourse of identity.

A fundamental question with regard to the social origin of the authors is how much it conditions the nature of their fiction. With regard to modern Assamese fiction, the role of social base can be most evident, for example, in ideology and in the plot and characterisation of a text. Compared to many other parts of South Asia, one of the most remarkable absences in modern Assamese fiction is landed aristocracy. The absence is not as a descriptive category. It is as a conceptual category. The contrast, especially from the neighbouring Bengali literature, is most evident. For example, in the literature of Rabindranath Tagore (Bangla literature) or Sarat Chandra Chatterjee (Bangla literature), landed aristocracy or zamindars exists as a conceptual category. The social world and ideology of the aristocracy is a powerful presence in the ideology as well as the plot and characterisation of the texts. Such a presence of the landed aristocracy is also evident in Urdu works, such as of Ismat Chughtai (for example, *Dil Ki Duniya*, The Heart Breaks Free, 1966).

However, with regard to Assamese fiction, the absence is evident. The only exception is possibly Mamoni Raisom's (Indira Goswami) fiction. Her classic *Datal Hantir Une Khowa Howdah* (The Moth Eaten Howdah, 1988) is an example of such an exception. Further, the novel deserves mention because herein one can locate a plot that not only relies on psychoanalysis, i.e., the individual as central to interpretation or exploration of the social, but also on the antagonism between the monastic landed aristocracy (the *satradhikar*s) and the landless peasants or sharecroppers as a social

---

*This essay has been reproduced to given an idea of my position in my doctoral research.

context that explains the mind of the individual. The twin approaches to the same subject is especially notable in the case of the *satradhikar* family. Whether it be the *satradhikar* (headman), other men of the household, the Brahman widows or the servants associated with service to the family, the social and the individual differ, but converge into a whole as a context (and plot in the case of the novel) as is amply clear in *Datal Hantir Une Khowa Howdah*. According to the author, the fact that she too belongs to a *satradhikar* family had a great role to play in writing the novel. It was her understanding of the life of the *satradhikar* household and of its relation to society that got expressed in the novel (Goswami 1992).

The difference in Mamoni Raisom's approach is evident when compared to that of the other writers. For example, in Abdul Malik's *Surajmukhir Sapna* (The Sunflower Dream, 1960), the plot, though based on land relations, revolves around the expansion of the village/rural frontier by reclaiming forests and establishing new settlements. There is no presence of landlord in the process. Similarly, Homen Borgohain's *Halodhiya Soraye Bau Dhan Khai* (The Harvest, 1972) is based on the opposites of landlessness of peasants and illegal land ownership of village moneylenders, but not of 'landlords'. Therefore, the exception of Mamoni Raisom's *Datal Hantir Une Khowa Howdah* could be taken as an example of the role that the social origin of authors plays in the structure and meaning of text.

Assamese fiction has dealt with the rural, urban, caste, tribe, family and, in a limited way, women. More than these concerns, it is the way in which these concerns emerge into plots that indicates the role of the social base of the authors in/upon the text. In the case of authors like Borgohain, it is both substantive and symbolic. A socialist, he has characters that are class-oppressed or even 'subaltern'. Yet, his plots are reformist rather than being revolutionary. There are oppressed characters like Subala or Rasheswar, respectively, in his fiction like *Subala* (1963) or *Halodhiya Soraye Bau Dhan Khai*. They suffer due to class or in terms of gender. Yet, the plot does not end on a revolutionary note. There is only a plea for change. As in the case of *Halodhiya Soraye Bau Dhan Khai* the landless peasant (Rasheswar) could not identify the moneylender/'landlord' as his class enemy. This is starkly different from Mamoni Raisom's *Datal Hantir Une Khowa Howdah*, where landless peasants could identify the *satra* institution as its class enemy and organised themselves under the communist party.

Thus, in the case of Bargohain, though his characters are victims of class oppression in the authorial commentary (the novel is written in the third person), the characters themselves remain unaware of it. Importantly, nothing happens in the plot as well that makes the characters conscious of their 'class' status. In other words, the author, plot and characters remain un-integrated as part of the same textual structure.

Such lack of integration, however, is not seen when the middle-class worldview conditions all the elements of the textual structure. The fundamental feature of this Assamese middle-class worldview is the universality in the identity of Assamese nationhood, and order is located within this universality. In texts like *Aghari Atmar Kahini* (Rootless Soul, 1969) by Abdul Malik, the characters are acutely aware of the problems of morality and materiality that affect their bourgeois life. Family and order, central to bourgeois life, are also central in the life of the characters of the text. The problematic that the text engages with is when such 'order' gets destabilised due to the very incongruities within the structure of the 'order'.

In *Aghari Atmar Kahini*, the rupture between the author (through his/her narration), the plot and the characters that was evident in Bargohain's texts like *Halodhiya Soraye Bau Dhan Khai* is absent. The author, plot and characters are equally conscious of the problematic that forms the subject matter of the text. In other words, whereas texts like *Halodhiya Soraye Bau Dhan Khai* do not arrive at a conclusion in terms of textual structure, the same is not true for texts like *Aghari Atmar Kahini*. Such alignment of ideology and plot is also evident in texts that exist within the Assamese middle-class worldview, even though the social base in the text may be different. For example, in texts like *Seuji Patar Kahini* (The Story of Green Leaves, 1959) or *Iaruingam* (People's Rule, 1960), though they have plots based on tea plantations or the Naga 'tribe', there is no visible rupture between the author, plot and characters. This is because unlike texts like *Halodhiya Soraye Bau Dhan Khai*, they do not seek to identify and expose the economic or social divisions within the society. Rather, they seek to show the universality of experience/worldview/identity in (Assamese) society. In the former, though the text attempts to expose the rupture within the universal (on the basis of class) it fails to create a textual structure that could correspond to the ideology. But in the case of the latter, the success of its textual structure lies in its very conformity to the predominant ideology of identity and society. The difference, once again, as evident emerges from the social origin of the authors.

The other bourgeois character of Assamese fiction is the role of or its focus upon the hero/heroine in the plot. They stand apart from the masses rather than being part of the masses. In other words the plot, rather than being based on the social or general, is based primarily on the individual lives of these prime characters. These characters stand apart from the masses because they are either special or their story is the specialty of the narrative. They do not exist as a representative case (in the text) of the masses, but as a peculiarity within it that needs to be or is highlighted. For example, Bargohain's *Halodhiya Soraye Bau Dhan Khai* can again be a revealing example of the point. Though the plot in the text opens with Rasheswar being a landless peasant oppressed by the money lender (Sanatan) of the village, as the plot progresses, it becomes increasingly a case of how Rasheswar handles the situation based on the peculiarities of his personality or thoughts. The role of the mass gradually diminishes into the background. The same can be said of his texts like *Matsyagandha* (Fish Daughter, 1987) or of Malik's *Surujmukhir Sapna*.

To be noted is that the concept of hero or heroine is different from the central characters of a story. For example, in Bibhuti Bhusan Bandyopadhyaya's *Pather Panchali* (The Song of the Little Road, Bangla literature, [1928] 1990) or Manik Bandopadhyaya's *Padma Nadir Majhi* (The Boatman of Padma, Bangla literature, [1948] 1973), the central characters do not exist as heroes or heroines, though the plot progresses based on their lives. They exist as representative of the class or society that they come from. In contrast, in the Assamese texts cited above, the plot progressively gets individu-alised, distanced from the social. Associated with the focus on hero and heroines, most Assamese texts end with a conclusion in terms of the story. The conclusion signifies that the problem a text is dealing with has come to be resolved. Most Romantic texts are seen to have the twin features of hero and heroine and conclusion. Resolution of the problem of these prime characters also is the resolution of the problem that the text is dealing with. The conclusion of a narrative, however, needs to be differentiated from the conclusion of a textual structure. As already noted, even though the story in *Halodhiya Soraye Bau Dhan Khai* concludes, the structure of the text itself is unable to reach a conclusion.

Nevertheless, there have been few writers in whose texts the role of the hero or heroine remain minimal in the plot, if not absent. One of them was Lakshminath Bezbarua (1868–1937). Even though his plots had prime characters and the narrative revolves around the lives of these characters, the plot never gets individualised. The characters continue to remain representative or part of the mass. A fine example of such an approach is his short story *Bhadari*. In the story, Sisuram (farmer/husband) mercilessly beats his wife Bhadari over a trivial issue. Yet, the initial part of the plot is the build up to the reasons, as the author perceives, and the act of beating in this given social context.

Sisuram is angry because he has fasted the previous night, he is poor and has never had enough to eat, because his bullocks were difficult to handle that day and because the sun was very hot for one to work in the field that day (but he had to work for being a poor farmer). When he reaches home hungry, he gets angry because his wife has not yet prepared the meal and because she retorts when Sisuram scolds her for not preparing the meal in time. Bhadari is angry because she has suffered enough trying to make fire from damp wood that Sisuram had brought for the hearth. Though usually a quiet woman, that day she cannot take it, for the smoke from the damp wood has left her coughing and tearful. Thus, the act of beating the wife mercilessly was not merely a problem between a husband and wife, but a problem in a family of poor farmers.

The conclusion of the story is also worth taking note of. Bhadari has to be hospitalised, taken care of by Sisuram's younger brother, while Sisuram is jailed for his act. Bhadari is sad that her husband has been jailed, even if it was for beating her. But Sisuram is happy for he looks forward to his imprisonment as atonement for beating his beloved wife. However, Bezbaruah does not make the point the conclusion of the story. The first phase of the conclusion is the irony of their life — that Bhadari is sad and Sisuram happy. This contrast of happiness and sorrow that is reflective of their social/marital life (as Bezbaruah thought) was the irony and a conclusion of the story for him. The second stage of the conclusion was that he (the author) had told the readers a story and finally the story has come to an end, so the listeners can now disperse. It is typical of Bezbaruah's aesthetic wherein traditional (oral) forms of storytelling were incorporated into the text. But through the method, the author also clearly distinguishes between himself and the people/masses that he is narrating about. The distinction between narration and the narrative is highlighted, and that the conclusions of the two differ is also exemplified.

Further, the differences between the author and of the social base in the text are evidently spelt out. In other words, the ideological (or class) differences between the author and of the characters in the plot are not silenced through the textual structure. As seen in the case of texts like *Seuji Patar Kahini* or *Halodhiya Soraye Bau Dhan Khai*, such differences are either sought to be silenced or denied (even though a close study of the structure of such texts reveals the ruptures that emerge as a result of such attempt). However, through the story *Bhadari*, when seen in the larger context of Bezbaruah's aesthetic and writings, it becomes evident that his was a particular aesthetic that without denying or diluting the peculiarity of the specific, it is possible to convey the perspective of the universal. In the process, even though a plot is made up of central characters to carry forward the story, the characters do not exist as heroes or heroines; rather they exist as representatives of the class or of the society that they come from.

A similar characteristic is also seen in Mamoni Raisom's writings in terms of relation between central characters and their relation to the social base in the text. This is especially evident in novels like *Neelkanthi Braj* (The Blue Necked Braj, 1975), *Mamore Dhara Taruwal* (The Rusted Sword, 1980) or *Bikhar Patra Bhangi* (To Break the Begging Bowl, [1990] 1998). In these novels, the central characters do not emerge as heroes or heroines through whom the plot progresses or the problematic of the plot is resolved. For example, in *Neelkanthi Braj*, the widows (living in Vrindavan), whose lives constitute the cases being explored in the text, do not stand beyond the social of which they are representative. The dilemmas that they face and their helplessness in living life or making choices in living life are acutely conditioned by the fact of them being widows and living in the temples and other accommodation in Vrindavan. When Saudamini finally commits suicide, it is because of her inability to resolve the problem of her moral/sexual obligation as a widow, i.e., whether or not she should start a fresh life with a new man, a new lover, despite being already a widow. Like most of the other characters in the novel the central characters do not resolve the basic problematic of their life, viz. that they live a life that has frozen with the death of their husbands and would have to spend the rest of their lives as outcasts of the society they belong to or were born into. Even life spent in religion and devotion in the holy city of Vrindavan does not bring any changes to their lives.

Similarly, in *Bhikhar Patra Bhangi*, the lives of the three women (mother and her two grown-up daughters) of the family caught up in the web of poverty and militancy are more representative of the social milieu than being an individualised story of a family in rural Assam. The fact that the son of the family becomes a militant, that they lose their land to the village moneylender and are living in abject poverty, that the younger daughter has to work as a construction labourer in the nearby town for economic sustenance of the family or the fact that help from the women's organisation (from the town) does not materialise (organisation/women members) for it could not overcome class difference and comprehend the problems of the family — all the reasons are part of the social milieu of which the three women of the family remain only representatives. The problem that the life of the women constitutes in the text is that of context. Importantly, the problem does not get resolved in the text. Like *Neelkanthi Braj*, the central characters do not exist outside the social. Their engagement with the problem (or context) is not as individuals, but as social beings, as part of others like them.

In *Mamore Dhara Taruwal*, the central characters once again do not become heroes/heroines. The fact that the novel emphasises is the claustrophobic subsuming of the personal (such as Narayani, Shibu Dhasal, Jaswant, Lisu and others) into the social of being Dalit industrial workers. It is made evident throughout the novel, whether in terms of gender or of class. Two of the most significant dimensions of the novel are the relation between individual and the social/class and between gender/patriarchy and class among the Dalit industrial working class (in the novel). These two kinds of relations can be seen in the two characters Jaswant and Narayani. Jaswant is the only Dalit who is a member of the trade union leadership. But increasingly, he finds that he can achieve little for his community/class because he can exercise little power with regard to the workers' strike and their welfare. Finally, he gives up his position as a leader and returns to the people. His return to the community/class is a significant indicator of the approach of the text, viz. that the individual is subsumed in the social and it is the latter that defines the existence of the former. One important point in the relation is that the category of working class, when seen in terms of leadership, could also be a discursive construct (the problematic of Dalit as working class).

The other kind of relation that the text focuses on is that of gender and class. Narayani, one of the women Dalit workers, not only becomes an industrial worker but also sleeps with her upper-caste/class superior (Thakur Sahab) so as to feed her starving family (due to the ongoing strike). The dilemma that the novel raises is whether Narayani's need to sleep (i.e., sex) with her superior is an example of class or gender exploitation. When she is criticised in the community, she argues that she has every right to use her body in the way she likes. This position can be seen as an intense feminist standpoint. But it can also be seen as one of class 'alienation' (i.e., sex as labour). Further, though Narayani argues for her control over her body and exercises that right, she herself too does not get over the dilemma if what she is doing is morally right. It is this dilemma that leads to her act of killing her superior. But once again, even in this act, it is the coming together of class and gender that gets highlighted.

Therefore, one commonality among all the texts discussed above is that they do not have a conclusion. If the conclusion is seen as resolving the problematic the text begins with or engages with, then in the texts of Mamoni Raisom discussed above, that problematic does not get resolved. Unlike in the texts, for example, by Bargohain or Malik, the central characters in Mamoni Raisom's fiction continue to be a part of the social. More than being heroes or heroines, they exist as representatives of the social milieu, wherein the problem lies. In other words, the plot does not get individualised.

With regard to the relation between the characters, plot and author, it is important to mention here Jyotiprasad Agarwalla's unfinished novel *Amar Gaon* (Our Village, [1950] 1996). Unlike the texts of Bezbaruah or Mamoni Raisom, in *Amar Gaon*, the hero gradually merges into the mass. The plot opens with the focus on the hero Abhinava Baruah, with his personal angst and resolve to transform. But as the plot progresses the hero becomes one among the people and the focus shifts from the individual to the social (in the village) and to attempts at reconstitution of the social.

Agarwalla passed away before he could complete the novel. Therefore, it is not possible to consider if as a plot or as a textual structure *Amar Gaon* would have been a 'people's text', wherein the people or the mass and not the hero or the prime characters become central to the plot (Agarwalla was one of the leading Progressives of his times). However, in the unfinished novel, one can locate an attempt at producing a 'people's text'. One fundamental difference between Bezbaruah's and Mamoni Raisom's texts on the one hand and Agarwalla's *Amar Gaon* on the other that needs to be emphasised is the relation between the individual and the social in the plot. In the former, there are no transitions that occur in the relation between the individual and the masses in the plot. Throughout the plot, the nature of the relation remains constant. But the notable difference with *Amar Gaon* is the transition that occurs in the nature of the relation. Though the plot begins with the individual, it gradually shifts to the popular. It is open to debate (because it is unfinished) if that is also reflective of an attempt in the space of single work of art to achieve a structural transition from bourgeois to socialist art.

In conclusion, one can say that Bezbaruah's or Agarwalla's or Mamoni Raisom's fictions stand more as exceptions if the collective body of modern Assamese fiction is taken into account. In other words, the bourgeois character of modern Assamese fiction is evident both in terms of the nature and use of plot and relation between characters and plot.

Section II

The social origin of authors is also crucial to understanding the nature of an author's engagement with the discourse of identity. Assamese fiction of the late 19th and throughout the 20th century can be seen in terms of nationalism conceived through a bourgeois worldview. One of the indices of the bourgeois character is the nature and content of 'order' that is reflected through fiction. For example, the novel *Dawar Aru Nai* (The Clear Sky, 1955), though based on the plantation society, focuses primarily on the middle-class Assamese (families) that were part of that society, mostly as clerical staff. In the novel, the workers exist but as incidental to the life of the Assamese people in the plantations. *Dawar Aru Nai* is one of the few novels that highlight the impact of World War II on the Assamese middle class.

Further, the bourgeois character of the novel is also evident in the centrality of the bourgeois peculiarity of a simultaneous fetish for moral values and materialism. The novel emphasises the sanctity of the institution of family as symbolising 'order'. But it also shows how a factor intrinsic to the bourgeois character, i.e., simultaneous fetish for moral values and materialism, could break the very 'order' upon which it survives. The novel ends in tragedy. The destruction of Bakhar's family results from an inability to resolve the opposite pressures of morality and materialism operating in the context of World War II.

Another significant novel on plantation society is Umakanta Sharma's *Ejak Manuh Ekhan Aranya* (A Crowd and a Forest, 1986). It is significant because it focuses on the fundamental social constituent of the plantations, viz. the workers. The novel is about the severe economic exploitation of the workers. Nevertheless, it is ironical that despite the sympathy shown for the sufferings of the workers, there is no ideological challenge to the economic order that produces that condition for the workers.

In the case of another novel based on plantation life, viz. *Seuji Patar Kahini*, the focus is balanced between all the social groups that constitute the plantation social world. The British planters and their wives, the Assamese clerical staff, the workers, the local villages and the villagers living in areas neighbouring the plantations or the children born of the (unmarried) union between British planters and 'coolie' workers — they all exist in the novel and are integral to the plot of the text. Yet, when seen in terms of nationalist ideology, it is evident that the role of the bourgeois worldview is emphatic.

In all the novels, one of the fundamental evidence of the bourgeois worldview as the content of the imagination of the 'Assamese' is that difference of class does not figure as a factor in the formation or construction of identity. More than novels that are based on social units that are relatively homogeneous, it is novels such as those noted above in this section that reflect the class character of identity upon which the text is premised. In plantation society, class difference is paramount. In fact, even in postcolonial Assam, plantation politics was one of the very few politics that was class-based rather than being based on ethnicity.

It is significant that in none of the noted novels, class exists as a problematic. In other words, class is not recognised as a problem. *Ejak Manuh Ekhan Aranya* is a novel that came to identifying it the closest. However, the focus in the novel is diffused into poverty and the sufferings of poverty rather than the structure of governance or of the social order that makes possible the poverty. Therefore, there is also no emphasis on the transformation of the structure of that social order or of governance that could eradicate the context of poverty.

There are attempts at creating fiction where the class character of society is recognised, as in Bargohain's *Halodhiya Soraye Bau Dhan Khai*. However, as already discussed, the text fails to incorporate that problematic into the structure of the text. The dichotomy between the plot, the authorial narration and that of the characters and their consciousness is reflective of that failure. One of the notable dimensions of *Seuji Patar Kahini* is that all the different constituents of Assamese identity come together to form one universal unit. In the text, it is achieved not by recognising the differences among the constituent social groups. Rather, it is achieved by the superimposition of uniformity (through the textual mechanism of universal language) on the text. In other words, the language of narration (by the author) and of conversation (among the characters) remains the same, viz. the dominant Sibsagar variant of Assamese. This is despite the fact that the communities/classes that constitutes the social world of the novels communicate in different language variants which are both substantive and symbolic markers of their social differences. In contrast to these novels, in Mamoni Raisom's fiction, the facility of direct (among the characters) and indirect speech (narration by the author) is successfully used to highlight social diversity and conflict in terms of languages that a given social unit practises. In other words, whereas these texts make visible only the universe (of 'Assamese' identity), Mamoni Raisom's fiction highlights the specific that comprises the larger universal construct. However, in Raisom's fiction, the universe is not invalidated. The validation is made possible by the language of the authorial narration that sutures the plot and narrative progression, viz. the dominant Sibsagar variant of Assamese. In this regard, it may be noted that Mamoni Raisom draws her social origin from both eastern and western Assam. Her paternal lineage is from western Assam (Kamrupi variant) while her maternal lineage is from eastern Assam (Dibrugarh, i.e., dominant Sibsagar variant).

In modern Assamese literature, the role of the social origin of authors on their texts can be seen as a process, i.e., in terms of the changes that a historical context undergoes and thereby the nature of an author's engagement with the historical process as an individual. For example, such a process in the engagement of an author with the discourse of identity over a period of time is evident in the writings of Agarwalla (1901–50). Through the decade of the 1940s, it may be possible to argue that there was a shift, however inconclusive, from nationalist to socialist art in his literary works. The play *Labhita* ([1943] 1996) and the incomplete novel *Amar Gaon* can be taken as two poles in this transformative process.

Labhita is a nationalist play because the structure of the text is an emphatic clarion for the cause of nationalism. Whether it is the author's narration, ideology, plot and nature of characterisation or the use of songs and language, the entire play forms a composite whole of nationalism. The play uses the concept of hero/heroine, not to romanticise the play but as a means towards easier communication of nationalism to the audience. It is important to note that in the play, the story of Labhita (the central character) does not stand out from the social milieu. Labhita's is constantly conditioned by the historical context of the society. In other words, the plot is not individualised. Therefore, it would also be difficult to locate the text in the Romantic genre. It is realism through the ideology of nationalism.

But his last and incomplete novel *Amar Gaon* (Our Village, 1950) does not appear a nationalist text in the same way as the play *Labhita*. There are two dimensions to *Amar Gaon* as a text, viz. its structure and its ideology. Precisely because of its incompleteness, it is difficult to locate *Amar Gaon* in a particular method or ideology. But as previously discussed, its textual structure appears an attempt at formulating socialist art. In terms of plot and characterisation, and in terms of the emphasis of the author (in his narration), there is a clear shift in focus from the individual (protagonist) to the social. There is gradual drift through the text in the 'individual' becoming one among the 'social'. Through the example of the structure and ideology of *Labhita* and *Amar Gaon*, it is possible to show how texts are related to their respective historical contexts. But it is also possible to show how the process of change that the ideology or consciousness of authors undergoes plays a role in the structure of the text. It is important to note that this change is not merely a result of change in the historical context. It also needs to be treated as a change in the nature of the author's engagement with the historical context. Acknowledging the agency of the author (in the exercise of his/her rational consciousness) is important to highlight the differences in the response of different authors to the same historical context.

For example, if in the post-Independence period the challenge was national reconstruction, the response of Birendra Kumar Bhattarcharjya differed sharply from that of Agarwalla's. Whereas in the case of Agarwalla the change was from a nationalist to a possible socialist imagination of an identity (from *Labhita* to *Amar Gaon*), in the case of Bhattacharjya it became almost the reverse, i.e., from socialist to nationalist. This is evident from his two novels *Rajpathe Ringiyai* (The Road Beckons, 1955), to *Iaruingam*. From a socialist reconstruction of the post-Independence national life in the former, there is a clear shift to a nationalist reconstruction of the national life in the latter, though the exact nature of the nationalism in *Iaruingam* is not elaborated. Whether it is Agarwalla or Bhattacharjya, in either case what becomes evident is the role of the change that an author undergoes in his/her ideology or consciousnesses in relation to the historical context upon the text. Such textual differences, rather than emphasising only the primacy of context, also help one identify the agency of the author in the relation between text and context.

Another significant dimension pertaining to the social origin of authors is the role that consciousness (or awareness) of one's class position (by the author) plays in the nature of the text. This becomes evident in a comparison of literary works by Agarwalla and Mamoni Raisom. In Mamoni Raisom's *Datal Hantir Une Khowa Howdah*, it is possible to locate the role that consciousness of one's class position plays in the text. Towards the end of the text, the benevolent landed aristocrat (*satradhikar*) Indranath is killed by the peasants who organised under the communists and fight for land rights. In the text, this class opposition exists as part of the plot. Yet, the text is ambiguous with regard to the killing of the aristocrat. The text is not opposed to the land rights of the peasants, neither does it exhibit or offer any critique against the communist mobilisation of the peasants against the traditional landed aristocracy. In fact, the text shows that such mobilisation could be considered genuine. What it does reflect upon is whether such organising of peasants and their political act resolves their problem of landlessness. In other words, the text is unable to decide on a perspective as to whether class opposition or class cooperation *ought* to be the way out to resolve the problem.

This dilemma in *Datal Hantir Une Khowa Howdah* could be traced to the author's own class background. One could argue that the author is aware of the causation of class conflict, but is unable to decide how to respond to it ideologically. Such dilemmas are, however, difficult to locate in Agarwalla's writings. Agarwalla belonged to the industrial bourgeoisie, an affluent family of tea planters. If one considers his unfinished novel *Amar Gaon* as an example, one of the most evident aspects that emerge is the transformation occurring in the class character of the people, especially of the protagonist. He (Abhinava Baruah) attempts to transform from bourgeois to being one of the 'masses'. In the process, as already discussed, the aesthetic of the text also undergoes a transformation, viz. from bourgeois to socialist. In other words, classes do not stand in opposite relation to each other; rather they move towards a composite whole.

This feature in Agarwalla's text where class differences dissolve is unique to his writings in Assamese fiction. In the case of other writers as well, it is possible to identify how differences get dissolved into a composite whole. For example, this has been shown in the case of Bezbaruah (*Bhadari*) or Birinchi Baruah (*Seuji Patar Kahini*) and others. However, the text itself does not undergo a (class) transformation, as is seen (or is attempted) in the case of Agarwalla's *Amar Gaon*. In conclusion, therefore, one may argue that though it is possible to identify a pattern in the role that the social origin of an author plays in the nature of the text, it is also possible to identify exceptions, such as *Amar Gaon*, wherein there is a conscious attempt by and through the agency of the author, to overcome the limits to aesthetics that social origin as a factor can play in the text. *Amar Gaon* may be taken as an example of an aesthetic wherein is also inscribed the process of change in the author's engagement with the historical context.

(b) Translations of Essay and Letters Published in *Bahni**

Excerpts from 'A Few Words on the Assamese Language' (Axomiya Bhaxar Xamparke Aaru Duiaxarman Kotha) by Lakhminath Bezbaruah, Bahni, 1 (2), 1911

The issues that I will cover in today's lecture are the branches from my previous lecture. It should not have been this way; but since that is how it has happened, it is a duty to do justice to it. In the course of delivering the previous lecture, some of our friends had brought up issues which were not linked directly to the topic of the lecture. Nevertheless, I would have still liked to share my opinions on those issues had it not been for lack of time. But the president of that meeting and my friend Barkakoti Dangoria, had replied in brief on those issues. Today, in support of his replies, I would like to say a few words.

There were things that I heard in the lecture the other day on what is after all Assamese language, and I must say that those who raised it seemed indeed to be very confused about it. Has Assamese language in use today been produced with a lot of words from the Ahom Assamese prevalent in upper Assam or after effecting changes in the Kamrupi Assamese of lower Assam? This Assamese in use today, has it been produced to sound the drums of the victory of Ahom Assamese or to blow the conch shell at the deathbed of Kamrupi Assamese? These are the questions which they have not been able to answer till now. In fact, they have been sitting with their hands folded over the questions, in a way. This situation is certainly surprising, especially given all the movements that had to be waged for the sake of the language. The language which, after such a struggle through all these years, after finally escaping from omens, has gained its feet to find a place in the university today, has found a place in the quarters of the government, has recently managed to get bedecked in a few books, and has found across Assam its children who call it their mother tongue and worship — to create such problems for this language at this juncture is certainly surprising. We can understand what is at the root of their confusion. It is that they do not try to analyse the issues using their own

---

*Translations mine.

mind. On the contrary, they analyse it using the thinking and conclusions given by others.

Assamese language is neither of upper Assam alone nor of lower Assam alone, it is the language of entire Assam. The language in which books have been written since the days of Sankardeb, Madhabdeb and Kandali, the language in which the people of Assam, especially the elites, have been exchanging their views and thoughts everyday and continue to do so, that is the Assamese language. It may be that in that language there is a predominance of upper Assam, there is a greater scope to express the words and feelings of upper Assam and there is less such scope for lower Assam, but still there is no doubt on the fact that it is indeed the real Assamese language of Assam. It may be that there was a time when the language of lower Assam too had as proud a history as of upper Assam, it may be that had that language received the patronage of kings and support from the masses, it need not have had to leave maximum space for the language of upper Assam. But the fact cannot be denied that in the struggle of language, it got left behind and had to retreat. By the languages of upper Assam and lower Assam, I am not referring to language per se, I am referring to dialects. Having received a proper growth, it is natural that some dialects of a given place establish their supremacy over the other dialects which could not become as strong. One particular group slowly gains predominance over the neighbouring groups and, over time, transforms into society in the process. Similarly, a dialect too transforms thus into a language over time. There is no need to look too far for evidence. The present-day Bangla or English languages are examples in this regard. Nadia language was the language of Bengal and then Calcutta; Bangla added greater glory to it. The Anglo-Saxon language established its predominance over the Celtic, Scots, Wales and Norman languages. In the same way, our Assamese language too established its predominance over the Bodo, Barahi, Cutiya, Ahom languages. Usually, that the language of the capital in course of time becomes the language of the entire state can be considered a given. It is due to that same reason that the present-day Bangla language is shaped by the influence of Calcutta. If our King's language would have been Bangla, then entire India would have been swept by Bangla. It was in the same way that Akbar's camp language Urdu later swept entire India. Sometimes, the language of religion can have such power of influence. That is why there is a predominance of Gurmukhi in Panjabi language of the Sikh people, and it was the same way in which Pali developed in the south. If a language is strong, everyone contributes to make it fertile and more developed. In such a language, it is natural that the local element is more prominent. It is also the root reason why in Assamese, the preponderance of speech forms of the Sibsagar district is to be found. Give and take will always be there in everything. No language can live self-contained. Even a Napoleon of language cannot live that way. Therefore, a language with a larger share of speech forms of upper Assam has to borrow from lower Assam too. It has borrowed and would continue to do so. Without such exchanges no living language, living community and creation can carry on with its existence. In this process, it always happens that both the strong and the weak undergo transformation in their nature and form. A language which is growing will borrow and imbibe ideas and words into its own self; only a language which is going to die cannot do so. If a foreigner comes and start living in my house, I can stay aloof from him in my pride only in the beginning. But when he becomes a permanent member of my house, the situation will force me to mix with him. The situation will not listen to any of my complaints, if I have any, in that case.

Upper and lower together makes Assamese *jati* (people/nation) and Assamese language. Sankardeb and Madhabdeb are the pride of Assamese, their writings gave an eternal life to the language. But they were from lower, not upper, Assam. If Sankardeb himself was from Bordua in upper Assam, his favourite disciple Madhabdeb was from lower Assam, and it was in Barpeta in lower Assam that Madhabdeb wrote his immortal *ghoxa* and submerged the whole of Assam in the river of Bhakti. That is why we say that in today's time, it brings benefit to none to start a debate on Assamese of lower and upper Assam, and those who indulge in such issues will never succeed.

Assam is no longer a remote corner like before that we can remain satisfied with whatever little we have. We are now caught up in the whirlpool of international conflicts. Therefore, in this scenario, if we want to stand our language on its feet with pride and honour, we have to get rid of our internal squabbles, overlook our differences and get united by the common thread of unity. Otherwise our destruction is inevitable.

If we are under one king and have to fight on behalf of the king, then we will have to get united under one general and abide by his orders. Only then there will be victory. On the other hand, if we fight according to our own wishes for the king, even if we fight till eternity, there will never be any victory. The whole of Bengal does not speak the same. But today northern Bengal, southern Bengal, western Bengal, they have all accepted the leadership of Calcutta Bangla, and under its leadership are striving for development, and have indeed achieved it in a short span of time. Kaliprasanna Ghose of Dhaka moves forward under the leadership of Calcutta's Dhizendranath Thakur; he has not tried to pose his colourful Dhaka Bangla against the developed Calcutta Bangla and waste energy in the process. The place of mother tongue is like the Jagannath Temple of Puri or the Kabah of Mecca. All the good sons should give up their narrowmindedness and pride and enter with a sublime purity. Will the pilgrims to Puri or Mecca not make pilgrimages to these shrines thinking that there is a local preponderance in these sites of pilgrimage? The way in which in temples or sites of pilgrimage there is no place for multiple views, even in the temple and site of pilgrimage of the mother tongue there should not be any upper and lower or Ahom and Kamrupiya views. Always remember that those who worship their mother tongue can never stay away from offering the flowers of pure heart and devotion to it. The Assamese people of lower Assam can keep alive their speech forms in their own lives, we have no complaints on that count. In fact, through this way, their love for their language will get expressed. But they should keep aside these speech forms from the common Assamese language of the Assamese people. They should not raise these forms against the common Assamese language and create a mindset of opposition — this is my humble request. When Scots speak English, they retain a few Scot pronunciations. They pronounce the English A as A' as is pronounced in their country. But through it, they only express their love for their country, not animosity towards the English language; in fact, they have made English their own mother tongue and wish good for the English language. On many occasions, the people of Yorkshire speak English retaining a lot of their own speech forms, yet their lives placing English on the throne of their mother tongue. If the people of Nagaon call Aanhath as Aaxath or *tenga* curry as *xaak*, it does not harm the Assamese language. As people can contribute to the national life despite while retaining their local uniqueness, similarly it is possible to contribute towards the national language despite local speech uniqueness. If one has to attain larger freedom, one has to give up small freedoms. Similarly, to attain a larger language, one has to give up small speech forms and their peculiarities. National language is like an ocean. Before reaching the ocean, the different rivers and tributaries flow with their own uniqueness. But the moment they empty into the ocean, these differences disappear. In the same way, local speech forms can survive to an extent with their peculiarities. But when they reach the national language, they cannot retain them, and dissolve into the ocean of the national language. This is the mantra of development. At this, someone may comment that are we not going back to the earlier problematic situation of one written and another spoken language? I say we will not have that problem. This will not happen because the peculiarities which I have said that people of an area can retain in their language use are not sufficient to make a full-fledged language. These peculiarities are retained only as bonds with our localities.

    I would like to ask one question to my Assamese friends: How long are we going to keep trying to prove again and again that Assamese is not an offshoot of another language, that it is an independent language, that it is an indigenous language of Assam? Is it not enough when our earlier experts have already given us conclusive answers to these questions that we need to keep on discussing them without end? Great scholars of Assam like Anandaram Dhekial Phukan, Hemchandra Baruah and Gunabhiram

Baruah or foreign scholars like William Robinson, Nathan Brown, Gait, George A. Grierson and others have left behind incontrovertible evidence on these questions. Their studies are enough to give us light to move ahead. Then why do we still need to look for a lantern for light on these questions? When we have reached the middle of the path of development of Assamese language, why do we have to return back again the distance that has already been covered on these questions? Rather than taking 'promotions' and 'double promotions', why do we have to 'degrade' and drop to first or second standard in school? As some of our writers say, why do we have to get demoted? Not to speak of what others are doing, what about us ourselves? The government has allowed Assamese to be taught at the university. But rather than trying to learn and teach the language better, we are trying to hide our lack of effort in this regard by questioning the very legitimacy of the language in the name of what is Assamese language.

It would be good if India has only one language. But India is a nest of hundreds of languages. There is still a lot of time for these hundreds of languages to become one language. But do we have to show our large-heartedness in this matter by sacrificing our language for the sake of this one language? Like the Dadhisi sage, to make the weapon with the help of his own bones which can destroy the hundreds of languages in India and create in its place into one language like Bangla or Hindi may be a matter of piety in the other world, but it certainly can be postponed for now in this world. I make this humble petition to those Assamese who take the lead in creating one language in India. Rather than feeding smaller animals to a huge python and making the python even bigger, I believe it is better to let the smaller animals live in this world so that the greatness of the creator can be better appreciated. Else the creator would not have created the smaller animals in the first place. He would have just created one huge python. After creating one python, he would have call it a day in creation. The numerous smaller language states in India should be allowed to survive and they should all come together into a larger union of language states with each language state enjoying its life. That is how the arrangement ought to be. In the larger interests of the empire all can come together, but for domestic purposes everyone can retain their own individuality. Such an approach certainly is not reprehensible. Yes, it is important that the Indian empire should have one common lingua franca. But for the sake of it, there is no need for the smaller languages to sacrifice their lives. I believe that despite having a common lingua franca, it will be possible for the many smaller languages to live together without dispute and differences among them. These days, many Indian languages are growing in the shadow of India's lingua franca English.

... Linguistic differences or similarity do not depend on the similarity or differences in a dozen or so words. It can only be determined from rules of grammar. Therefore, if someone tries to show similarity of our Assamese language with some other language and our Assamese friends get frightened and abandon their seat for the others, it is only those Assamese friends who will fall. Nothing will happen to the Assamese language. It is clear to anyone who has deeply studied Assamese and the Bangla, that the relation that Dhaka or Mymensing speech forms share with Bangla is very different from that of Assamese. The rules of grammar of Assamese are quite different from Bangla. If despite this fact of difference someone tries to force the point of similarity, it only reflects on one's attempt to force one's views using muscle power or that one has not applied one's analytical mind to the question.

'Old Wine in New Bottle' (Purani Kathat Natun Rang) by Padmanath Gogain Baruah, Bahni, 1 (7), 1911

This letter to the editor was in response to a couple of Lakhminath Bezbaruah's articles in Bahni *on the Ahoms and their socio-cultural life and history. Bezbaruah was also the editor of* Bahni.

For about a month or so, a few sharp articles on the Ahoms have been published in *Bahni*. When observed closely, there is nothing new in the articles; things which have been discussed earlier have only been repeated. But some sharp views have put a new colour to the issues, seeking to hurt the feelings of a major section of the people of Assam. What would be its result? As in the west and in Bengal, where Brahmans, Kshatriyas, Vaishyas or Kayasthas have formed their own separate societies, or as a result of the Hindus and Muslims developing their differences of opinion and India getting weaker, it is my apprehension that this growing Assamese *jati* (nation) would also suffer a same fate of becoming weaker due to differences of opinion between Ahoms (who are today more than half of the total population of Assam) and the Brahmans of Assam. I have no desire to elaborate on the issue. Thoughtful readers can read for themselves and the writer who wrote articles such as 'Maidam', the editorial remarks on 'Ahom Scriptures on the Origin of the World', 'Ahom' published in *Bahni* and would understand on their own what is the apprehension I am indicating. Anyone who can read between the lines will understand that 'Maidam' is only a figment of the writer's imagination. The kind of pleasure that the writer has expressed over the annihilation of the Ahom royal families, the criticism that has been heaped on the Ahom scriptures or the kind of remarks being made on the 'Ahom roots in Assam', a mere reading of these writings will make it amply clear to readers what the basis of my views against these writings is.

It was only the other day (not even a hundred years have passed), when Assam had spent 600 years under Ahom rule, people still proudly display their royal titles received during Ahom rule, innumerable Brahman,

Mahanta and Goswami families survived and still survive on the *brahmottar* and *devottar* grants from the Ahom rulers, how come this joy at the destruction of the same Ahom royalty! There was a time when the Ahoms were referred to with so much respect, and now they are being referred to as mere this and that!

In any religious text, there will always be some supernatural descriptions. Hindu texts are no exception to it. Then why this selective impatience toward Ahom scriptures?

In the olden days some Cutiya, Barahi and Kacari people went out with the Ahom army to fight the Koch by wearing the sacred thread. But the battle was won without even them having to fight. After the battle was over, these people could not forgo the attraction of the sacred thread. That is how they have added to a population of the Brahmans in Assam. In the same way, many local people have also expanded the Ahom population. But today, in reality, it is some Goswamis who are increasing the population figures of Ahom in the hope of getting some disciples. Just like the way the number of pure Brahmans and Kayasthas coming to Assam was very low, the figure for pure Ahoms coming to Assam is also very low. Both the peoples have increased their population through the same process. Therefore, no one in Assam is pure in that sense today.

Impressionistic history is not acceptable. To ignore such histories is the prevalent practice today. Buddhism is dated to around 600 BC. The forefathers of the Ahoms left Syam province of Burma around the 6th century AD (i.e., around 1,200 years after the spread of Buddhism), and entered Soumar around 1200 AD (i.e., after nearly 1,800 years after the spread of Buddhism). In such a context, to say that Buddhism spread to Burma only after the Ahoms had left Burma certainly must have required a great deal of strength and effort from the writer. The history of the Ahoms is systematically written in Ahom language. Without knowing Ahom language, it is better to leave Ahom history in the dark than writing its history with materials from here and there.

In conclusion, I hope that the views I have expressed do not cause much pain to the writer of articles like 'Ahom' in *Bahni*. It is in fear that such articles will make a river flow between the Ahoms and the Brahmans in this growing Assamese *jati* (people or nation) that I had to write so much here.

'For Our Friends of Lower Assam' (Aamar Namoni Aaxamar Bandhu Xakalar Prati), *editorial remark by Lakhminath Bezbaruah in Bahni, 2 (2), 1913*

The editorial is in response to the criticism that was leveled against Bahni *for publishing the poem* 'Ha Mur Kapal!' *(My Luck!) in Kamrupi language in which the poet expressed how the speech form and its speakers seem to have been reduced to a laughing stock, and how they are finding it difficult to express their thoughts in the 'standard' Assamese of the day.*

We sincerely regret that some of our friends of lower Assam have been hurt by the poem '*Ha Mur Kapal!*' that we had published in *Bahni* in our previous issue. We had not published it to cause pain to them or anyone or to make fun of those from lower Assam. Neither did we have any intention of showing that Assamese and Kamrupi are two different languages. Why would we do it? They are not two languages. Assamese language means Kamrupi language and Kamrupi language means Assamese language. I think had we not written in that issue that it is a poem in Kamrupi language and had only written that it is a poem in lower Assam speech forms, the problem would not have arisen. Anyone who has read the article by honorable Bholanath Kakoti in the previous issue would surely understand our views on this issue. Beautiful poems can be written in the speech forms of lower Assam. Those who have read the poem '*Ha Mur Hari*' in this issue will certainly realise it. If something is written with dialectical peculiarities of a speech form, it does not mean that we are trying to belittle the speech form or are trying to raise it as an opposition to the main language. We have never heard that the intention of Burn's poetry is to raise it as a banner of opposition against English language. We hope that our friends will think over the matter deeply and will not misunderstand our intentions. Beautiful literature, whether old or new, in speech forms of lower Assam should be a matter of appreciation for all of us. We feel enriched reading Kaliram Baruah's '*Radhika Kalanka Bhanjyan*' in this regard. Should such literature be eliminated? If such language forms exist like stars around the moon of Assamese language, it will only make the sky of Assam brighter. We do not know how have friends of lower Assam have taken these words as they are. But it is true that our intentions are noble. We too have been pained by the way they have been pained thinking that we are wrong.

Bibliography

Agarwalla, Jyotiprasad. (1943) 1996. *'Labhita'*, in idem, *Jyotiprasad Racanavali* (Writings of Jyotiprasad), pp. 187–229. Guwahati: Publication Board Assam.
———. (1950) 1996. *Amar Gaon* (Our Village), in idem, *Jyotiprasad Racanavali* (Writings of Jyotiprasad), pp. 346–58. Guwahati: Publication Board Assam.
———. 1996. *Jyotiprasad Agarwalla Rasanavali* (Collected Works of Jyotiprasad Agarwalla). Guwahati: Assam Publication Board.
Ahmad, Imtiaz. 2008. 'State Formation and Consolidation under the Ujjainiya Rajputs in Medieval Bihar: Testimony of Oral Traditions as Recorded in the *Tawarikh-i-Ujjainiya*', in Surinder Singh and I. D. Gaur (eds), 2008, *Popular Literature and Pre-Modern Societies in South Asia*, pp. 74–85. Delhi: Pearson/Longman.
Antrobus, H. A. 1957. *A History of Assam Company 1839–1953*. Edinburg: T & A Constable Ltd.
Ao, Temsula. 2006. *These Hills Called Home*. New Delhi: Penguin Books India.
Bandopadhyaya, Manik. (1948) 1973. *Padma Nadir Majhi* (Padma River Boatman). Trans. Barbara Printer and Yuan Lovelock. Queensland: University of Queensland Press.
Bandyopadhyaya, Bibhuti Bhusan. (1928) 1990. *Pather Panchali* (The Song of the Little Road). Trans. T. W. Clark and T. Mukherji. Delhi: Rupa & Co.
Baruah, Gunabhiram. (1892) 2001. *'Kamrupir Patra'* (A Letter from a Kamrupi), in Nagen Saikia (ed.), *Jonaki* (Omnibus Collection), pp. 518–19. Guwahati: Asam Sahitya Sabha,.
———. (1911) 2001.*'Purani Kathat Natun Rang'* (Old Matters in New Colour), in Jatindranath Goswami (ed.), *Bahni: Part One* (Omnibus Collection), pp. 219–21. Jorhat: Asam Sahitya Sabha,
Baruah, Hem. 1900. *Hemkosh*. Guwahati: Hemkosh.
Baruah, Manjeet. 2007. 'Women Characters in Assamese Ramayanas'. New Delhi: Indira Gandhi National Centre for the Arts. Unpublished.
———. 2008. 'The Problematic of Space and Historiography on Tea Plantation in Upper Brahmaputra Valley', 23rd ICHR Lecture. Guwahati: Indian Council of Historical Research.

Baruah, Manjeet. 2009. 'Guerrilla Space as Literary Plot', paper presented at international seminar on 'Region in South Asia'. Delhi: University of Delhi. 24–27 November.

———. 2010. 'Assamese Language, Narrative and the Making of North East Frontier of India: Beyond *Regional* Indian Literary Studies'. Unpublished.

———. 2008. 'Construction of "People" and Gender in Colonial and Post Colonial Assam: A Study in the Use of Literary Aesthetic as Historical Sources', in Shirin Banu (ed.), 'Proceeding Volume of UGC & ICHR sponsored National Seminar on Status of Women in Colonial Assam'. Guwahati: Pandu College.

Baruah, Navakanta. 1995. *Folkways in Literature: An Aesthetic Enquiry*. New Delhi: Sahitya Akademi.

Baruah, Rasna. 1959. *Seuji Patar Kahini* (The Story of Green Leaves). Nalbari: Journal Emporium.

Baruah, Sanjib. 1999. *India against Itself: Assam and the Politics of Nationality*. New Delhi: Oxford University Press.

——— (ed.). 2009. *Beyond Counter Insurgence: Breaking the Impasse in North East India*. New Delhi: Oxford University Press.

Baruah, Umeshchandra. (1911) 2001. '*Ha Mur Kapal!*', in Jatindranath Goswami (ed.), *Bahni: Part One* (Omnibus Collection), pp. 41–43. Jorhat: Asam Sahitya Sabha.

Belden, Jack. 1949. *China Shakes the World*. New York: Harper.

Bezbaruah, L. (1895) 2001a. '*Assamiya Bhasa*' (Assamese Language) in Nagen Saikia (ed.), *Jonaki* (Omnibus Collection), pp. 638–45. Guwahati: Asam Sahitya Sabha.

———. (1895) 2001b. '*Assamiya Bhasa*' (Assamese Language), 2nd Lecture, in Nagen Saikia (ed.), *Jonaki* (Omnibus Collection), pp. 621–28. Guwahati: Asam Sahitya Sabha.

———. (1897) 2001.'*Assamiya Bhasa*' (Assamese Language), 7th Lecture, in Nagen Saikia (ed.), *Jonaki* (Omnibus Collection), pp. 815–21. Guwahati: Asam Sahitya Sabha.

———. (1910) 2001. '*Assamiya Bhasar Samparke Aaru Duaasarman*' (A Few More Words on Assamese Language), in Jatindranath Goswami (ed.), *Bahni: Volume One* (Omnibus Collection), pp. 42–52. Jorhat: Asam Sahitya Sabha.Bezbaruah, Lakhminath. 2003. *Comedy of Spark and Other Stories*. Trans. Manjeet Baruah. Delhi: Rupa & Co.

Bhattacharjya, Birendra Kumar. (1952–53) 2007. *Ramdhenur Sampadakiya* (Editorials of Ramdhenu). Guwahati: Banalata.

———. 1955. *Rajpathe Ringiai*. Guwahati: Mani Manik Prakash.

———. 1960. *Iaruingam*. Guwahati: Lawyer's Book Stall.

Bhuyan, Surjya Kumar (ed.). (1920) 1958. *Jaymati Akhyan* (Episode of Jaymati). Guwahati: DAHS.

——— (ed.). 1924. *Barphukanar Geet* (Song of Barphukan). Guwahati: DAHS.

Bibliography   195

Bhuyan, Surjya Kumar (ed.). 1932. *Asamar Padya Buranji* (Verse Buranjis of Assam). Guwahati: DAHS.

———. (1935) 2007. *Saurjya Kumar Bhuyanr Jibani Sahitya* (Biographical Writings of Surjya Kumar Bhuyan. Guwahati: Assam Publication Board.

Blackburn, Stuart. 2003–2004. 'Memories of Migration: Notes on Legends and Beads in Arunachal Pradesh', *European Bulletin on Himalayan Research*, 25/26: 15–60.

Bordoloi, Nirmalprabha. 1986. *Devi*. Guwahati: Sahitya Prakash.

Bordoloi, S. S. (1895) 2001. '*Assamiya Bhasa Unnati Sadhini Sabhar Karjya Bibaran*, 5th–7th Year' (An Account of the Activities of the Society for the Development of Assamese Language 5th–7th Year), in Nagen Saikia (ed.), *Jonaki* (Omnibus Collection), pp. 660–63. Guwahati: Asam Sahitya Sabha.

Borgohain, Homen. 1963. *Subala*. Jorhat: Bookland.

———. (1972) 1988. *Halodhiya Soraye Bau Dhan Khai* (The Harvest). Guwahati: Student's Stores.

———. 1987. *Matsyagandha* (Fish Daughter). Guwahati: Student's Stores.

Braman, Sivanath (ed.). 2007. *Prasannalal Choudhury Rasanavali* (Collected Works of Prasannalal Choudhury). Guwahati: Assam Publication Board.

Brown, Nathan. 1848. *Grammatical Notices of the Assamese Language*. Sibsagar: American Baptist Missionary Press.

Calvino, Italo. 2009. *The Paths to the Spiders' Nests*. New Delhi: Penguin Books India.

Choudhury, Prasannalal. 2007. *Prasannalal Choudhuryr Rasanavali* (Complete Works of Prasannalal Choudhury), pp. 627–30. Ed. Sivanath Barman. Guwahati: Publication Board Assam.

Choudhury, Prasenjit. 2006. '*Bhasik Durjog aaru Oitihasik Punorusandhan*' (Problem of Language and Historical Reconsideration), in Bijanlal Choudhury, (ed.), *Sahityar Bikhyan*, pp. 177–207. Guwahati: Natun Sahitya Parishad.

Choudhury, Rita. 2010. *Makam*. Guwahati: Jyoti Prakashan.

Choudhury, Satish Chandra and Pradip Bhuyan (eds). 2008. *Asom Sahitya Sabhar Bhaxanavali* (Lectures of Asom Sahitya Sabha). Dhemaji: Kiran Prakashan.

Chughtai, Ismat. (1966) 1993. 'The Heart Breaks Free', in idem, *The Heart Breaks Free and the Wild One*, pp. 3–71. Trans. Tahira Naqvi. New Delhi: Kali for Women.

Das, K. C. (ed.). 1994. *Durgabori Ramayana*. Guwahati: Bani Prakash.

Das, J. 1955. *Dawar Aru Nai* (The Clear Sky). Guwahati: Sunabhil.

de Certeau, Michel. 1984. *The Practice of Everyday Life*. London and New York: University of California Press.

Devy, Ganesh N. 1992. *After Amnesia: Tradition and Change in Indian Literary Criticism*. Delhi: Orient Longman.

Dutta Baruah, Hari Narayan (ed.). 1978. *Katha Guru Charit*. Nalbari: Dutta Baruah and Co.
Dutt, Uddipan. 2004–2005 'Growth of Print Nationalism and the Formation of Assamese Identity in Two Early Magazines: *Arunodoi* and *Jonnaki*', Sarai Newsletter. http://www.sarai.net/fellowships/independent/archival-submissions/fellowships-04-05/uddipan-dutta-the-growth-of-print-nationalism-and-assamese-identity-in-two-early-assamese-magazines/the-growth-of-print-nationalism-and-the-formation-of-assamese-identity-in-two-early-magazines-arunoloi-and-jonnaki. Accessed 12 July 2011.
Eaton, Richard. 1994. *The Rise of Islam in the Bengal Frontier, 1206–1760*. New Delhi: Oxford University Press.
Evans, Geoffrey and Antony Brett-James. 1962. *Imphal: A Flower on Lofty Heights*. London: Macmillan.
Fishman, Joshua A. 1989, '"Nothing New under the Sun": A Case Study of Alternatives in Language and Ethnocultural Identity', in idem, *Language and Ethnicity in Minority Sociolinguistic Perspective*. Cleveland and Philadelphia: Multilingual Matters Ltd.
Gait, Edward. (1905) (1926) 1994. *A History of Assam*. Guwahati: LBS.
Gentzler, Edwin. 2008. *Translation and Identity in the Americas: New Directions in Translation Theory*. London: Routledge.
Gohain Baruah, Padmanath. (1971) 2008. *Padmanath Gohain Baruah Rasanavali* (Collected Works of Padmanath Gohain Baruah). Guwahati: Assam Publication Board.
———. (1902) (1971) 2008. 'Jaymati', in *Padmanath Gohain Baruah Rasanavali* (Collected Works of Padmanath Gohain Baruah), pp. 39–98. Guwahati: Publication Board Assam.
Gohain, Hiren. 1985. *Assam: The Burning Question*. Delhi: Spectrum.
———. 1987. *Asamar Jatiya Jibanat Mahapuruxiya Prabhab* (The Impact of Vaishnava Saints on the National Life of Assam). Guwahati: Lawyers Book Stall.
Goswami, Hemchandra. (1891) 2001. 'Assamiya Bhasa' (Assamese Language), in Nagen Saikia (ed.), *Jonaki* (Omnibus Collection), pp. 365–70. Guwahati: Asam Sahitya Sabha,.
Goswami, Indira. 1991. 'Indian Epic Values: Ramayana and its Impact', proceedings of the 8th International Ramayana Conference. Leuven. 6–8 July.
———. 1992. *I and my Writings*. Delhi: Department of MIL & LS, University of Delhi.
Goswami, Jatindranath (ed.). 2001. *Bahni: Volume One* (Omnibus Collection). Jorhat: Asam Sahitya Sabha.
Goswami, Mamoni Raisom. (1975) 2001. *Neelkanthi Braj*, in idem, *Collected Works of Mamoni Raisom Goswami*, pp. 167–243. Guwahati: Students Stores.

Goswami, Mamoni Raisom. (1980) 2001. *Mamore Dhara Taruwal*, in idem, *Collected Works of Mamoni Raisom Goswami*, pp. 167–243. Guwahati: Students Stores.

———. 1988. *Datal Hantir Une Khowa Howdah*. Guwahati: Bani Prakash.

———. (1990) 1998. *Bikhar Patra Bhangi* (To Break the Begging Bowl), in idem, *Mamoni Raisom Goswami Upanyas Samagra*, pp. 785–816. Guwahati: Student's Stores.

Goswami, Sabita. 2009. *Man Gangar Teerat*. Guwahati: Anwesha.

Griffiths, P. 1967. *The History of the Indian Tea Industry*. London: Weidenfeld & Nicolson.

Guha, Amalendu. 1977. *Planter Raj to Swaraj*. New Delhi: ICHR.

———. 1982. 'The Medieval Economy of Assam', in Irfan Habib and Tapan Raychowdhury (eds) *Cambridge Economic History of India*, vol. 1, pp. 478–505. New Delhi: Cambridge University Press.

Hussain, Nikumani (ed.). 2008. *Syed Abdul Malikar Aprakashita Rasanavali aru Diary* (Unpublished Works and Diary of Syed Abdul Malik). Guwahati: Chandra Prakash.

Iyengar, K. R. Srinivasa (ed.). (1983) 2003. *Asian Variations in Ramayana*. New Delhi: Sahitya Akademi.

Kakati, Banikanta. (1925) (1991) 2006. '*Jatiya Cetana*' (National Consciousness), in, Maheswar Neog (ed.), *Banikanta Kakati Rasanavali* (Collected Works of Banikanta Kakati). Guwahati: Publication Board Assam.

———. (1941) 1995. *Assamese: Its Formation and Development*. Guwahati: LBS.

Kakati, Saroj. 2000. '*Axomiya Anchalik Upanyas*' (Assamese Regional Novels), in Nagen Thakur (ed.), *Exa Basarar Axomiya Upanyas* (Hundred Years of Assamese Novel). Guwahati: Jyoti Prakashan.

Kar, Bodhisattva. 2009. 'When was the Post Colonial?' in Sanjib Baruah (ed.), *Beyond Counter Insurgence: Breaking the Impasse in North East India*, pp. 49–77. New Delhi: Oxford University Press.

Klein, Kerwin Lee. 1997. *Frontiers in Historical Imagination: Narrating the European Conquest of Native America 1890–1990*. California: University of California Press.

Kumar, Sanjay. 2007. 'Foliated Identity: The Case of the Nagas', in P. C. Pattanaik and D. Bora (eds), *Tribes of India: Tradition, Culture and Lore*, pp. 218–32. Guwahati: Angik Publishers.

Lefebvre, Henri. 1961. *Critique of Everyday Life, Vol. 2*. London and New York: Verso.

Mackenzie, Alexander. (1884) 1989. *The North East Frontier of India*. Delhi: Mittal.

Mahanta, Anuraag. 2007. *Aulingar Zui*. Sibsagar: Basudeb Publication.

Mahanta, Puna. 2007. '*Nocte Janagosthi aaru Anyana Janagosthir Dharma Sanskritir Prasarat Saliha Bareghar Satrar Bhumika*' (The Role of

Bareghar Satra in the Spread of Dharma Culture among Nocte and Other Communities), in Pradip Hararika (ed.), *Srimanta Sankardeb aaru Uttar Purbanchalar Janagosthi* (Srimanta Sankardeb and North East Communities). Guwahati: Purbanchal Prakash.

Malik, Abdul. 1960. *Surujmukhir Sapna* (The Sunflower Dream). Jorhat: Sarali Puthighar.

———. 1969. *Aghari Atmar Kahini* (Rootless Soul). Guwahati: Guwahati Book Stall.

Malik, Syed Abdul. 2008. *Syed Abdul Malikar Aprakashita Rasanavali aru Diary* (Unpublished Works and Diary of Syed Abdul Malik). Ed. Nikumani Hussain. Guwahati: Chandra Prakash.

Misra, Udayan. 2000. *The Periphery Strikes Back: Challenges to the Nation State in Assam and Nagaland*. Shimla: Indian Institute of Advanced Studies.

Mitchell, J. (1883) 1973. *The North East Frontier of India*. Delhi: Mittal.

Moral, Dipankar. 1992, 'Phonology of Asamiya Dialects: Contemporary Standard and Mayong', PhD dissertation. Pune: Deccan College.

Neog, Dimbeswar. 1963. *Mahapurusism: A Universal Religion*. Guwahati: Xuwani Prakashan.

Neog, Maheswar (ed.). 1961. *The Language Question*. Jorhat: Assam Sahitya Sabha.

———. (1974) 2008. 'Presidential Address of the Asam Sahitya Sabha (at Mongoldoi), *Asam Sahitya Sabhar Bhasanavali* (Presidential Addresses of the Asam Sahitya Sabha), p. 88. Eds S. C. Choudhury and P. Bhuyan. Dehemaji: Kiran Prakashan.

——— (ed.). (1991) 2006. *Banikanta Kakati Rasanavali* (Collected Works of Banikanta Kakati). Guwahati: Assam Publication Board.

Orunudoi. 1850. 'Purani Asom Buranji', (1). August.

———. 1851. 'Purani Asom Buranji', (12). July.

———. August 1850–August 1852. 'Purani Asom Buranji' (Deodhai Buranji). Sibsagar: American Baptist Press.Pathak, Suryasikha. 2010. 'Tribal Politics in India', *Economic & Political Weekly*, 45 (12): 61–69. 6–12 March.

Pemberton, R. B. (1835) 1979. *Report on the Frontier of India*. Delhi: Mittal.

Pollock, Sheldon. 2006. *Language of God in the World of Men*. California: University of California Press.

Pujari, Anuradha Sarma. 2007. *No Man's Land*. Guwahati: Pratidin.

Rabha, Bishnu. (1962) (1989) 2008. *Sunpahi*, in idem, in *Bishnu Prasad Rabhar Rasanavali* Vol. 1 (Collected Works of Bishnu Prasad Rabha), pp. 564–642. Ed. Jogesh Das. Nagaon: Rabha Rasanavali Prakashan Sangha.

Rabha, Bishnu. (1989) 2008a. *Bishnu Prasad Rabhar Rasanavali*, vol. 1 (Collected Works of Bishnu Prasad Rabha). Ed. Jogesh Das. Nagaon: Rabha Rasanavali Prakashan Sangha.

Rabha, Bishnu. (1989) 2008b. *Bishnu Prasad Rabhar Rasanavali*, vol. 2 (Collected Works of Bishnu Prasad Rabha). Nagaon: Rabha Rasanavali Prakashan.
———. (1989) 2008c. '*Na Prithvir Natun Jug*', in idem, *Bishnu Prasad Rabhar Rasanavali*, vol. 1 (Collected Works of Bishnu Prasad Rabha), pp. 282–97. Ed. Jogesh Das. Nagaon: Rabha Rasanavali Prakashan Sangha.
———. (1989) 2008d. '*Simanta Soinik*' in idem, *Bishnu Prasad Rabhar Rasanavali*, vol. 1 (Collected Works of Bishnu Prasad Rabha), pp. 446–60. Ed. Jogesh Das. Nagaon: Rabha Rasanavali Prakashan Sangha.
———. (1989) 2008e. '*Mukti Deul*' in idem, *Bishnu Prasad Rabhar Rasanavali* vol. 1 (Collected Works of Bishnu Prasad Rabha), pp. 270–81. Nagaon: Rabha Rasanavali Prakashan Sangha.
Raichoudhury, Ambikagiri. (1920) 2009. 'India's Self Rule and Assam's Self Rule', Editorial, *Chetana*.
———. 2009. '*Jatiya Jagaran*' (National Awakening) in idem, *Ambikagiri Raichoudhury Rasanavali* (Collected Works of Ambikagiri Raichoudhury), p. 742. Ed. S. Sarma. Guwahati: Publication Board Assam.
———. (1935) 2009. '*Dexor Mati he Aasol*' (One's Land is the Most True), in idem, *Ambikagiri Raichoudhury Rasanavali* (Collected Works of Ambikagiri Raichoudhury), pp. 538–40. Ed. S. Sharma. Guwahati: Publication Board Assam.
Ramanujan, A. K. 2004. *The Collected Essays by AK Ramanujan*. Ed. Vinay Dharwadker. New Delhi: Oxford University Press.
Ray, Rajat Kanta. 2008. 'Creating a Secret Universe: Love and Syncretism in the World of an Eighteenth Century Fakir', in Surinder Singh and I. D. Gaur (eds), *Popular Literature and Pre-Modern Societies in South Asia*, pp. 192–204. Delhi: Pearson/Longman.
Reid, Robert. 1942. *A History of Frontier Areas Bordering on the Province of Assam*. Shillong: Government Press.
Robb, Peter. 1997. 'The Colonial State and Constructions of Indian Identity: An Example on the North-east Frontier in the 1880s', *Modern Asian Studies*, 31 (2): 245–83.
Said, Edward. 2001. 'Arabic Prose and Prose Fiction after 1948', in idem, *Reflections on Exile and Other Literary and Cultural Essays*. New Delhi: Penguin Books India.
Saikia, Nagen (ed.). 2001. *Jonaki* (Omnibus Collection). Guwahati: Asam Sahitya Sabha.
Saikia, Rajen. 2001. *A Social and Economic History of Assam, 1826–1921*. Delhi: Manohar.
Saikia, Utpal. 2005. 'Socio-Economic and Political Consequences of Bangladeshi Immigration in India', paper presented at XXV International Population Conference, International Union for the Scientific Study of Population. Tours, France. 18–23 July.

Saikia, Yasmin. 2004. *Fragmented Memories: Struggling to be Tai Ahom in India*. Durban and London: Duke University Press.
Sarma, Phani. (1976) 2003. *Phani Sarma Rasanavali* (Collected Works of Phani Sarma). Guwahati: Assam Publication Board.
Sarma, Satyandranath (ed.). (1986) 2008. *Ambikagiri Raichoudhury Rasanavali* (Collected Works of Ambikagiri Raishoudhury). Guwahati: Assam Publication Board.
Sarma, Umakanta. 1986. *Ejak Manuh Ekhan Aranya* (A Crowd and a Forest). Pathsala and Guwahati: Bani Prakash.
Sharma, Nabin Chandra. 2009. *Bharatar Uttar Purbancalar Paribesya Kala* (Performing Arts of North East India). Guwahati: Banalata.
Satyanath, T. S. 2008. 'Religions Crossing Borders: On the Emergence of Translation Traditions in India', paper presented at the Third Asian Translation Traditions Conference: (Ex)Change and Continuity in Translation Traditions. Istanbul: Boğaziçi Universitesi. 22–24 October.
Scott, James C. 2009. *The Art of Not Being Governed: An Anarchist History of Upland South East Asia*. CT: Yale University Press.
Shimray, U. A. 2004. 'Socio-Political Unrest in the Region Called North East India', *Economic and Political Weekly*, 39 (42): 4637–4643.
Siddiqui, Mohd. Abu. 1990. *Evolution of Land Grants and Revenue Policy of Government: The Growth of the Tea Industry of Assam 1834–1940*. Calcutta: Asian Publishers.
Smith, Ian. 2008. 'Pidgins, Creoles, and Bazaar Hindi', in Braj B. Kachru, Yamuna Kachru and S. N. Sridhar (eds), 2008, *Language in South Asia*, pp. 253–67. Cambridge and New York: Cambridge University Press.
Sridhar, S. N. 2008. 'Language Contact and Convergence in South Asia', in Braj. B. Kachru, Yamuna Kachru and S. N. Sridhar (eds), *Language in South Asia*, pp. 235–52. Cambridge and New York: Cambridge University Press.
Subrahmanyam, Sanjay. 2005. *Explorations in Connected History: From the Tagus to the Ganges*. New Delhi: Oxford University Press.
Terang, Rong Bong. (1981) 2010. *Rongmilir Hanhi*. Guwahati: Publication Board Assam.
Truett, Samuel and Elliot Young. 2004. *Continental Crossroads*. London: Duke University Press.
Turner, Frederick Jackson. (1920) 2010. *The Frontier in American History*. BiblioBazaar.
Waddell, Lawrence, Augustine. (1901) 2001. *The Tribes of the Brahmaputra Valley*. Delhi: Logos Press.
Williams, Raymond. 1977. *Marxism and Literature*. Oxford: Oxford University Press.
Wrobel, David M. 1996. 'Beyond the Frontier–Region Dichotomy', *Pacific Historical Review*, 65 (3): 401–29. August.

About the Author

Manjeet Baruah is Assistant Professor, School of Translation Studies and Training, Indira Gandhi National Open University, New Delhi. His publications include *The Problematic of Space and Historiography on Tea Plantations in Upper Brahmaputra Valley* (2008); *Ravana: Myths, Legends and Lore* (co-edited, 2009); and *The Comedy of A Spark and Other Stories* (trans., 2003).

Index

Adi Kanda, 67, 70
Agarwalla, Jyotiprasad, 101–102
agrarian system, 7
Ahmad, Imtiaz, 7
Ahom, 6; *khat* policy of, 26–27; migration to Brahmaputra Valley, 17; origin of, 45; *paik* system (*see Paik* system)
Ahom movement: eastern valley, in, 88
Ahom royal, 17
All Assam Students Union (AASU), 147
All India Radio, 141
Armed Forces Special Powers Act, 9
Asomiya Bhasa Unnati Sadhini Sabha, 86
Asom Sahitya Sabha, 145; aim of, 88; Das presidential address during 51st Congress, 93; Gohain presidential address, in first congress, 113, 115; Neog presidential address, 152–53
Assam, 16 *see also Katha Guru Charit*
Assam Association, 78–79, 88
Assam *desh*, 16–17 *see also Katha Guru Charit*
Assamese: pre-colonial period, in, 88
Assamese fiction, 174; bourgeois character of, 175
Assamese identity formation, 122
Assamese language, 186; historical significance of: Baptist missionary role, in development of Sibsagar variant, 77; grammar development, for language, 78; missionaries and colonial, establishment of, 78–79; Kakati views on, 120–21; pre-colonial history of, 77; variants of: eastern valley, 76; western valley, 76
Assamese literature, 115; Bhattacharjya on need for generation, of new content, 142; Kakati views on, 120–21
Assamese nationhood, 145
Assam movement, 147
Assam valley, 15 *see also* Brahmaputra Valley
Axomiya, 77

Bahni, 89, 115
Barak Valley, 3
Barphukanar Geet, 17–18, 51
Baruah, Gohain, 113
Baruah, Gunabhiram, 115
Baruah, Hemchandra, 115
Baruah, Padmanath Gohain, 110, 113
Bengal frontier, 7–8
Bezbaruah, Lakhminath, 87, 89, 110, 191–92; criticism to elite, by using everyday language, 119
Bhakti movement, 73; influence on trans-creation process, in South Asia, 80
bhasa literature, 80
Biswesar Bidyadhip, 46–47 *see also* Buranji chronicles
Blackburn, Stuart, 19–20

Index ~ 203

Bodo community: demand of, 88
Bodoland Autonomous Council, 144
border, 7; Sixth Schedule of Indian Constitution, institutionalisation in, 8–9
Bordoloi, S. S., 86
Brahmaputra Valley: erosion of shared domains, 6; formation of, 3, 15; highway of migration, 80; identity discourses in: study on, 6–7; pre-colonial period, 15–17; north-east India as misnomer, 20; policy of colonial regime, 21–22; trans-created literature, 81; Waddell views on, 4
Buranji chronicles, 12, 17, 41 *see also* Neo-Vaishnava literature; mapping of social–spatial relations: Ahom origin myth, 42; Biswesar Bidyadhip (*see* Biswesar Bidyadhip); Dutiram Hazarika (*see* Dutiram Hazarika); features of, 43; issues, 41; notion of foreigners, 45; private possession, of families, 41; Purani Asom Buranji (*see* Purani Asom Buranji); Tai-Ahom language, written in, 41; us and them, framework of, 43–44

central variant *see* Nagaon variant
Chatterjee, Sarat Chandra, 173
Chinese Aggression (1962), 145
colonial government: Brahmaputra Valley, in: introduction of order, 24; peasant settlement policy, 25; settlement of *char* areas, 24; tea plantations, 25
colonial revenue collection, 30
culture formation: process of, 76

Datal Hantir Une Khowa Howdah, 156, 158–59, 173–74, 183
democracy: Bhattacharjya's on language in, 141
Devy, Ganesh N., 80
dialectical understanding of frontier, 10
dialectics: emphasis on historical processes, 3; focus of, 3
Dutiram Hazarika, 46–47 *see also* Buranji chronicles

Eastern Frontier of Bengal, 21
eastern variant *see* Sibsagar variant
Eaton, Richard, 7–8, 83
ethnographic debate, in Valley: over language, 89–91

foothills: classification of, 24

Gandhian nationalism *see* Iaruingam
Gentzler, Edwin, 7
Gill, K. P. S., 148
Goalparia variant, 77
Goswami, Hemchandra, 87
Goswami, Mamoni Raisom, 156, 158–59, 167
Goswami, Sabita, 147

Hazarika's Buranji, 47–48, 52
hills: relationship between valleys and, 32–33
Hinduisation, 31

Iaruingam, 148–50
identity politics: Assam, in, 143–48
Imphal Valley, 3
Inner Line Regulation (1873), 27–28, 36

Jagara Mandalar Premar Akhyan, 116–17

janajatiya areas: Assam, of, 120
Jaymati, 113–16
Jaymati, legend of: Buranji tradition appropriation, into Indo-Gangetic worldview, 52; historical significance, 55–56
Jonaki, 86, 89, 115

Kakati, Banikanta, 110, 120
Kamrupi Assamese, 47
Kamrupi variant, 77, 157
Kar, Boddhisattva, 36–37
Katha Guru Charit, 15, 25–26, 67
Khat policy, 26–27
Koch tribe, 29
Kumar Bhuyan, Surjya, 17
kun-how, 17, 29

Lailik Buranji, 56
language: role in Assam politcal life, 146; variants of: Goalparia variant (*see* Goalparia variant); Kamrupi variant (*see* Kamrupi variant); Nagaon variant (*see* Nagaon variant); Sibsagar variant (*see* Sibsagar variant)
language agitation, 144; Assamese nationhood (*see* Assamese nationhood)
language modernisation, 76; using of language, as cultural resource, 79
language shift, 76
literature, in pre-colonial period: characteristic modes of, 79
Look East Policy, 34
loukik culture, 83

Mahabharata, 47, 58, 61, 80
Mahila Samiti, 158
Malik, Abdul, 134–35
Mitchell, John, 22
Mizo politics, 144

modern Assamese language: colonial period, in, 109; ethnographic contradiction, 88–96
modern Assamese literature, 12
morong ghar, 83
Mukti Deul, 130, 132

Naga nationalism, 149
Nagaon variant, 77
Naga politics, 144
nagara music, 82
Na Prithivir Natun Jug, 127
Nara kingdom, 43
National Highway 39 (NH 39), 28
NEFA area: imposition of Hindi language, by Indian government, 141
Nellie massacre, 147
Neo-Vaishnava literature: Brahmaputra Valley, in, 81; emergence of, 67; pre-colonial period, of, 5; trans-creations of; *Bhagavada Gita*, 80; puranas, 80
Neo-Vaishnava Movement, 81; ethnic rebellion against Ahom monarchy, 84–85; indigenised trans-creations in, 82
Neo-Vaishnava tradition, 84
No Man's Land, 161–62
north-east India frontier, 3; Shimray's critique of, 20
NSCN, 164, 166

Order, 7, 24

Paik system, 26; abolition by British government, 27
Pemberton, R. B., 21
Plain Tribal Council of Assam (PTCA), 88
Plain tribe, 6
politics: identity in Assam, of, 143–48

Purani Asom Buranji, 44 *see also* Buranji chronicles; Indo-Gangetic worldview, appropriation of, 49; marriage alliances, recording of, 44–45; narrative of, 47; opposition to ruling King, 45; recovery from Baptist missionaries, 42

Purani Kathat Natun Rang, 90, 190–91

Quit India movement, 149–50

Rabha, Bishnu, 12, 34, 94, 96, 101, 109–10, 120, 146, xii
Ramanujan, A. K., 79
Ramayana, 51, 67–68
Ramdhenu, 11, 118, 140
Region, 8
Revolutionary Communist Party of India (RCPI), 123, 134
Rongmilir Hanhi, 160–61

Saikia, Yasmin, 17
Sankari culture, 26; Bezbaruah role in, 118; Sanskritisation and mapping relations in, 67–69; challenges, 69
Sanskritisation: through Shakti sect, 81

Satyanath, T. S., 79
Scott, James C., 31–32, 35
Seuji Patar Kahini, 98–99, 102
Shimray, U. A., 20
Sibsagar variant, 41; Baptist missionaries' role in, 77; as communicator of narrative, 133
Simanta Soinik, 129
Simon Commission, 88
Subrahmanyam, Sanjay, 36, 45–46, 65

Tagore, Rabindranath, 173
tea plantations, 22, 24 *see also Seuji Patar Kahini*; land reclamation into colonial order, 25
Treaty of Yandaboo (1826), 18

ULFA, 148
Uttara Kanda, 67, 70

valley: relationship between hills and (*see* hills, relationship between valleys and)

Waddell, Lawrence, Augustine, 1, 4–6, 9, 21, 130, 170
western variant *see* Kamrupi variant

For Product Safety Concerns and Information please contact our EU representative GPSR@taylorandfrancis.com
Taylor & Francis Verlag GmbH, Kaufingerstraße 24, 80331 München, Germany

www.ingramcontent.com/pod-product-compliance
Lightning Source LLC
Chambersburg PA
CBHW052111300426
44116CB00010B/1619